Rethinking Institutions, Processes and Development in Africa

Africa: Past, Present & Prospects

Series Editors: Toyin Falola (University of Texas at Austin) and Olajumoke Yacob-Haliso (Babcock University)

This series collates and curates studies of Africa in its multivalent local, regional, and global contexts. It aims fundamentally to capture in one series historical, contemporary and multidisciplinary studies which analyze the dynamics of the African predicament from deeply theoretical perspectives while marshalling empirical data to describe, explain, and predict trends in continuities and change in Africa and in African studies.

The books published in this series represent the multiplicity of voices, local and global in relation to African futures. It not only represents diversity, but also provides a platform for convergence of outstanding research that will enliven debates about the future of Africa, while also advancing theory and informing policy making. Preference is given to studies that deliberately link the past with the present and advances knowledge about various African nations by extending the range, breadth, depth, types and sources of data and information existing and emerging about these countries.

The platform created proceeds from the assumption that there is no singular "African experience", nor is it possible to, in any way, homogenize the identities, histories, spaces and lives of African people.

Titles in the Series

Ghanaian Politics and Political Communication
Edited by Samuel Gyasi Obeng and Emmanuel Debrah

Beyond History: African Agency in Development, Diplomacy and Conflict Resolution
Edited by Elijah Nyaga Munyi, David Mwambari and Aleksi Ylönen

Reflections on Leadership and Institutions in Africa
Edited by Kenneth Kalu and Toyin Falola

Imagining Vernacular Histories: Essays in Honour of Toyin Falola
Edited by Mobolanla Ebunoluwa Sotunsa and Abikal Borah

Insights into Policies and Practices on the Right to Development
Edited by Serges Djoyou Kamga and Carol C. Ngang

Guerrilla Radios in Southern Africa: Broadcasters, Technology, Propaganda Wars, and the Armed Struggle
Edited by Sekibakiba Peter Lekgoathi

Identities, Histories and Values in Postcolonial Nigeria
Edited by Adeshina Afolayan

A Tight Embrace: Narratives and Dynamics of Euro-African Relations
Edited by Marco Zoppi

Promoting Gender Equality in Political Participation: New Perspectives on Nigeria
Damilola Taiye Agbalajobi

Rethinking Institutions, Processes and Development in Africa
Edited by Ernest Toochi Aniche and Toyin Falola

Rethinking Institutions, Processes and Development in Africa

Edited by Ernest Toochi Aniche
and Toyin Falola

ROWMAN & LITTLEFIELD
Lanham • Boulder • New York • London

Published by Rowman & Littlefield
An imprint of The Rowman & Littlefield Publishing Group, Inc.
4501 Forbes Boulevard, Suite 200, Lanham, Maryland 20706
www.rowman.com

86-90 Paul Street, London EC2A 4NE, United Kingdom

British Library Cataloguing in Publication Information Available

Library of Congress Cataloging-in-Publication Data

Names: Aniche, Ernest Toochi, 1978– editor. | Falola, Toyin, editor.
Title: Rethinking institutions, processes, and development in Africa / edited by Ernest Aniche and Toyin Falola.
Other titles: Africa: past, present & prospects.
Description: Lanham : Rowman & Littlefield, 2021. | Series: Africa: past, present & prospects | Includes bibliographical references and index.
Identifiers: LCCN 2021020656 (print) | LCCN 2021020657 (ebook) | ISBN 9781538151129 (cloth) | ISBN 9781538151136 (ebook)
Subjects: LCSH: Economic development—Africa. | Africa—Economic conditions.
Classification: LCC HC800 .R46446 2021 (print) | LCC HC800 (ebook) | DDC 338.96—dc23
LC record available at https://lccn.loc.gov/2021020656
LC ebook record available at https://lccn.loc.gov/2021020657

™ The paper used in this publication meets the minimum requirements of American National Standard for Information Sciences – Permanence of Paper for Printed Library Materials, ANSI/NISO Z39.48–1992.

Contents

About the Contributors

Ifeanyichukwu Michael Abada is a senior lecturer in the Department of Political Science, University of Nigeria, Nsukka (UNN) and was the former head of the department. He earned his PhD from UNN. His research interests include public administration, public policy, peace and conflict studies, development administration, civil-military relations and urban development.

Bamidele Omotunde Alabi holds a BSc (Hons.) degree in sociology from the then Ondo State University Ado-Ekiti and MSc (Hons.) degree in marketing, and in sociology from the University of Lagos. He holds an MBA degree from the University of Lagos. Bamidele is a Chartered Accountant – Associate member of the Institute of Chartered Accountants of Nigeria (ICAN). He is presently a full-time doctoral student in the Department of Sociology, University of Lagos. His research interest is migration, on which he has published a number of research works and participated in several local and international conferences.

Ernest Toochi Aniche earned BSc, MSc and PhD degrees from the Department of Political Science, University of Nigeria, with bias in international relations. He is currently a senior lecturer in the Department of Political Science, faculty of social sciences, Federal University Otuoke, Bayelsa State, Nigeria. He was the acting head, Department of Political Science, Hezekiah University, Umudi, Imo State, Nigeria (2017–2019).

Toyin Falola is the Jacob and Frances Sanger Mossiker Chair Professor in the humanities and a distinguished teaching professor at the University of Texas at Austin. A celebrated scholar of global stature, Professor Falola has published numerous books and essays in diverse areas. He has received various awards and honours, including the Jean Holloway Award for Teaching Excellence, the Texas Exes Teaching Award and seven honourary doctorates. He is the series editor of Carolina Studies on Africa and the Black World, among several others.

Obinna Innocent Ihunna earned his BSc MSc degrees in political science from the University of Ibadan, Ibadan, Nigeria. Currently teaching at the Federal University of Technology, Owerri, Imo State, Nigeria, his research interests span African studies, feminist epistemology, democratic studies, federalism, and indigenous political structures. He has a number of domestic and international scholarly publications to his credit.

Emeka C. Iloh is associated with the Department of International Relations, Madonna University Nigeria, Okija Campus. He has also worked as a senior researcher with the African Heritage Institution, Enugu. He holds a PhD in political science with specialization in international relations from the UNN. He has published in reputable local and international journals, and contributed chapters to numerous edited books. His research interests cut across international political economy, regional integration, migration and politics of food security.

Gaius Jatau is a lecturer in the Department of History, Kaduna State University, Kaduna, Nigeria.

Ifeanyi P. Maduechesi is a doctoral candidate with the Department of Economics, University of Abuja. He is a corporate financial expert with extensive experiences in commercial and investment banking. He is currently engaged in projects in transportation and infrastructure development. His research interest encompasses maritime, seaport efficiency and Nigeria's trade competitiveness.

Ngozi Joy Maduka is a lecturer in the Department of Educational Psychology/Guidance and Counselling, Alvan Ikoku Federal College of Education Owerri, Imo State, Nigeria. She has academic qualifications in the following areas: PhD and MEd in guidance and counselling from Imo State University Owerri, Nigeria; BEd in guidance and counselling from UNN; and NCE in home economics from University of Benin, Nigeria (Agbor Campus). She is a member of Teacher's Registration Council of Nigeria (TRCN) and a long standing member of Counselling Association of Nigeria (MCASSON), Women in Colleges of Education (WICE), Nigeria Psychologist for Educational Psychologists (NISEP) and Gender Studies Association of Nigeria (GSAN). Dr Maduka is actively involved in professional counselling in and out of school settings. She has authored and co-authored chapters in several books and articles in numerous peer-reviewed journals.

Jerry Mmanoko Mathekga is a senior researcher at the Human Sciences Research Council (HSRC), in South Africa, and a sociology PhD candidate at Rhodes University, Grahamstown, South Africa.

Chukwuemeka V. Muoneke is a lecturer in the Department of International Relations, Madonna University Nigeria, Okija Campus. He is also a doctoral candidate with the Department of Political Science, UNN. His research interests include political economy, international terrorism and peace and conflict studies.

Christopher Ewuzie Obianagwa is a lecturer in the Department of Political Science, UNN. He received his master's degree from the same university and currently a doctoral student there. His research interest is in political economy.

Cinderella Temitope Ochu is a lecturer in the Department of History and Strategic Studies, University of Lagos, Akoka, Yaba, Lagos State, Nigeria. Her contact: cindyamos1@yahoo.com.

Timothy Olusola Ogunfuwa's doctorate degree is in fine art, specializing in painting. He worked in the print journalism and advertising industries before practising as a full-time studio artist and graphic design consultant for two decades. Ogunfuwa teaches drawing, graphic design and painting in the University of Lagos, Nigeria. His recent drawing and painting exercises are expressions of inner freedom pivoted on his principle of overlapping geometrics to achieve contents and themes that metamorphose from accidentals. His theoretical studies and writings focus on conflict and resolution in art and artists. He has participated in several joint and group exhibitions.

Nneka Ifeoma Okafor is a lecturer in the Department of Philosophy at the UNN. She received her doctorate from the University of KwaZulu-Natal, South Africa. Her areas of specialization are ethics, international relations and development administration.

Paul Hezekiah Omeh is a lecturer in the Department of Political Science, UNN. He received his master's degree from UNN and is currently a doctoral student in the same university. His research interests are political economy and public administration.

Introduction: Institutions and Development in Africa

Ernest Toochi Aniche and Toyin Falola

BACKGROUND

There seems to be an unending debate on the nexus between institution and development in Africa. Indeed, in recent years in Africa, the link between the two has become a significant and a growing field of academic and policy research, in social sciences generally. Hence, there is increasing attention on the role of institutions on development in Africa. Thus, various empirical research have emerged attempting to provide additional evidence of the impact of institutions on development as well as the processes through which institutions may affect development.[1]

However, this increasing emphasis on the role of institutions and governance on economic development cannot be completely dissociated from the third wave of democratization in Africa. Most scholars have through their empirical researches concluded and insisted that institutions matter for growth in Africa. In other words, literature attributes development crisis to weak institutions in Africa abounds.[2]

Institution is therefore a concept widely used to analyse the development of African economies.[3] Analytically, chapter contributors in this book dealt with democratic institutions, processes and development but more profoundly with democratic institutions and development in Africa.

CONCEPTUALIZING INSTITUTION AND DEVELOPMENT

The two major concepts in this book need to be further conceptualized. In other words, the objective of this section is to conceptualize and clarify the twin concepts of institution and development.

Institution

Human institutions can be classified into the following sets of institutions: international and national institutions, traditional and modern institutions, public and private institutions, political, economic, social, and religious institutions, formal and informal institutions, governmental and non-governmental institutions, democratic and non-democratic institutions, and more.

From economics point of view, institutions are seen as structures that describe the 'rules of the game' and the conditions under which economic agents operate in an economy. Thus, North defines an economic institution as 'a set of rules, compliance procedures and moral and ethical behavioural norms designed to constrain the behaviour of individuals in the interests of maximizing the wealth or utility of principals'.[4] In trying to modify this definition, Pande and Udry sees institutions as sets of rules, regulations, regimes, procedures or norms that limit or restrain behaviour.[5]

There is difficulty in measuring and quantifying institutions. Indeed, the definition of institutions is naturally vague. In other words, institutions are the rules of engagement in a society or, more formally, are the artificially created constraints that condition human interactions.[6] It means inherent constraints, official rules and enforcement architectures.[7] Hence, an institution is a distinct form of social configuration that involves possibly codefiable and evidently normative rules of interpretation and behaviour. Institutions are seen as a socially entrenched system of rules.[8]

However, following from the perspectives of various chapter contributors of this book, institutions can be defined as those formal political, economic and social structures of governance which carry out legislative, executive, administrative, bureaucratic, judicial, regulatory and enforcement functions. The primary roles of institutions of social, economic and political governance within structural-functional input-output matrix include rule-making, rule-implementation and rule-adjudication.

Development

Development, on the other hand, is a process not an event. It is a continuous process. Every country is developing. Development is a process and underdevelopment does not necessary mean absence of development. It is also multi-dimensional in terms of economic, social, human and political development, and can be measured with economic, social and human political indicators.[9]

Development usually means improvement, either in terms of the integral condition of the system, or in some of its component elements.[10] Economic development, for example, refers to growth accompanied by qualitative changes in the productive structure generally referred to as structural change.[11] Economic development is improvement of the way resources and goods and services are utilized within the system or by the system to generate new goods and services in order to produce increasing consumption and investment opportunities to the members of the system. It has often been strictly associated with the concept of economic growth, in turn, defined as an increase in the economic indicators like per capita income, gross domestic product (GDP) and so on. Other economic development indices include standard of living, adequate infrastructures, wealth creation, income level and employment rate.[12]

The aforementioned economic conception of development needs to be interrogated because it focuses more on availability of infrastructures than accessibility of citizens to infrastructures, income level than income equality and wealth creation than wealth distribution. It sees development as a thing or a project, and therefore, conceives development as acquisition of artefacts or economic resources. This approach to the study of development therefore thingifies or materializes development such that inability to acquire these artefacts is considered to be under-development. In other words, thingification of development is taken to mean availability of infrastructures and social amenities whilst underdevelopment is conceived as lack or inadequacy of them. This conception of development is thing-centred.[13]

This notion of development needs to be problematized because it alienates man. There should be emphasizes on humanistic approach to development which upholds that man should be not only the end but also the means and agents of development. The focus of human development is on developing the man. This approach posits that development should be man-centred. Man should be the centre or object of development, because development is made for man and not for development.[14]

Whilst economic development reifies the materialization of development, human development elevates humanization of development. Economic development dehumanizes development, whereas development should have a human face.[15] Indeed, man should be the means to development. Thus, development becomes participatory when it is people-centred.[16]

Therefore, human capital development entails investing in man or human resources through human capacity training and enlightenment; increasing access to quality education and healthcare; equal opportunities and empowerment; promotion of human welfare, dignity and respect; and protection of human rights. It connotes training man to be able to protect his right and assert himself to the society. It is only through this way, he will be able to make a meaningful contribution to the overall wellbeing and advancement of his society. Human development indices (HDIs) and human poverty indices (HPIs) include life expectancy, poverty level, and inequality gap.[17]

Human development and economic development are not necessarily parallel or mutually exclusive for they are actually mutually inclusive in that without the latter, the former may not be achieved. Without economic growth and development, any attempt to redistribute income, achieve equality, minimize poverty and reduce inequality may amount to sharing poverty.

INSTITUTIONS AND DEVELOPMENT IN AFRICA

As noted earlier, most of the studies in the economic literature that tried to interrogate the nexus between institutions and development see development as economic growth and development. Also, most of earlier studies focused on the link between political institutions and economic development, which were measured through indices of political crisis, instability and violence.[18] Whereas, the more recent studies emphasized the relationships between economic institutions and economic development.

Thus, the institutional view asserts that poorly performing institutional structures (e.g. institutional incapacity, weak institutions, inadequate constraints on the executive, ineffective property rights protection, inefficient legal and court systems, etc.) are the ultimate causes of underdevelopment.[19] In the same vein, Aloysius Amin argued that the absence of strong institutions has been a major cause of Africa's slow economic growth.[20] This is because strong institutions are the recipes for sustainable development in the development process.[21] For advocates of this view therefore economic performance is essentially shaped by the prevailing set of institutions.[22] Institutions define the incentives that condition economic choices in any society.[23]

Similarly, the institutional quality thesis argues that economic development is affected by the institutional framework within which the economic actors interact with one another in an economy. Institutions matter in defining the prevailing explicit and implicit behavioural norms and their ability to create appropriate incentives for desirable economic behaviour. This thesis explores the relationship between institutional factors (like civil liberty, human rights, rule of law, economic and political freedom) and economic performance. This point of view argued that countries will prosper once they create the requisite institutions that drive entrepreneurship, savings and investments.[24]

A number of studies have demonstrated that institutions that promote more political freedom lead to less income inequality and economic prosperity. This shows that countries with greater civil liberties have lower levels of income inequality. Whilst, more recent studies have shown that that institutions that promote economic freedom have a positive impact on economic performance. In other words, countries with economic freedom and consistent policies that guarantee security of property, non-confiscatory taxes and enforcement of contracts promote development and engender better economic performance. By positively affecting investment, economic freedom promotes economic prosperity.[25]

Institutional characteristics that matter in promoting economic growth and development in Africa include improvement in the quality of institutions; regulatory quality and rule of law; political freedom, public accountability and political stability; increase in investment in physical and human capital; and openness and reduction in population growth.[26] The point being made is that if political institutions can allocate power to groups that encourage and guarantee property rights enforcement, create constraints on power holders and capture a few rents by power holders, economic growth is simulated.[27]

However, it has been argued that politically accountable and inclusive governments can lead to improved economic outcomes. But they are likely to adopt economically desirable policies that are unpopular with the populace. This tends to increase the risk of political disorder in Africa, which may ultimately be growth-inhibiting. In other words, this view contended that the recent attempts to democratize Africa may not lead to the expected improved growth and development outcomes unless successful attempts at reducing political instability can be attained.[28]

From the institutional point of view, therefore, it has been argued that prevailing existing institutions are the cause of Africa's poor economic performance.[29] This is because inefficiency of extractive institutions has been recipes for exploitation which are disincentives for productive economic engagement. Acemoglu, Johnson and Robinson linked the ineffective post-colonial institutions to colonialism when they pointed out that in most of the African colonies, the colonial governments set up weak extractive institutions that were just enough to enable the expropriation of resources to Europe.[30]

There was totally a disconnection between government and the governed where government institutions were designed to intimidate and harass the citizens and to serve the government. During this period of colonial rule, the primary role of setting up police force was to protect the colonial officials, while its secondary role was the intimidation and subjugation of the people. Public institutions and processes were not meant to serve the people, but to extract resources from them for the benefit of the colonial administration.[31]

For Kenneth Kalu, European colonial administrative and governance institutions in Africa were predatory and parasitic, and thus laid the foundations for Africa's predatory state-society relations.[32] This created extractive institutions, which, in turn, nurtured mutual distrust between state and citizens. These perverse predatory-prey relations continued to keep most Africans away from meaningful engagement or involvement in the political and economic affairs of their countries. Kalu further argued that Africa's economic and governance institutions are fundamentally extractive in nature. These institutions created perverse incentives as they fostered exploitation and rent-seeking on the part of the public officials and their cronies.[33]

Consequently, most states in Africa have been unable to achieve political stability and meaningful economic development. The pervasive extractive institutions coupled with the increasing mistrust between the state and its citizens and the predatory state-society relations continue to undermine every effort to establish real development in the continent. Even with the wave of democratization in Africa in the 1990s, the outcome has been anything but developmental.[34] Given the low level of democratization, most African states are still predatory rather than being developmental.[35]

Kalu concluded that crisis of development in Africa is basically an institutional problem. This is because the region's economic and political institutions cannot produce real development.[36] This prevailing form of predatory relations has produced miserably very poor and extremely unequal societies, with some public officials living in affluence or opulence, while the majority wallow in abject poverty. No wonder, Africa has produced more sit-tight rulers than has any other region. Given the exploitative character of the governance institutions, African societies have been characterized by gross exploitation of the masses by the ruling elite. Africa's development challenge is thus a result of predatory state-society relations, and the types of institution this structure generates.[37]

Unfortunately, African scholarship concerning the nexus between institutions and development is still dominated by economic perspective of development despite the emergence of humanistic perspective of development. Not only that human development is a more embracing, encompassing and comprehensive view of development than economic development, but it also offers a better explanation of African situation than economic development. This is because development viewed from humanistic perspective is an aspect or part and parcel democracy, and therefore co-extensive with it.[38] From this point of view, therefore, it is not even necessary to examine the relationships between democratic political institutions and human development.[39]

Just like development, democracy is also a process. Africa states are still democratizing and thus characterized by low level of democratization in which democracy or democratic culture is yet to be institutionalized due to nascency of democracy and incessant military intervention in politics. In effect, institutions of democracy are still weak and need to be strengthened.

All available information or indicators like human development index (HDI) suggest that the most African states have failed in developing their citizens and do not consider investing on their citizens a worthwhile venture. This shows the reason why the African states have been treating their citizens with disdain thereby elevating social injustice to the level of state policy. African states, therefore, do not invest in the development of human resources in which their citizens could be the primary beneficiaries. Rather, what abounds is social injustice which does not provide an enabling or conducive environment for human resources development.[40] It is instructive that the recent report by World Poverty Clock ranked Nigeria the world poverty capital or headquarters of extreme poverty in the whole world.

A developed man should be able to afford at least basic needs of life like food security or sufficiency; shelter; and physical, human and environmental security. A state should endeavour to provide its citizenry minimum conditions or requirements of existence. Such a welfare state is a just society, because it provides an enabling environment for development of man. A society where men are given their dues and the role for which their natural endowment fits them; people are likely being able to realize their potentials and hence developed themselves.[41]

LAYOUT OF THE BOOK

The book is divided into two sections. The first section contains chapters that focus on democratic institutions and processes in post-independence Africa. The contributors tried to examine the political institutional processes in post-colonial Africa. The section dealt with workings of various institutions like education, bureaucracy, interest groups, trade unions, and problems of enforcements in Africa. It also discussed the relevance of creative arts for political socialization as well as the role of privatization on service delivery in contemporary African societies.

The first chapter by Jerry Mmanoko Mathekga focuses on the role of the two main labour federations in democratic South Africa and Namibia such as the Congress of South African Trade Unions (COSATU) and the National Union of Namibian Workers (NUNW), respectively. He argues that as much as these federations try to deal with social, political and economic issues, they have been effectively involved in accumulating capital. Mathekga also observes that the two trade unions have played a key role during the South African and Namibian struggles for liberation. He however notes that both federations continue to be affiliated to the ruling parties; while the COSATU is affiliated to the African National Congress (ANC), the NUNW is affiliated to the South West Africa People's Organization (SWAPO).

In chapter 2, Ngozi Joy Maduka asserts that education and bureaucracy are the needed ingredients or catalyst for an all-round nation building. From the point of a counsellor, she sees education as one that must expose and improve positively peoples' latent abilities. She suggests that African countries like Nigeria should re-engineer their education industry to a more political and economic developmental standpoint that will engender the manifestation of leadership style devoid of indices of retardation and corruption so as to facilitate improved growth.

In chapter 3, Ifeanyi Michael Abada, Nneka Okafor and Christopher Obi-anagwa recognize the fact that electricity remains the catalyst for economic growth and everyday living. They state that the rationale for unbundling and privatizing power sector in Nigeria was due to abysmal state of electricity supply and revenue losses of low operational capacity. They also note that privatization reduces the fiscal and administrative burdens of a large public enterprise sector but also to spur private sector development. They ethically appraise the post-reforms effects of the power sector on the Nigerian economy and concluded that despite the reforms, the electricity sector in Nigeria has continued to wallow in endemic corruption and impunity and degenerated from darkness to darkness. They therefore recommend among other things that Nigerian Electricity Regulatory Commission (NERC) and other regulatory bodies should endeavour to eliminate weak operational capacity in the sector.

In chapter 4, Timothy Ogunfuwa advances the economics of artistic creativity as it affects a people's political socialization process using the Nigerian cultural and rich spatial dimension as a typological case. He notes that the fundamental structure of political socialization extends beyond a set of people's generational value circumstances and the peculiar application of these to the political atmosphere of their immediate and extended cultural and environmental boundaries. He concludes that some arts can be studied through their economics of creativity to determine a depth of transmission of political socialization, and also that art and the artist qualify as equal agents of this transmission.

The second section contains essays that focus on democratic institutions and development challenges in post-independence Africa. The themes of this section revolve around historicizing post-colonial institutions and crisis of development in Africa thus problematizing Western development models. The authors of the various chapters in this section examine the infrastructural challenges and development trajectory in Africa.

In chapter 5, Toyin Falola notes that democratic institutions, values and culture are evolving in Africa despite several challenges. He identifies the prospects of these emerging democratic institutions, values and culture in the continent.

In chapter 6, Cinderella Ochu points out that the period after the Second World War was marked by expansive development programmes and policies in Africa. The author traces the history of development planning in Nigeria to the 1946 Ten-Year Plan of Development and Welfare, which continued after independence with other four development plans and independence, Nigeria has had four development plans and initiatives. She argues that the current state of economic downturn in the country can be traced to the colonial era and suggested that Nigeria needs to locally design a policy tailored towards transforming the colonial economic structure into an economy that is internally oriented.

In chapter 7, Nneka Okafor, Ifeanyi Abada and Paul Hezekiah Omeh emphasize the role of local government in addressing grassroots developmental challenges, its relationship with the state and disposition to its financial obligations. They recognize the transformative roles of local government in grassroots development. They concluded that weaknesses and challenges of local government in discharging its functions are holistically tied down to the joint account operation of state and local governments. For them, this intergovernmental fiscal relation has undermined the local government financial autonomy in Nigeria. They recommend that local governments should have their own separate accounts upon which statutory allocations, grants and other payments shall be paid for effective operations.

In chapter 8, Obinna Ihunna examines state institutions, its agents and agencies, and the place of the citizenry in a continuing, contagious and dissuasive neocolonial project in Nigeria. He investigates the tenacious hold of tenacious hold on that society on Nigeria and other African countries.

In chapter 9, Bamidele Omotunde Alabi examines the dynamics, mechanisms and outcomes of the recent urban redevelopment initiative of the Lagos state government. He argues that urban redevelopment is a mere metaphor for gentrification in this part of the world. Bamidele states that a good reference of relics of colonisation in Africa is the preponderance of urban redevelopment schemes, wherein gentrification is often cloaked with the garb of urban redevelopment, the execution of which is often achieved through forcible evictions, typified by intimidation, coercion and violence. He concludes that the regeneration of Otodo Gbame and Ebute Ikate at this time is indeed a replacement of an impoverished population by others with greater economic resources.

In chapter 10, Gaius Jatau focuses on the role of the railways in the economic transformation of Kafanchan, Kaduna State, by highlighting how it brought various positive changes to the area, while also acknowledging its negative impacts in the period 1927–1993. He notes that railway transport infrastructure has been indispensable vehicle for socio-economic transformation in Africa. He also emphasizes the impact of the railway system on the growth in size, population and changes in direction and structure of the social and economic status of Kafanchan.

In chapter 11, Ernest Toochi Aniche notes that economic, social, and political indices show that there is widening international inequality between developed and underdeveloped countries of which Africa belongs to the latter. He therefore concludes that extreme inequality of international politics as embedded in international political economy deepens crisis of African developmental regionalism. He recommends post-neo-functionalism or post-neo-nationalism as a panacea for crisis of African integration and development.

In chapter 12, Emeka C. Iloh, Ifeanyi P. Maduechesi and Chukwuemeka V. Muoneke explore the link between preferential trade agreements and intra-regional trade in West Africa in the prevailing World Trade Organization (WTO)'s regime. They examine the impacts of preferential trade agreements such as the Economic Partnership Agreements (EPAs) and the African Growth and Opportunity Act (AGOA) on intra-regional food trade and food security in the sub-region. Iloh, Maduechesi and Muoneke demonstrate that the existence of these agreements within the framework of the WTO has diverted food trade from West Africa to other parts of the world, thereby undermining food security in West Africa. They show that food trade is often diverted to the European Union and the United States under the EPAs and AGOA arrangements. They conclude that food security in West Africa is undermined.

CONCLUDING REMARKS

It has been noted that political independence in Africa failed to transform the governance structures and economic institutions that evolved during the centuries of slavery and colonialism. These perverse governance institutions nurtured mutual suspicion and popular resentment and led to the evolution of predatory state-society relations, where the provision and maintenance of public goods was not a government priority.[42] This exploitative governance institutions lack the institutional characteristics or qualities, like participatory and inclusiveness; political and economic freedom; public accountability and political stability; increase in investment in physical and human capital; and openness and reduction in population growth, to engender development in Africa. In effect, the predatory state-citizen relation is not inclusive enough to galvanize the citizens towards development of their societies.

More fundamentally, there is need to rethink the predominant institutional view in the existing literature which interrogates the relationships between institutions and development from economic view of development. This will entail mainstreaming humanistic approach to development by problematizing the link between democratic governance institutions and human development. Hopefully, the chapter contributors of this book will address these concerns and more.

NOTES

1. Rasha Osman, Constantinos Alexiou and Persefoni Tsaliki, 'The Role of Institutions in Economic Development: Evidence from 27 Sub-Saharan African Countries', *International Journal of Social Economics* 39, no. 1 (2011): 142–60.

2. A.A. Kilishi, H.I. Mobolaji, M.A. Yaru and A.T. Yakubu, 'Institutions and Economic Performance in sub-Saharan Africa: A Dynamic Panel Data Analysis', *Journal of African Development (JAD)* 15, no. 2 (2013): 91–120.

3. Colnot Louis, Patel Arpit and Strang Stephen, *Institutions and the Economic Development of Africa* (Atlanta: Georgia Institute of Technology, 2015).

4. Douglass North, *Structure and Change in Economic History* (New York: Norton & Co, 1981).

5. R. Pande and C. Udry, 'Institutions and Development: A View from Below' (working paper, Yale University Economic Growth Center, Yale, 2006).

6. Daron Acemoglu and James Robinson, 'The Role of Institutions in Growth and Development' (working paper no. 10, The World Bank Commission on Growth and Development, Washington, DC, 2008).

7. Louis, Arpit and Stephen, *Institutions and the Economic Development of Africa.*

8. Geoffrey Hodgson, 'What Are Institutions?', *Journal of Economic Issues (JEI)* XL, no. 1 (2006): 1–25.

9. Adam Szirmai, *The Dynamics of Socio-economic Development: An Introduction* (Cambridge: Cambridge University Press, 2005).

10. Lorenzo Bellù, *Development and Development Paradigms: A (Reasoned) Review of Prevailing Versions* (Rome: Food and Agriculture Organization, 2011).

11. Szirmai, *The Dynamics of Socio-economic Development.*

12. Bellù, *Development and Development Paradigms.*

13. Ernest Aniche, *A Modern Introduction to Political Science* (Onitsha: Desvic Publishing, 2009).

14. Ernest Aniche and Victor Ukaegbu, 'Crisis of Human Rights and Social Justice in Nigeria: Implications for Human Development', *Journal of Development and Contemporary Studies (JODACS)* 1, no. 1 (2014): 32–41.

15. Aniche, *A Modern Introduction to Political Science.*

16. Aniche and Ukaegbu, 'Crisis of human rights'.

17. Ibid.

18. Osman, Alexiou and Tsaliki, 'The Role of Institutions'.

19. Stelios Michalopoulos and Elias Papaioannou, 'National Institutions and Subnational Development in Africa' (working paper no. 18275, NBER, Cambridge, MA, 2013).

20. Aloysius Amin, 'Africa's Development: Institutions, Economic Reforms and Growth'. *International Journal of Economics and Financial Issues* 3, no. 2 (2013): 324–36.

21. Osman, Alexiou and Tsaliki, 'The Role of Institutions'.

22. Douglass North, *Institutions, Institutional Change and Economic Performance* (Cambridge: Cambridge University Press, 1990).

23. Kenneth Kalu, 'State-Society Relations, Institutional Transformation and Economic Development in sub-Saharan Africa', *Development Policy Review* 35 (2017): 234–45.

24. Osman, Alexiou and Tsaliki, 'The Role of Institutions'.

25. Ibid.

26. Kilishi, Mobolaji, Yaru and Yakubu, 'Institutions and Economic Performance'.

27. Louis, Arpit and Stephen, *Institutions and the Economic Development.*

28. Augustin Fosu, Robert Bates and Anke Hoeffler, 'Institutions, Governance and Economic Development in Africa: An Overview', *Journal of African Economies* 15, no. 1 (2006): 1–9.

29. D. Acemoglu, S. Johnson and J. Robinson, 'Institutions as a Fundamental Cause of Long-Run Growth', in *Handbook of Economic Growth*, eds. P. Aghion and S.N. Durlauf (Amsterdam: Elsevier, 2005), 1369–401.

30. D. Acemoglu, S. Johnson and Robinson, 'The Colonial Origins of Comparative Development: An Empirical Investigation', *The American Economic Review* 91, no. 5 (2001): 1369–401.

31. Kalu, 'State-Society Relations'.

32. Kenneth Kalu, *Foreign Aid and Future of Africa* (New York: Palgrave Macmillan, 2018).

33. Kalu, 'State-Society Relations'.

34. Ibid.

35. Ernest Aniche, 'Africa's "Big Men" in the Continent's Democratic Experiments', in *Africa's Big Men: Predatory State-Society Relations in Africa*, eds. K. Kalu, O. Yacob-Haliso and T. Folala (New York: Routledge, 2018).

36. Kalu, 'State-Society Relations'.

37. Kenneth Kalu, 'Postcolonial African States and Its Citizens', in *Africa's Big Men: Predatory State-Society Relations in Africa*, eds. K. Kalu, O. Yacob-Haliso and T. Folala (New York: Routledge, 2018).

38. Claude Ake, *Democracy and Development in Africa* (Washington, DC: Brookings Institution, 1996).

39. Claude Ake, *The Feasibility of Democracy in Africa* (Dakar: CODESRIA, 2000).

40. Aniche and Ukaegbu, 'Crisis of Human Rights'.

41. Ibid.

42. Kalu, 'State-Society Relations'.

BIBLIOGRAPHY

Acemoglu, D., S. Johnson and J. Robinson. 'The Colonial Origins of Comparative Development: An Empirical Investigation'. *The American Economic Review* 91, no. 5 (2001): 1369–401.

Acemoglu, D., S. Johnson and J. Robinson. 'Institutions as a Fundamental Cause of Long-Run Growth'. In *Handbook of Economic Growth*, edited by P. Aghion and S.N. Durlauf, 109–39. Amsterdam: Elsevier, 2005.

Acemoglu, Daron and James Robinson. 'The Role of Institutions in Growth and Development'. Working Paper No. 10, World Bank Commission on Growth and Development, Washington, DC, 2008.

Ake, Claude. *Democracy and Development in Africa*. Washington, DC: Brookings Institution, 1996.

Ake, Claude. *The Feasibility of Democracy in Africa*. Dakar: CODESRIA, 2000.

Amin, Aloysius. 'Africa's Development: Institutions, Economic Reforms and Growth'. *International Journal of Economics and Financial Issues* 3, no. 2 (2013): 324–36.

Aniche, Ernest. *A Modern Introduction to Political Science*. Onitsha: Desvic Publishing, 2009.

Aniche, Ernest. 'Africa's "Big Men" in the Continent's Democratic Experiments'. In *Africa's Big Men: Predatory State-Society Relations in Africa*, edited by K. Kalu, O. Yacob-Haliso and T. Folala, 236–255. New York: Routledge, 2018.

Aniche, Ernest, and Victor Ukaegbu. 'Crisis of Human Rights and Social Justice in Nigeria: Implications for Human Development'. *Journal of Development and Contemporary Studies (JODACS)* 1, no. 1 (2014): 32–41.

Bellù, Lorenzo. *Development and Development Paradigms: A (Reasoned) Review of Prevailing Versions*. Rome: Food and Agriculture Organization (FAO), 2011.

Fosu, Augustin, Robert Bates and Anke Hoeffler. 'Institutions, Governance and Economic Development in Africa: An overview'. *Journal of African Economies* 15, no. 1 (2006): 1–9.

Hodgson, Geoffrey. What Are Institutions? *Journal of Economic Issues (JEI)* XL, no. 1 (2006): 1–25.

Kalu Kenneth. 'State-Society Relations, Institutional Transformation and Economic Development in sub-Saharan Africa'. *Development Policy Review* 35 (2017): 234–45.

Kalu, Kenneth. *Foreign Aid and Future of Africa*. New York: Palgrave Macmillan, 2018.

Kalu, Kenneth. 'Postcolonial African States and Its Citizens'. In *Africa's Big Men: Predatory State-Society Relations in Africa*, edited by K. Kalu, O. Yacob-Haliso and T. Folala. New York: Routledge, 2018.

Kilishi, A.A., H.I. Mobolaji, M.A. Yaru and A.T. Yakubu. 'Institutions and Economic Performance in sub-Saharan Africa: A Dynamic Panel Data Analysis'. *Journal of African Development (JAD)* 15, no. 2 (2013): 91–120.

Louis, Colnot, Patel Arpit and Strang Stephen. *Institutions and the Economic Development of Africa*. Atlanta: Georgia Institute of Technology, 2015.

Michalopoulos, Stelios, and Elias Papaioannou. 'National Institutions and Subnational Development in Africa'. NBER Working Paper No. 18275, Cambridge, MA, 2013.

North, Douglass. *Structure and Change in Economic History*. New York: Norton & Co, 1981.

North, Douglass. *Institutions, Institutional Change and Economic Performance*. Cambridge: Cambridge University Press, 1990.

Osman, Rasha, Constantinos Alexiou and Persefoni Tsaliki. 'The Role of Institutions in Economic Development: Evidence from 27 sub-Saharan African Countries'. *International Journal of Social Economics* 39, no. 1 (2011): 142–60.

Pande, R. and C. Udry. 'Institutions and Development: A View from Below'. Yale University Economic Growth Center Working Paper No. 928, Yale, 2006.

Szirmai, Adam. *The Dynamics of Socio-economic Development: An Introduction*. Cambridge: Cambridge University Press, 2005.

Part I

INSTITUTIONS AND PROCESSES IN AFRICA

Chapter 1

Reflections on Powers of Trade Union Federations in Democracies: A Comparative Discourse

Jerry Mmanoko Mathekga

INTRODUCTION

Trade union federations have a significant role to play in South Africa and Namibia's development projects and in protecting the workplace rights of its members and improving their economic status. Workers expect trade union federations to be more involved in promoting social change and justice, promoting workplace harmony and human resource development, as well as playing active roles in civil society. However, these tasks have proved more difficult for the Congress of South African Trade Unions (COSATU) and the National Union of Namibian Workers (NUNW). The COSATU and the NUNW have failed to be strategic and independent in its relationship with the African National Congress (ANC) and the South West Africa People's Organization (SWAPO), respectively. These labour federations have been actively involved in campaigning for both political parties during elections. COSATU is in formal alliance with ANC and NUNW is in formal alliance with the SWAPO. Most literature on trade unions in Africa, more specifically in South Africa and Namibia, discuss the role played by labour federations during the struggle for liberation, the role they played in amending labour legislations, and in advocating and protecting the interests of their member.[1]However, there is not much literature on trade unions as sites of capital accumulation. By being owners of shares and properties, labour federations are accumulating much capital, and are becoming key players in the South African and Namibian economies. This chapter is divided into four sections. The first section gives a brief rationale as to why the chapter focuses on South Africa and Namibia, the second section give an overview of both the COSATU and the NUNW, the third section gives a critical reflection and analyses of how the COSATU and the NUNW accumulate capital and its impact, and the fourth section is the conclusion.

WHY THE FOCUS ON SOUTH AFRICA AND NAMIBIA?

In both South Africa and Namibia, fundamental socio-economic changes took place towards the end of the twentieth century through mediated and controlled decolonization processes by the previously settler-dominated societies.[2] Briefly, South Africa's and Namibia's independence and democracy was the result of negotiated settlements. Both countries promoted socio-economic policies of compromise. This was a consequence of much pressure being exerted by the international community on both the colonial powers and the liberation movements, the ANC and the SWAPO, respectively. In so doing, the ANC and the SWAPO found themselves inevitably engaged in compromises, in that, they both formally ascended to power, but they did so without securing adequate control over wide swathes of society and the economy.[3] South Africa and Namibia have moved progressively towards economic liberalization, and their states have been reengineered in favour of democratic and decentralized participation.[4] Their neoliberal policies have made little progress in solving both countries' economic problems. Inequality in Namibia is too high, and it can be traced back from the colonial period to the neoliberal policy pursued by the black majority government after independence.[5] The same applies to South Africa where the levels of poverty and inequality are too high.[6]

As a result, the structural legacy of settler colonialism remained alive. Consequently, their projects of effective social and economic transformation were always going to be a long drawn out processes. The same applies to profound changes to political culture towards the consolidation of democracy in both countries. Apart from the structural legacy of settler colonialism, vested interests have been re-established, and originally formulated goals of social transformation have been either compromised or even totally abandoned in favour of the interests of the new black elite, rooted mainly in the sphere of a new nationalism and definition of power.[7] Both the COSATU and the NUNW are chosen because they have been actively involved in the struggle for liberation.

COSATU AND NUNW: AN OVERVIEW

The COSATU is the main union federation in South Africa. It was formed in 1985 as a result of a merger of the early political 'congress' unionism of the South African Congress of Trade Unions (SACTU), 'workerism' of the Federation of South African Trade Unions (FOSATU) and numerous independent trade unions.[8] The federation formally allied to the African National Congress (ANC) in the 1990s. The COSATU developed into a socio-political trade union federation. The federation's lobby for working-class interests was defined broadly as the fight against apartheid.

The federation worked for political and economic rights through networks and partnerships with community organizations, churches and other civil formations that were against apartheid.[9] The federation's strategy was mass mobilization and international sanctions. The main aim of the COSATU was and it is still a non-racial democracy with strong public participation.[10] During its early years, within formation, the COSATU had a membership base of approximately 500,000, and the number rose to 1.26 million in 1991. In 2014, COSATU's membership was around 1,875,238.[11] The COSATU is still the biggest trade union federation in South Africa. Table 1.1 shows COSATU affiliated unions and membership figures in 2014.

The NUNW had two phases of establishment. It was first founded by the SWAPO in April 1970 in Dar es Salaam, Tanzania. It contributed to the SWAPO Youth League's organization and mobilization of the great contract workers' strike of 1971 and 1972, respectively.[12] It disappeared from the workers' and political struggle scene for a few years, but re-emerged in 1978 as a general union organizing mine workers. Secondly, the NUNW existed in exile as the trade union wing of the SWAPO.

Table 1.1. COSATU affiliated unions with estimated membership in 2014

Unions	*Membership*
Chemical, Energy, Paper, Printing, Wood and Allied Workers' Union (CEPPWAWU)	80,331
Communications Workers' Union (CWU)	22,007
Democratic Nursing Union of South Africa (DENOSA)	81,319
Food and Allied Workers' Union (FAWU)	127,000
National, Education, Health and Allied Workers' Union (NEHAWU)	277,317
National Union of Mineworkers (NUM)	270,649
Public and Allied Workers' Union of South Africa (PAWUSA)	13,745
Police and Prison Civil Rights Union (POPCRU)	149,339
South Africa Catering, Commercial and Allied Workers' Union (SACCAWU)	120,352
South African Clothing and Textile workers union (SACTWU)	85,000
South African Democratic Teachers' Union (SADTU)	25,3039
South African Football players' Union (SAFTU)	592
South African Medical Association (SAMA)	8166
South African Municipal Workers Union (SAMWU)	161,490
South African State and Allied workers' Union (SASAWU)	6099
The Finance Union, formerly the South African Society of Bank Officials (SASBO)	66,539
South African Transport and Allied Workers' Union (SATAWU)	152,254
Total	**1,875,238**

Source: Ashman (2015), 50–51.

In 1989, these two, the internal and external wings, merged to form a strong federation for SWAPO. Both, exile and internal members were integrated into the federation's new structure, the NUNW. The NUNW is the World Federation of Trade Union (WFTU) affiliate. The WFTU offered the NUNW an opportunity to connect to socialist countries. The objectives of the NUNW are the protection of Namibian workers from exploitation; creation of unity and solidarity; preparation for involvement in the government of an independent Namibia; participation in the complete transformation of the existing social, economic and political conditions; fight against tribalism and ethnic particularism, as well as any forms of discrimination, and the total abolition of all mechanisms of alienation.[13]

The NUNW is still the largest trade union federation with a membership of about 84,900.[14] It is affiliated to SWAPO. Trade unions that are NUNW affiliates include the Namibian Food and Allied Workers Union (NFAWU), the Namibian National Teachers Union (NNTU), the Namibian Public Workers Union (NPWU), the Namibian Transport and Allied Workers Union (NTAWU), the Metal and Allied Namibian Workers Union (MANWU), and the Mineworkers Union of Namibia (MUN).[15] The NUNW has huge support in Namibia and it has played a leading role in ensuring SWAPO's national election victories since 1989. It is still influential in Namibian politics. Table 1.2 shows the NUNW affiliate unions and membership figures.

The history of both the COSATU and the NUNW is very similar in the sense that they both played prominent roles during the liberation struggles in their respective countries. They were key federations in terms of mobilizing the majority of the black populations against colonial and apartheid rule.[16] Both federations linked workplace struggles with the broader struggle for political independence and they both formed connections with other civil organizations such as students and women organizations. These federations

Table 1.2. The NUNW affiliated unions with the estimated membership in 2017

Unions	*Membership*
Metal and Allied Namibia Workers Union (MANWU)	8,000
Mineworkers Union of Namibia (MUN)	8,000
Namibia Financial Institutions Union (NAFINU)	4,500
Namibia Food and Allied Workers Union (NAFAU)	12,000
Namibia National Teachers Union (NANTU)	16,000
Namibia Public Workers Union (NAPWU)	25,000
Namibia Transport and Allied Workers Union (NATAU)	4,000
Namibia Music Industry Union (NAMIU)	400
Namibia Farm Workers Union (NAFWU)	7,000
Total	**84,900**

Source: Jauch (2018), 23.

understood their roles as that of social movements meant to address workers' issues and issues affecting the broader society.[17] Discrimination and exploitation at the workplace was connected to the broader struggles against racial and political oppression.[18] As such, these federations have been key players in the democratization process in South Africa and Namibia.

The NUNW has also played a key role in amending the new Labor Act of Namibia in order to ensure that Namibian workers are protected. The 1992 Labor Act constituted an important improvement compared to the then prevailing colonial and apartheid labour laws. The 1992 Act has given all workers in Namibia, especially farm, domestic and public service workers' rights and protection. The act promoted collective bargaining and workers' and trade union's rights, and it set out the procedures for legal strikes and provided protection to unfair labour practices.[19] However, the act did not meet all the NUNW's demands such as the provision of minimum wages as promised by SWAPO during its election campaign in 1989. The act did not guarantee paid maternity leave, and also did not provide for a forty hours working week and twenty-one days annual leave for Namibian workers.

The same applies to the COSATU which was influential in the development of the Labor Relation Act of 1995.[20] The act promotes freedom of association, organizational rights as well as workers' rights and protection. However, in the post-colonial and post-apartheid periods, both the NUNW and COSATU's attempt at influencing broader economic policies in favour of the poor and the working class have been difficult, especially in the face of neoliberal policies adopted by the ANC and the SWAPO.[21] In the same vein, South Africa and Namibia are a clear example of what the late Antonio Gramsci, an Italian Marxist philosopher and politician, called 'Bourgeois hegemony' where the interests of the poor and working class are taken less care of, and the interests of business are represented as constituting the national interests, and are accepted by the working classes and significant section of the trade union movements.

One of the major aspects of the relationship between the union federations and liberation political parties has been the movement of both the COSATU and the NUNW leadership to better remunerated and often high-profile positions in the corporate sectors, government departments, politics (mainly the ruling parties ANC and SWAPO) and junior- and middle-management positions in different companies.[22] For instance, in Namibia, NUNW leaders who left the federation for government include Ben Ulenga and Ya Otto who were elected to the constituent assembly in 1989. Three other NUNW top leaders who left the federation include Bernhardt Esau, Walter Kemba and John Shactonhodi for SWAPO's seats in the National Assembly.[23] In South Africa, three former general secretaries of the National Union of Mineworkers (NUM) which is affiliated to the COSATU have served or still serve in government. These former NUM general secretaries include the current president of South Africa, Cyril Ramaphosa, Gwede Mantashe, current minister of mineral resources and Kgalema Motlanthe who served as the deputy president and then as the third president of South Africa between 25 September 2008 and 9 May 2009, following the removal of the previous incumbent, Thabo Mbeki.[24]

However, there have been internal battles within the NUNW and the COSATU, which have raised concerns about these federations' effectiveness. For example, in Namibia, the battle between the NUNW and the Namibian government over the government Institution Pension Fund scandal in 2010–2011 created a new power struggle among union leaders and affiliates.[25] Leadership battles of the COSATU's resources have also created power struggles among union leaders.[26] Conflicts between the Namibian government and the NUNW have also caused leadership disagreement.

COSATU AND NUNW AS SITES OF CAPITAL ACCUMULATION

Capital Accumulation: What Does It Mean?

Capital accumulation refers to an increase in assets from investment or profit. It is a product of capital investment in different businesses and has to do with an increase in returns from investment. Companies, organizations and individuals can accumulate capital in different ways, some of which include investment purchases and investment savings. Returns from an investment can also lead to capital accumulation, specifically from occurrences such as investment profits, rent, interests or capital gains.[27]

The COSATU and the NUNW began the process of capital accumulation when they started to build their financial muscle through the collection of union membership fees and through the establishment of workers' provident funds. Union membership fees are the basic fees that workers, who belong to a particular union, pay on a monthly basis in order to obtain full representation, as well as full rights of membership such as the right to participate in voting during union elections and collective bargaining sessions. Whether or not workers who join a particular union utilize the services of the union, they are often compelled to pay membership fees every month. In most cases, unions deduct union membership fees directly from the worker's salary.

Membership fees differ from job categories and the sectors in which the unions organize workers. A worker's provident fund is the worker's managed retirement savings. Workers contribute a portion of their salary to a provident fund. In the same vein, trade unions have been very effective and busy investing the money collected from their members through the formation of companies called investment companies, through buying shares in different sectors of the South African economy. Consequently, unions have been more successful in accumulating capital. The next section gives a clear explanation of the processes of capital accumulation by the COSATU and the NUNW.

Processes of Capital Accumulation by the COSATU and the NUNW

The COSATU and the NUNW are no longer confined to their mandates of being revolutionary labour movements that lobby for workers' rights and protection. They have become sites of capital accumulation through investing in companies, owning shares, properties and companies, as well as administrators of workers' provident funds.[28] Briefly, unions have become extensively involved in business, accumulating as much capital as possible.[29] The move into business and the accumulation of capital started when trade unions established so-called investment arms or investment companies of unions.

The main reason for the establishing of investment companies by South African trade unions is to improve the lives of union members and their dependents through benefits such as funeral schemes, pension funds and education bursaries for workers and their children. Trade unions, affiliated to the COSATU, argue that originally the establishment of trade union investment companies was to address the development needs of union members. Unions state that as organizations for workers, they are not just looking for their members while working but to be able to look after their members after they are unemployed. To betray workers even more, unions invest in companies where they organize workers, making it far too difficult for union leaders to act fairly in the best interest of their members.[30] As for the NUNW, the federation's main reason for the move into business is that the federation wants to uplift workers by adding real value to their lives while affecting the Namibian economy.[31]

As for the COSATU, the federation started to accumulate capital when it set up an investment company called Kopano Ke Matla Investment Company (KKMIC). KKMIC Pty Ltd. is entirely owned by the Kopano Ke Matla Trust. 'Kopano Ke Matla' simply translates to mean 'Unity is power'. The Company was established in 1996 and the COSATU is the main beneficiary. KKMIC has over the years invested in the following economic sectors, namely, petroleum, media, mining beneficiation and extraction, financial services, social service benefits, infrastructure development and construction with different partner companies.

The KKMIC has subsidiary companies that focus on investing in specific targeted strategic areas with the aim to not only own shares in them but also participate in the value chain to extract as much value from investee companies.[32] The KKMIC has eleven subsidiary companies operating in different sectors. These subsidiary companies are as follows: KKM Review Publishing, iChoice, Sekunjalo Independent Media, Kopano Resources, KKM Property Development (Pty) Ltd. (worth R57.5 million), infrastructure joint venture, Tswelopele Minerals & Energy/Sasol, Kopano NMDC Minerals, Business Venture Investment 1677, and Consulate Property (Pty) Ltd. The KKMIC owns 3% of Raubex, the construction company tasked to improve the R21 freeway, which introduced e-tolls. The R21 freeway is situated in Kempton Park, Gauteng province. KKMIC's Raubex shares have a market value of R6.7 million.[33]

The NUNW started to accumulate capital when it established a business arm in 2007, called the Labor Investment Holdings (LIH), with the aim of creating wealth and generating opportunities and benefits for the NUNW and its affiliates. The NUNW owns 44% shares in a company called MobiPay. The LIH chief executive officer (CEO), Cleophas Mutjavikua, served as the chair of the MobiPay board. MobiPay is a service provider in Namibia and other African countries for mobile wallets, card issuing and acquiring, cardless monetary transactions as well as value-added services (VASs). MobiPay Company was founded in 2009 and was licensed by the Bank of Namibia in 2010 as a payment instrument issuer. MobiPay's main clients include retailers, financial institutions, banks and corporates. In addition, LIH has shares in various industries – these industries include mining and financial service companies, Epango Fishing Company, Bidvest, Craft Holdings and Avbob (Funeral Service Company).[34]

Most union officials sit on boards of companies for which they are paid attendance fees and benefits. This has brought about a layer of trade union bureaucrats whose material standards of living are significantly higher than those of the average trade union member, and who have entered companies' boards of directors, the latter as part of an unclear trade union investment strategy. This has contributed to the creation of a trade union bureaucracy that has a material interest in limiting the class struggle for reforms within capitalism. These union officials regard the interests of labour and capital as reconcilable and thus gradually spend less time on bargaining, so separating themselves from the workers they represent.

As trade union leaders entered and continue to enter company boards as part of a poorly defined union investment strategy, their views and interests increasingly converge with those of the businesses they have invested in. Furthermore, some trade union leaders are now occupying management positions in both public and private sectors, which contradicts the principle of worker control within unions. These developments point to a lack of clarity regarding the working-class base of the trade unions and whose interests they are meant to serve.

The trade union activities of the 1980s and 1990s that organized workers under extremely severe conditions, including threats to their lives, are gradually being substituted by union leaders who regard trade unionism as a career option or as a facilitator to greener pastures in the private sector, and as a site of capital accumulation. The notions of worker democracy, worker control and social transformation that emerged in the 1980s were not developed into coherent concepts within the labour movement and have been gradually substituted by more hierarchical and bureaucratic forms of organization in the democratic context.

CONCLUSION

Major changes in the South African and Namibian economies have taken place, and trade union federations are in the mix as investors and shareholders. The economies are no longer controlled by a single class – but by different classes united at both a structural level, through common interests, and interdependence. The union federations themselves are the big elephants in the economic room acting as sites of capital accumulation.

Investment unionism has opened a very fertile ground for corruption, maladministration, factionalism, jostling for posts, and self-serving interests. Workers' funds are exploited for the benefit of a few union officials. Workers do not trust their unions, and are running out of patience. These are signs that trade unions are becoming dysfunctional organizations. The most disturbing revelation is that it seems that the major businesses and union leaders jostling for positions that will allow them access to unions' investments and workers' funds gradually capture these unions. Trade union federations are the organizations that are supposed to be dealing with workplace issues, representing and taking care of their members' funds, and preventing disrepute and exploitation. Yet, it is the very same federations that are complicit in this degradation.

After more than twenty years of democratic functioning, the South African and Namibian trade union federations find themselves in deep crisis. Workers have realized that the changes after independence did not really lead to the expected socio-economic transformation. There are signs that trade union federations have lost their vision, and are struggling to develop strategies around how to play meaningful roles in the process of social change. Deep divisions within unions worsen this dilemma. These divisions undermine the power of trade union federations. Presently, many trade unions are unable to work together, and are unable to provide workers with strong organizational bases needed to advance a working class agenda.

Who will provide oversight for trade union federations? Who will regulate the COSATU and the NUNW in business? These are rather difficult questions to answer because now no one is able to look into the functionality of unions and whether they actually can or do accomplish what they are mandated to do. One of the biggest issues facing trade unions is the lack of accountability. In all of this, it is important to remember who is most affected by this widespread ineptitude and corruption in the labour movements. The poor, mostly black workers of South Africa and Namibia are condemned to lives of poverty and unemployment. That is the real tragedy here. Whether the formation of new breakaway unions will in itself solve workers' issues and the consequent problem of the fragmentation of trade unions remains to be seen.

NOTES

1. Godfrey Kanyenze, Timothy Kondo, and Jos Martens, *The Search for Sustainable Human Development in Southern Africa* (Harare: Zimbabwe, 2006), 159.
2. Henning Melber, *Limits to Liberation in Southern Africa: The Unfinished Business of Democratic Consolidation* (Cape Town: HSRC Press, 2003), 134.
3. Ibid., 134.
4. Herbert Jauch, 'Labor in Namibia: Important Lessons for South Africa', *South African Labor Bulletin* 26, no. 1 (2002): 22–35.
5. Herbert Jauch and Ellison Tjirera, 'The Need for Developmental State Intervention in Namibia', in *Towards Democratic Developmental State in Southern Africa*, eds. Godfrey Kanyenze, Jauch Herbert, Alice D. Kanengoni, Masego Madzwamuse and Deprose Muchena (Harare: Weaver Press, 2016), 135.
6. Thabileng Mothabi, 'The Need for Developmental State Intervention in South Africa', in *Towards Democratic Developmental State in Southern Africa*, eds. Godfrey Kanyenze, Jauch Herbert, Alice D. Kanengoni, Masego Madzwamuse and Deprose Muchena (Harare: Weaver Press, 2016), 91.
7. Ndeutala Hishongwa, *The Contract Labor System and Its Effects on Family and Social Life in Namibia: A Historical Perspective* (Windhoek: Gamsberg Macmillan, 1992), 14–15.
8. Sakhela Buhlungu, 'South Africa: The Decline of Labor Studies and the Democratic Transition', *Work and Organization* 36, no. 2 (2009): 145–61.
9. Pauline Dibben, 'Industrial Relations and Employment Security in South Africa: The Possibilities of Social Justice Unionism', in *Industrial Relations in South Africa*, eds. Chris Brewster and Geoffrey Wood (New York: Palgrave Macmillan, 2007), 113.
10. Elizabeth Lawrence, 'Trade Unions', in *Democracy and Participation: Popular Protest and New Social Movements*, eds. Malcolm J. Todd and Gary Taylor (London: Merlin Press, 2004), 135.

11. Ashman Sam, 'The Social Crisis of Labor and the Crisis of Labor Politics in South Africa', *Revue Tiers Monde* 4, no. 224 (2015): 47–65.

12. Herbert Jauch, 'Namibia's Labor Movement: Prospects and Challenges for 2017 and Beyond', *Pambazuka*, last modified 6 December 2007: https://www.pambazuka.org/democracy-governance/namibia%E2%80%99s-labour-movement-peospects-and-challenges-2017-and-beyond.

13. Henning Melber, 'The National Union of Namibian Workers: Background and Formation', *The Journal of Modern African Studies* 21, no. 1 (1983): 151–8.

14. Herbert Jauch, 'Namibia's Trade Union Movement: An Overview: History, Challenges and Achievements', FES, 2018, 23. https://cms.my.na › p1c5t3p3tcth2ap61nplhsv1jjs4.

15. Ibid., 23.

16. Godfrey Kanyenze, Timothy Kondo and Jos Martens, 'The Search or Sustainable', 159.

17. Herbert Jauch, 'Serving Workers or Serving the Party?' in *Trade Unions and Party Politics*, eds. Bjrn Beckman, Sakhela Buhlungu and Lloyd Sachikonye (Cape Town: HSRC Press, 2010), 171.

18. Ibid., 171.

19. Ibid., 181.

20. Dibben, *Industrial Relations*, 113.

21. International Labor Research and Information Group (ILRIG), *An Alternative View of Privatization* (Woodstock: Cape Town, 1999), 25–27.

22. Gretchen Bauer, 'Nothing to Lose but Their Subordinate to the State? Trade Unions in Namibia Fifteen Years after Independence', in *Trade Unions and the Coming of Democracy in Africa*, ed. Jon Kraus (New York: Palgrave Macmillan, 2007), 243.

23. Ibid., 243.

24. Andries Bezuidenhout, 'Labor beyond Cosatu, Other Federations and Independent Unions', in *Labor beyond Cosatu: Mapping the Rupture in South Africa's Political Landscape*, eds. Andries Bezuidenhout and Malehoko Tshoaedi (Johannesburg: Wits University Press, 2017).

25. John J. Grotpeter, William A. Lindeke and Victor L. Tonchi, *Historical Dictionary of Namibia* (London: The Scarecrow Press, 2012), 293.

26. Ibid., 293.

27. Dennis Brown Ebuware and Anuli Regina Ogbuagu, 'Capital Accumulation and Economic Growth in Nigeria "Endogenous growth approach"', *Journal of Economic and Finance* 26, no. 6 (2015): 49–69.

28. Matuma Letsoalo, Qaanitah Hunter and Mmanaledi Mataboge, '"Business Unionism" the Cause of Cosatu's Factional Battles', *Mail & Guardian*, 19 July 2015. https://mg.co.za/article/2015-07-09-business-unionism-the-cause-of-cosatus-factional-battles.

29. Jerry Mmanoko Mathekga, 'Fighting the Battles of the Mineworkers: The Emergence of the Association of Mineworkers and Construction Union (AMCU)', *South African Journal of Labor Relations* 39, no. 2 (2015): 190–204.

30. Jeremy Seekings and Nicoli Nattrass, 'Trade Unions, the State and 'Casino Capitalism' in South Africa's Clothing Industry', *Review of African Political Economy*, 43, no. 147 (2016): 89–106.

31. Theresia Tjihenuna, 'Investments Plans Proves Fruitful for Nam Workers', *Prime Focus Magazine*, April 2013.

32. Leonard Gentle, '"What about the Workers?" The Demise of Cosatu and the Emergence of the New Movement', *Review of African Political Economy* 46, no. 146 (2015): 666–77.

33. Letsoalo, Hunter and Mataboge, 'Business Unionism'.

34. Tjihenuna, 'Investments Plans Proves Fruitful for Nam Workers'.

BIBLIOGRAPHY

Bauer, Gretchen. 'Nothing to Lose but Their Subordinate to the State? Trade Unions in Namibia Fifteen Years after Independence'. In *Trade Unions and the Coming of Democracy in Africa*, edited by Jon Kraus. New York: Palgrave Macmillan, 2007.

Bezuidenhout, Andries. 'Labor beyond COSATU, Other Federations and Independent Unions'. In *Labor beyond COSATU: Mapping the Rupture in South Africa's Political Landscape*, edited by Andries Bezuidenhout and Malehoko Tshoaedi. Johannesburg: Wits University Press, 2017.

Buhlungu, Sakhela. 'South Africa: The Decline of Labor Studies and the Democratic Transition'. *Work and Organization* 36, no. 2 (2009): 145–61.

Dibben, Pauline. 'Industrial Relations and Employment Security in South Africa: The Possibilities of Social Justice Unionism'. In *Industrial Relations in South Africa*, edited by Chris Brewster and Geoffrey Wood. New York: Palgrave Macmillan, 2007.

Ebuware, Dennis and Regina Ogbuagu. 'Capital Accumulation and Economic Growth in Nigeria "Endogenous Growth Approach"'. *Journal of Economic and Finance* 26, no. 6 (2015): 49–69.

Gentle, Leonard. '"What about the Workers?" The Demise of COSATU and the Emergence of the New Movement'. *Review of African Political Economy* 46, no. 146 (2015): 666–77.

Grotpeter, John, William Lindeke and Victor Tonchi. *Historical Dictionary of Namibia*. London: The Scarecrow Press, 2012.

Hishongwa, Ndeutala. *The Contract Labor System and Its Effects on Family and Social Life in Namibia: A Historical Perspective*. Windhoek: Gamsberg Macmillan, 1992.

International Labor Research and Information Group (ILRIG). *An Alternative View of Privatization*. Cape Town: Woodstock, 1999.

Jauch, Herbert. 'Labor in Namibia: Important Lessons for South Africa'. *South African Labor Bulletin* 26, no. 1 (2002): 22–35.

Jauch, Herbert. 'Serving Workers or Serving the Party?' In *Trade Unions and Party Politics*, edited by Bjrn Beckman, Sakhela Buhlungu and Lloyd Sachikonye. Cape Town: HSRC Press, 2010.

Jauch, Herbert. 'Namibia's Labor Movement: Prospects and Challenges for 2017 and Beyond'. *Pambazuka*, last modified 6 December 2007: https://www.pambazuka.org/democracy-governance/namibia%E2%80%99s-labour-movement-peospects-and-challenges-2017-and-beyond.

Jauch, Herbert. 'Namibia's Trade Union Movement: An Overview, History, Challenges and Achievements'. FES, 2018, 23. https://cms.my.na › p1c5t3p3tcth2ap61nplhsv1jjs4.

Kanyenze, Godfrey, Timothy Kondo and Jos Martens. *The Search for Sustainable Human Development in Southern Africa*. Harare: Zimbabwe, 2006.

Lawrence, Elizabeth. 'Trade Unions'. In *Democracy and Participation: Popular Protest and New Social Movements*, edited by Malcolm Todd and Gary Taylor. London: Merlin Press, 2004.

Letsoalo, Matuma, Qaanitah Hunter and Mmanaledi mataboge. 'Business Unionism: The Cause of Cosatu's Factional Battles'. *Mail & Guardian*, 19 July 2015. https://mg.co.za/article/2015-07-09-business-unionism-the-cause-of-cosatus-factional-battles.

Mathekga, Jerry. 'Fighting the Battles of the Mineworkers: The Emergence of the Association of Mineworkers and Construction Union (AMCU)'. *South African Journal of Labor Relations* 39, no. 2 (2015): 190–204.

Melber, Henning. 'The National Union of Namibian Workers: Background and Formation'. *The Journal of Modern African Studies* 21, no. 1 (1983): 151–58.

Melber, Henning. *Limits to Liberation in Southern Africa: The Unfinished Business of Democratic Consolidation*. Cape Town: HSRC Press, 2003.

Mothabi, Thabileng. 'The Need for Developmental State Intervention in South Africa'. In *Towards Democratic Developmental State in Southern Africa*, edited by Godfrey Kanyenze, Jauch Herbert, Alice D. Kanengoni, Masego Madzwamuse and Deprose Muchena. Harare: Weaver Press, 2016.

Chapter 2

Nigerian Education, Industry and Bureaucracy: The Counsellor's Perspective

Ngozi Joy Maduka

INTRODUCTION

The first assumption of this chapter is that there is a tripartite and close relationship between a nation's educational system, industry and bureaucracy (government/leadership). The second assumption is that guidance counsellors have vital roles to play in bringing about a synergy between a nation's education industry and bureaucracy. Indeed, no nation can develop its economic and industrial sectors, technology and governance beyond what its educational system can offer. By extension, leadership and governance of a nation will succeed or fail depending on the quality of its formal and informal education. For example, most African countries including Nigeria are facing many problems of poor infrastructure, lack of industrialization, unemployment, underemployment, hunger, high rate of mortality, diseases, poverty and other developmental challenges partly as a result of the quality of education in these countries.

One can argue that guidance counsellors are in a good position to perceive, analyse and proffer positive suggestions/strategies that can enhance the quality of education in these countries. This is because of the counsellors' training, orientation, professional ethics and specializations as human or social engineers, behaviour modification strategists and bridge builders in human relationships. Against the aforementioned background, this chapter explores dynamics of Nigeria's educational system and its relationship to industry and bureaucracy. The chapter proffers recommendations on how best to enhance the educational system to ensure it is able to train leaders with the requisite skills and motivation to work for the development of country.

CONCEPT OF BUREAUCRACY

The term 'bureaucracy' in the popular mind has tended to be a pejorative term but equated with massive organizational structures through which faceless bureaucrats regulate the lives and control the thought processes of an unwitting populace. In today's society especially in Nigeria, bureaucracy has become an indispensable tool of governance. Despite its shortfall, most developed democracies all over the world insist on bureaucracy.[1]

The rules that regulate the functioning of organizations make bureaucracy a basic characteristic of most enterprises whether in the public or in the private sectors. For bureaucracy to emerge within an organization, certain elements must be developed. The first element or ingredient of bureaucracy is graded authority, a strict system of rank of office and hierarchy.[2] The second is a carefully maintained system of written records which document the functions, place and status of persons at various bureaucratic levels. The third element is the presence of a system of employment and advancement based on merit and performance rather than on the mere personal whims of a superior. These three elements lend themselves particularly well to advanced capitalist economies as well as to stable democratic states. In other words, state bureaucracy can be described as institutionalized structures through which activities of government are realized in the most efficient manner.

In Nigeria, bureaucracy is used synonymous with state civil service and public service or administration. State bureaucracy is known to be part and parcel of the executive branch of government. This means that they are institutions charged with the responsibility of formulating and implementing policies and programmes of the government. In other words, it is the duty of political executive to determine and direct the focus of state policies while the state or civil service is the administrative machinery through which the activities of government are realized. It is thus not an overstatement to claim that bureaucracy as typified by civil service is about the most significant single institution that affects the lives of the nation's citizenry.

There are two main contending views on bureaucracy. First, bureaucracy is viewed as a large-scale, complex, hierarchical and specialized organization designed to attain rational objectives in the most efficient and effective manner.[3] The goals and objectives are expected to be attained through formalism and impersonality in the application of rules and regulations in the management of organizations, including hierarchy, and division of labour anchored on specialization. It also involves a policy of promotion and recruitment based on merit. In addition to impersonality in the conduct of official duties, security of tenure and strict observance of rules and regulations are all common features.

The second school of thought sees bureaucracy as barely an instrument of oppression, exploitation and damnation in the hand of dominant class who control and manipulate the state and its apparatus.[4] More specifically, bureaucracy is conceived as instrument usually employed by the ruling class to accumulate wealth and maintain their domination and control of the state. According to this view, the principal driving force of bureaucracy is usually concealed by both the dominant class and the bureaucrats as efforts are made constantly and continuously to project bureaucracy as a neutral and as an instrument that work for the interest of the citizens. According to this view, the future and interest of bureaucracy are closely inter-linked with those of the ruling class and the state political leadership.

The Nigerian Constitution 1999 which is currently in place has made bureaucracy mandatory for all institutions of governance as outlined in chapter 5 under the title – the executive part 1(0) and part 2(c). This has provided for bureaucracies at both federal and state levels of government, including other public institutions like national and state assemblies, the judiciary, the police, armed forces, paramilitary agencies, parastatals, extra-ministerial departments and agencies (including social services), commercially-oriented agencies, educational institutions and research institutions, among others. The constitution has conferred on the executive leadership with enormous powers that can be misused and manipulated in the guise of fair application of the laws of the land.[5]

CONCEPT OF EDUCATION

Education is seen as the delivery of knowledge, skills and information from teachers to students.[6] While the aforementioned metaphor – education as a delivery system – sounds reasonable, it misses a very important component of true education. How the delivery of knowledge can be achieved is the root problem in mainstream education in Nigeria and across several other African states. This conception of education contributes to harming students by driving policy makers to insist on accounting for the 'units' of information that students demonstrate knowledge on tests.

Proper definition of education is complicated by the fact that there is no clear consensus about what is important about being educated. Some people believe that the importance of education lies in future job prospects, to some, it is the quality of citizenship and yet others just want literacy, critical thinking or creativity. Above all the differences of opinion, one may argue that true education is someone who is fully guided to exhibit and understand his or her inner potentials through accurate perception, thinking and contribution to national goals without being forced to do so.

The structure of educational institutions determines educational productivity. Educational outputs must be enduring, with ideas and morals to the advantage of teachers and students. Education is viewed as leading in bringing moral qualities in humans and in the suppression of the animal qualities that can also be exhibited by humans. As a counsellor, the major goal of education should be geared towards holistic preparation of the students for useful living within the society. High quality education must offer diverse curricula to carter for differences in talent, aptitude, opportunities and roles. No curriculum should be made to feel inferior or rejected.[7]

CONCEPT OF INDUSTRY

An industry is defined as a basic category of business activity. It is sometimes used to describe a very precise business activity which is related to the raising, producing, processing or manufacturing of products. The product can be consumer goods or producer goods. The consumer goods are finally used by the consumers for instance grains, textiles, cosmetics and cars, among others. Whereas, the producer products are goods used by the manufacturers to produce other goods example tools, equipment and machinery, among others. Furthermore, industry is seen as the manufacturing or technically productive enterprises in a particular field, country region or economy.[8] A single industry is often named after its principal product. For statistical purpose, industries are categorized generally according to a uniformed classification codes such as Standard Industry Classification (SIC).[9] In simple term, industry can be any general business activity or commercial enterprise that can be isolated by others. An industry can be seen to have a purpose and structure aimed at making profit and satisfying its teaming customers and therefore not just anybody can be hired to manage such an enterprise.

Governments and private individuals engage extensively in business or industrial enterprises or activities. In many cases, the government primarily dictates the tune and directs the affairs through policies, laws and so forth for the survival of industries in their countries. One of these is the state infrastructures including roads, energy, transport, uniform enforcement of standards and quality assurance to conform to international practices.

Categories of industries are as follows:

1. Primary Industry: Nature oriented and require very little human effort for example agriculture, farming, fishery, forestry and horticulture, among others.
2. Genetic Industry: Reproduction and multiplication of certain species of plant and animals with the aim of earning profit from the sale example cattle rearing, nurseries, poultry and cattle breeding.

3. Extractive Industry: Concerns with drawing out goods from the soil, air, water. Most products of extractive industries are in raw form and used by manufacturing and constructive industries for producing finished products, for example, mining, coal mineral, oil, iron ore, timber and rubber from forest.
4. Manufacturing Industry: This type of industry is involved in transforming raw materials into finished products with the help of machine and manpower. The finished products can either be consumer goods or producer goods, for instance, chemicals, sugar, textile, and paper, among others.
5. Construction Industry: Mainly engage in construction activities such as buildings, bridges, road, dams and canals. While other types of industries produce goods which can be sold at another place. Goods of construction industries are erected used at one place.
6. Service Industry: The modern trend of economic development of nations has brought into focus the service industry which includes hotel industry, tourism industry, and entertainment industry, among others.[10]

It can be inferred that industries are very complex and require to be developed and managed to maximize their economic potential. The industrial sector of any nation confers on it the level of economic growth and development. All levels of entrepreneurs are critically linked to their nation's industrial growth.

CONCEPT OF COUNSELLING

The complex/busy nature of the world today has brought with it stress and tension which have bottled up people with experiences that they find difficult to cope with. To solve these problems, they adopt talking therapy by confiding on people around them. These may include but not exclusively: family members, trusted neighbours, friends, priests and family doctors. Often the piece of advice from these people may not be sufficient. Many people are ashamed of sharing their problems for several reasons and this is where professional counsellors come in as a useful option. The counsellor has been referred to by many writers as the helper, facilitator, therapist and mind mender, among others. Characteristics of a professional counsellor include sociable, intelligence, interested in people, enterprising, sincere, stable, objective, calm, broad minded and so forth.[11] Apart from the above characteristics, a counsellor must be a trained personnel in the field of counselling. Professional counselling are services sought by people in distress or some degree of confusion who wish to discuss and resolve their problems in relationship which is more disciplined and confidential than friendship and kinsmen. Counselling stimulates an individual to achieve the following:

- Evaluate himself and his opportunities
- Make feasible choice in the light of his unique characteristics and opportunities
- Accepts responsibilities for his choice
- Initiate a course of action consonant with his choice so that he or she could become more effective and actualized in his society.[12]

Counselling is defined as a learning process or developmental process possibly aimed at achieving a positive change in behaviour.[13] It is also a service available to student to facilitate his or her academic success in school, to help him or her better understand his or her strength and limitation, to identify his or her interests, to aid his or her planning for attaining realistic goals.[14] In furtherance, counselling is an education process that helps individuals to have better understanding for themselves and their environment in other to have the opportunity of normal or better human growth and development.[15]

UNESCO further emphasized that counselling focuses on prevention and early intervention as ways of forestalling more serious problems that will develop if not attended to. It is therefore in controvertible that counsellors are heavily implicated in the growth of society through active promotion of their wellness and healthy lifestyle. A society so well built up is likely to have a very low percentage of deviance and high percentage of well-developed and disciplined individuals that anchor their thoughts on positivity such as adaptive behaviours, good norms, discipline, peace, growth and development of nationhood among others.

A combination of 'guidance' and 'counselling' package propel individuals to higher heights of acceptability, stability and growth since its principle emphasizes on the worth and dignity of man. In effect, guidance and counselling should be work seen as helping tool for behaviour modification of individuals for the betterment the society.

RELATIONSHIP BETWEEN EDUCATION, INDUSTRY AND BUREAUCRACY

The concepts of education, industry and bureaucracy have been outlined. There is no doubt all of them are inter-linked, connected and largely dependent on each other. Their combined effects affect any national development and economic growth. The leadership of nations need not underrate their contributions in both developing and developed economy. Bureaucracy has remained the centre point of governance in many nations of Africa including

Nigeria. This has been adopted into all sectors of the economy for running all business both private and public. The industrial sector which is the economic hub of any nation has focus on economic outcome as main objective.

The goals of any enterprise include but not limited to:

- efficiency Maximization;
- optimal use of employees to perform set duties;
- innovations to follow evolution in modern technological trend;
- profitable, cost friendly and quality product;
- competitiveness in global market;
- promotion of merit to ensure enterprise mandate and goals are achieved; and
- trainings to improve on consumer products.

Education is seen as an institution of learning and research to develop and remodel the institution of bureaucracy according to national interest economic growth and productivity. The primary expectations of educational institutions are not far from those in industrial sectors viz maximization of efficiency, optimal duty performance, innovations in teaching and research, human capacity building and professionalism, innovations in technological trends for specialization and trainability of its products for end users.

Education is a right and a foundation for a sustainable social and economic development. Poverty cannot be alleviated without education. In developing countries such as Nigeria, quality education remains the only instrument needed to manage sustainable societies; efforts on installing the needed institutional structures remains the only hope for emancipation of poverty, strife and diseases.

Education is a 'process, a product and a discipline'. As a product, it refers to change whether overt or covert, implicit or explicit, which education is expected to bring about. The product of education is the educated man, who in the African context is one 'who shows evidence of a well-integrated personality; he is economically efficient, socially and publicly competent, morally acceptable and intellectually and culturally sophisticated'. If this quality must be ascribed to an educated man and just as industrial products must be consumer or producer friendly, educational institutions like industries cannot be managed by mediocre or misfits.

HISTORICAL REVIEW OF EDUCATION, INDUSTRY AND BUREAUCRACY

History of education dates back to millions of years and began to be discussed at the end of 1770. Education as a science cannot be separated from the traditions that existed before. Adults train the young in their society in the knowledge and skills they need to master and eventually pass on. The depth and breadth of knowledge that could be passed soon increased exponentially. Formal education and schooling eventually followed. In almost all developed and developing countries, education is now compulsory to all at certain levels so that more people will receive formal education in the next thirty years than in all human history.[16]

Technology recently has improved access to education for people living in impoverished areas and developing countries. In Africa, the new partnership for Africa's development launched an 'e-school programme' to provide all 600,000 primary and high schools with computer equipment, learning materials and internet access within ten years.[17] In 2004, the Indian space agency Indian Space Research Organisation launched Edusat, a communication satellite providing access to educational materials that can reach more of the country's population at a greatly reduced cost. Today education and learning has been globalized to the extent that one can have easy access to class materials and lecture files. In this era of information communication technology (ICT), globalization of education has become even more simplified.

The term *bureaucracy* was invented by Monsieur de Gournay in 1845 and later developed by German sociologist.[18] He used bureaucracy to describe a rationalistic and efficient management of government organizations and industry. It is clearly seen in state administration, business education, science, military organizations and even religious groups. Not minding the criticisms, bureaucracy was defined as a model of carefulness, precision and effective administration.[19] The industrial revolution of the nineteenth century triggered evolution in the education and training process which produced relevant officers to effectively manage the size of industries and other business enterprises. It can be seen that education, bureaucracy and industries evolved side by side in time and space.

BY-PRODUCTS OF POOR-QUALITY EDUCATION IN AFRICA: INADEQUATE INDUSTRIALIZATION AND POOR GOVERNANCE IN NIGERIA

Nigeria is often referred as the giant of Africa owing its large population and economy. With approximately 186 million inhabitants, Nigeria is easily the most populous black nation. Moreover, Nigeria has the third-largest youth population in the world after India and China. It has over 500 different languages. In the past years, Nigeria has failed to use its human and natural resources to manage this large population, especially the youth and women. The vast untapped land has also received little or no attention in the areas of agriculture, mining and industry which are key areas of employment for the unemployed.

Tertiary education in Nigeria comprises universities, polytechnics, monotechnics, colleges of education and other specialized higher institutions of learning and is given after secondary education. The goals of tertiary education are as follows:

1. To contribute to national development through high level relevant manpower training
2. To develop and inculcate proper values of the survival of the individual and the society
3. To develop the intellectual capability of individuals to understand and appreciate their local and external environments
4. To acquire both physical and intellectual skills which will enable individuals to be self-reliant and useful members of the society
5. To promote and encourage scholarship and community service
6. To forge and cement national unity and
7. To promote national and international understanding and interaction[20]

These goals are being pursued through teaching, research and development, generation and dissemination of knowledge and maintenance of minimum education standard through appropriate agencies, among others. The policy stated that internal organization and administration of each institution shall be its responsibility. They are to select their students, appoint their staff, teach and select areas of research and determine the content of their courses as well as supplement government funding. In effect, institutions have every freedom to efficiently manage their affairs and nurture activities to effectively meet the needs and expectation of Nigeria as a nation. Today, Nigeria has over one hundred universities including federal, state and private. It was argued that universities are neither kindergarten schools, nor primary schools and there are limits to the rate at which you can create new universities without totally crippling the system as a whole.[21] Nigeria in particular and Africa in general long ago crossed these limits. The universities are now mere certification centres which have replaced the dissemination and reproduction of the unique kinds of knowledge traditionally purveyed by the universities.

The expansion may have been well intended, but the rapid expansion was unplanned, chaotic and opportunistic in creating undesirable cadres of teachers, lecturers and even professors that moved and are still moving into positions they are grossly ill equipped to handle.

Tertiary education are supposed to be centres where young Nigerians receive trainings to harness the natural resources and build a strength of character that will move the nation forward but Nigerian universities are today centres for indiscipline, rape, abortion, cultism, arson, hooliganism, gangsterism, armed robbery, assault, sexual harassment, murder, drug abuse, acquisition of certificates without competence and above all centres for educational wastage. The current certified Nigerian graduates lack acceptable level of competence in their areas of specialization. They cannot therefore fit into places where they finally find themselves in the society.[22] The problems in the secondary are even worse than those of the tertiary education. This work deliberately chooses to emphasize on tertiary education because their products are employed to control and steer the economic engine of the nation. The values of any society are inbuilt in the national education curriculum. It is very clear that entrants into tertiary education are not properly prepared. They lack rudimentary foundation from primary to secondary level. The lecturers at the same time are ill equipped to prepare our students whom upon graduation are expected to drive the society to greater height than they met it. Issues of poor conditions of service, lack of funding, cultism, examination malpractices lack and inadequate infrastructure and leadership are also fingered as cogs in the wheel of progress in our education system. It is only sensible to submit that continued neglect on education can bring disaster in all our governance structures including economic development. It is appropriate to agree that even our leaders need education. Public and private enterprises contribute a lot to national growth. When merits is driven down by mediocrity, such productive public enterprises may either decline or even close down due to non-performance. Poor-quality education and inadequate industrialization are all products of bad governance and leadership.

CONTRIBUTING FACTORS IN THE PERCEIVED FAILURE IN NIGERIAN EDUCATION, INDUSTRY AND BUREAUCRACY

Bureaucracy as a system of governance requires that leadership must put its priorities right to effect the needed change. The purpose of education is to ensure social conformity.[23] Sizeable number of industries viz primary, genetic extractive, and manufacturing, among others are located in the rural areas where the raw materials and other factors of production especially land are easily available.

Inadequate infrastructures activities in Nigeria have led to the closure or relocation of some key industries outside the country due to increased cost of production leaving youths idle and they tend towards alternate trades no matter how dangerous. Leadership can be described, as the ability of an individual to influence, motivate and enable others to contribute towards the effectiveness and success of a nation, organization or group of which they are members. A person who can bring about change therefore is one who has ability to be a leader.[24]

The realities of leadership is listed in three folds:

- Your nation can meet the goals you establish only if you lead the way by motivating and encouraging your bureaucrats to become a coordinated team focused on the destination.
- When you lead your nation into a new 'frontier' because neither you nor your bureaucrats have not been there before, mistake, miscues and inexperience add to the challenge and your leadership is key to meeting the challenges.
- You have to understand and be good enough to lead and to teach it to your employees both by example and by coaching.

The more leaders you can develop, the stronger the business will be, and the less you have to worry about how the business is operating. The problem with Nigerian economic development is leadership. Further, nobody can give what he does not have, rather can reduce all governance indices to his level.[25] What appears to be manifesting in Nigeria today are not cheering. Ethnicity, nepotism, religion, statism and party politics appear to be playing heavily against merits, hard work, excellence and industry. Quality leadership is one primary factor that is lacking in Nigeria and this has unfortunately imparted negatively on the growth and economic wellbeing of this nation due to poor and under application of available resources to the active sectors. The country's energy requirement was 7000 megawatts, while Nigeria was only able to provide 1500 megawatts in 2017.[26] This resulted in the energy rationing and shedding both for domestic and industrial uses.

Nigeria had a grand vision of becoming one of the world's twenty leading economies by the year 2020. It is also true that constant electric power supply is a catalyst and an indispensable factor in the production of affordable goods and services onto which national economic growth and development anchors. The former president Umaru Yar'Adua placed great losses due to poor electricity supply by Nigerian people at ₦10 billion.[27] It was further revealed that half of the 400 industrial establishments in Kano state alone have been forced to close down due to lack of electricity supply. The 75% of the more than 300,000 textile workforce have lost their jobs while many small-scale companies have closed down due to lack of electricity power supply and high cost of maintaining alternate power supply.[28] The negative effect of electricity supply disequilibrium in Nigeria is monumental and has dislocated the nation's economic development. The Manufacturers Association of Nigeria (MAN) disclosed unrelenting free fall in its membership due to the following:

- Dilapidated road network
- Absence of master plan for railway development
- Scarcity and persistent increase in the price of petroleum products and other energy sources
- Uncoordinated tax administration
- Smuggling and other trade malpractices
- Difficulty in accessing long term bank credits for small scale industries
- Failure to achieve one digit interest rate
- General insecurity of life and property
- Unsteady and inadequate power supply for productivity at industrial level[29]

The Organized Private Sector (OPS) has reacted to the ongoing effort by Ghanaian government to lure the nation's manufactures to Ghana and urged the government to take immediate proactive actions in solving these electricity problems.[30] It is no longer news that by 2009 many companies actually relocated to countries where ease of doing their businesses is better. Up till date, the problem of electricity supply disequilibrium still lingers with higher population and urbanization. Consequently, teaming unemployed and underemployed youths are ever increasing after graduation. There is unimaginable insecurity in the country involving but not limited to:

- Boko Haram insurgency especially in the North East, Nigeria;
- Herdsmen attack on the farms and communities leading to reduced production in the agricultural sector of the economy in the North Central, Nigeria;
- the Niger Delta militancy, destroying oil installations for alleged neglect and resource control question;
- Independent people of Biafra (IPOB) alleging marginalization of South East, Nigeria; and
- kidnapping, cultism, corruption and so on.

In all these, the economic indices of the nation are systematically being decimated with loss of human lives and displacement of men, women, youths and children. Houses, churches, mosques, schools, industries, farmlands and other investments are maliciously damaged and often burnt with impunity. This tends to question the credibility on the whole essence of governance. The list are unending, it is pertinent to note that there is a clear leadership question in this greatly endowed nation called Nigeria. There is also the gap in our educational system which would have been better fashioned to produce more quality young educated men as drivers of our bureaucratic norms in the various sectors of the economy which may have assuaged issues sounding these deviants now and in future.

THE GUIDANCE COUNSELLOR'S ROLES/STRATEGIES IN ENHANCING GOOD EDUCATION, INDUSTRY AND BUREAUCRACY IN AFRICA

- Identifying talents, interest and potentials in individual's through appropriate psychological instruments such as intelligent quotient (IQ) tests, Vocational Interest Inventory (VII) and Students Interest Inventory (SII), among others.
- Helping place or direct the individuals towards courses, institutions and programmes where their talents/ potentials will be adequately developed for the general good of the nation's education industry and governance.
- Identifying possible hindrances or problems that will militate against individuals in their bid to develop their potential.
- Helping counsel individuals against societal ills that run counter with national values, education, industry and bureaucracy such as cultism, armed robbery, prostitution, bribery, nepotism, election/examination malpractice, violence, insurgency, militancy, drug abuse and rape, ritual among others.
- Emphasizing skills acquisition, entrepreneurship, vocational education and so on to meet the educational and bureaucratic needs of the nation, that is, proper manpower, relevance and development.
- Organizing career day/week, seminars, conferences, workshop, orientation among others for parents, students, government officials, employment agencies, teachers on inter-disciplinary approaches to harnessing and mobilizing the nation's resources (human and nonhuman) towards quality education industry and bureaucracy.
- Taking care of constant evaluation and appraisal of governmental, industrial, technological and social programmes and provisions that enhance quality, manpower development and productivity.
- Managing rehabilitation counselling for school dropout and others affected by attributions in education, industry and governance.
- Forming healthy clubs and societies in schools and outside schools, for instance, war against indiscipline, war against indecent dressing, young scientist club, young farmers club, vigilante groups, good leadership and citizenship movement and cultural society, among others.
- Introducing role modelling and mentoring strategies using adults and youths.
- Introducing excursions essays and good governance, occupational files and work-school programmes.

CONCLUSION

Investments by individuals, private organizations and government on education and industry have been enormous and they are in expectation for both material and financial rewards on these investments. Unfortunately, past and present leaders in Nigeria have not given focus to actualizing these ultimate goals. It is clear from the brief analysis of this chapter that bureaucracy in Nigeria has been bastardized by non-focused leadership. Entrants to the universities are not given the required rudimentary trainings at both primary and secondary levels of education. The ill-equipped lecturers compounded education products as improperly trained managers of various economic sectors.

Industrial sectors went down due to poor and inadequate infrastructure like the roads, electricity, energy and so forth. Unemployment, underemployment and nepotism have taken the centre stage. Apparently issues like poor condition of services, lack of funding, examination malpractices and corruption strikes also constituted a huge barrier to the expectation of Nigerian society. Nigeria this time requires a serious generational shift to give birth to a well-trained, disciplined and corruption-free society. This is a mandate which relevant professionals like guidance counsellors and other relevant qualified professionals in Education should massively and aggressively be involved in raising young enterprising Nigerians to take over the new millennium march to nationhood.

RECOMMENDATIONS

1. The federal government should invest heavily in energy availability and sustainability through serious collaboration with developed international communities.
2. Roads and other forms of transport infrastructure should be put right to ease movement and evacuation of goods especially from the neglected rural areas.
3. Education at the tertiary level must be practical and functional where teaching and laboratory equipment should be provided to ensure that theory is not divorced from practical.
4. Government must come out heavily on the administration of tertiary levels of education to ensure that qualified intelligent, competent and hardworking lecturers are appointed for effective teaching, planning, organization monitoring and evaluation.
5. Guidance and counselling should be enforced at primary and secondary levels to catch and moderate youths early enough for the task of nation

building through ethical behaviour modification strategies and career opportunities.

6. Funding of education should target United Nations Education, Scientific and Cultural Organization (UNESCO) standards to help upgrade the low rating of Nigeria Education.
7. Merit and standard should be re-introduced and enforced as core values in all institutions of governance while playing down on federal character which often promotes mediocrity and poor economic growth and productivity.

NOTES

1. Jack Allen, 'Bureacracy in Education', A symposium. *Peaboy Journal of Education* 55, no. 1 (2009): 39.
2. Juliana Idiaghe, 'Bureacractic – Administrative Skills in Post-secondary Education System and national development', *Sky Journal of Education Research* 3 (2015): 003.
3. Allen Jain, 'Using the lens of Max "Weber's Theory of Bureaucracy" to examine E-Government Research', *Proceedings of the 37th Hawaii International Conference on System Sciences* (2004) 0-7695-2058-01/04 & 17.00 IEEE.
4. Allen Jain, *Using the Lens of Max*, 003.
5. Nigerian Constitution 1999.
6. Magnus Mahuta, 'Role of Education and Value Orientation in Attainment of Sustainable Development in Nigeria', *Knowledge Review* 19, no. 5 (2009): 92.
7. Melford Okilo, 'Forward' In *New Perspective in Moral Education*, eds. Onyema Nduka and Iheoma Okeke (Lagos: Academy Press, 2008).
8. Gaurav Akrani, What Is Industry? Image Credits Barrie Caveman (2011).
9. Ibid.
10. Standard Industry Classification (SIC).
11. Chris Gesinde, "Characteristics of a Professional counsellor," in *Effective Counselling Practicum* eds. Mike Ekwe and Patricia Nwamuo (Owerri: Palm Publishers, 2012).
12. Moshola Omoegun, *A Functional Approach to Practicum in Guidance and Counselling* (Lagos: Bab Shrift and Co., 2011).
13. Tambuwal Ali, 'Relationship among Guidance and Counselling Awareness, Study Habit, Attitude to School and Academic Performance of Secondary School Students in Sokoto Metropolis', *The Counsellor* 31, no. 2: 46.
14. Callista Akunna Ukoha and Chinonye Ugonna, 'Counselling towards Improved Longevity and Enjoyable Old Age', *Alvan School of Education Journal (ASEJ)* 7, no. 1 (2010): 95.
15. UNESCO, 'Inclusion Education, the Way of the Future', 2009. www.oropea nagency.orog. On 1/14/2018.
16. John Lenser, 'Democracy and Education', *The Free Press*, 2.

17. The Natural Learning Project. *Journal of Experiential Learning and Simulation* (Elseiver North-Holland, 2012), 1–8.

18. Idiaghe. 'Bureacractic – Administrative', 003.

19. Elisha Duru, 'The Role of Democracy in National Development: A comparative Analysis of the United States and Nigeria', *Journal of Social Science and Public Policy* 3, no. 1 (2015): 004.

20. Federal Republic of Nigeria, *National Policy on Education* (Lagos: NERDC, 2004).

21. Jeyifo, 'The thing caught in Nites' Trap', in *The Dilemma of Education in Nigeria*, eds. Roseline Nkereuwem Uganga and Nwaka Nneka (Onitsha: West and Solomon Publication, 2011).

22. Okunoha Omoregie, 'Quality Assurance in Nigeria University Education and Credentialing', in *The Dilemma of University Education in Nigeria*, eds. James Tarershima and Gideon Balogun (Ibadan: His Lineage Publishing, 2011).

23. Spring, *Bureaucracy in Modern Society* (New York: Random Press, 2009).

24. Aby Jain, 'Using the Lens of Max Weber's Theory of Bureaucracy to Examine E-Government Research', *Proceedings of the 37th Hawaii International Conference on System Sciences*, 2004.

25. Peter M. Blau and Marshall W. Meyer, *Bureaucracy in Modern Society*. New York: Random Press, 1971.

26. Losmos Nwaogwugwu, 'Energy Crisis and Nigerian's Economic Development: Conspiracy or enemy, within hypotheses, themes and perspective', *Social Sciences in Africa* 1, no. 1 (2010): 16.

27. *The News Magazine*, 'Yar'Adua Mounting Problems', vol. 32, no. 25–29 June, 2009.

28. Mba, Technological Development and Industrialization, 'Economic and Financial Digest', *Business Day*, 19 March, 2009.

29. Manufacturers Association of Nigeria (MAN), 'Consequences of Electricity Supply. Disequilibrium on Industrialization and Small Medium Enterprises', *Journal of Orient Education* 5, no. 2: 19.

30. Cosmos Uba, 'OPS Urges Federal Government to Stop Imminent Exodus of Nigerian Firms to Ghana', *Business World Magazines*, 6 July 2009.

BIBLIOGRAPHY

Akrani, Gaurav. 'What is industry?', 2011. https://kalyan-city.blogspot.com, accessed on 13/07/2017.

Ali, Tambuwal. 'Relationship among Guidance and Counselling Awareness, Study Habit, Attitude to School and Academic Performance of Secondary School Students in Sokoto Metropolis'. *The Counsellor* 31, no. 2: 46–7.

Armstrong, J. Scott. 'The Natural Learning Project'. *Journal of Experiential Learning and Simulation* 1 (1979): 5–12.

Dewey, John. *Democracy and Education*. London: The Free Press, 1997.

Duru, Elisha. 'The Role of Democracy in National Development: A comparative Analysis of the United States and Nigeria'. *Journal of Social Science and Public Policy* 3, no. 1 (2015): 1–5.

Federal Republic of Nigeria. '*National Policy on Education*. Lagos: NERDC, 2004.

Gesinde, Chris. 'Characteristics of a Professional counsellor'. In *Effective Counselling Practicum*, edited by Mike Ekwe and Patricia Nwamuo. Owerri: Palm Publishers, 2012.

Jack, Allen. 'Bureaucracy in Education: A symposium'. *Peaboy Journal of Education* 55, no. 1 (2009): 39–40.

Jain, Aby. 'Using the Lens of Max Weber's Theory of Bureaucracy to Examine E-Government Research'. *Proceedings of the 37th Hawaii International Conference on System Sciences*, 2004.

Jeyifo, 'The Thing Caught in Nites' Trap'. In *The Dilemma of Education in Nigeria*, edited by Roseline Nkereuwem Uganga and Nneka Nwaka. Onitsha: West & Solomon Publication, 2011.

Juliana, Idiaghe. 'Bureacractic – Administrative Skills in Post-Secondary Education System and National Development'. *Sky Journal of Education Research* 3 (2015): 001–5.

Mahuta, Magnus. 'Role of Education and Value Orientation in Attainment of Sustainable Development in Nigeria'. *Knowledge Review* 19, no. 5 (2009): 90–4.

Manufacturers Association of Nigeria (MAN), 'Consequences of Electricity Supply. Disequilibrium on Industrialization and Small Medium Enterprises'. *Journal of Orient Education* 5, no. 2: 19.

Mba, Technological Development and Industrialization. 'Economic and Financial Digest'. *Business Day*, 19 March, 2009.

Moghali, George. Channels Television Daily Sunrise Programme, viewed on 28/10/2017.

The News Magazine, '*Yar'Adua Mounting Problems*' 32, 25–29 June, 2009.

Nigerian Constitution 1999.

Nwaogwugwu, Losmos. 'Energy Crisis and Nigerian's Economic Development: "Conspiracy or Enemy, within Hypotheses, Themes and Perspective"'. *Social Sciences in Africa* 1, no. 1 (2010): 16.

Okilo, Melford 'Forward'. In *New Perspective in Moral Education* edited by Onyema Nduka and Iheoma Okeke. Lagos: Academy Press, 2008.

Omoegun, Moshola. *A Functional Approach to Practicum in Guidance and Counselling*. Lagos: Bab Shrift & Co., 2011.

Omoregie, Okunoha. 'Quality Assurance in Nigeria University Education and Credentialing'. In *The dilemma of University Education in Nigeria*, edited by James Tarershima and Gideon Balogun. Ibadan: His Lineage Publishing, 2011.

Peter M. Blau and Marshall W. Meyer. *Bureaucracy in modern society*. New York: Random Press, 1971.

Guibert, Bernard, Jean Laganier and Michael Volle. 'An Essay on Industry Classifications'. *Économie et statistique* 20 (1971): 23–26.

Uba, Cosmos. 'OPS Urges Federal Government to Stop Imminent Exodus of Nigerian Firms to Ghana'. *Business World Magazines*. July 6, 2009.

Ukoha, Callista Akunna and Ugonna Chinonye. 'Counselling towards Improved Longevity and Enjoyable Old Age'. *Alvan School of Education Journal (ASEJ)* 7, no. 1 (2010): 95–6.

United Nations Educational, Scientific and Cultural Organization (UNESCO). *Inclusive Education: The Way of the Future*. Geneva: UNESCO ED/BIE/CONFINTED 48/3, 2008, accessed from http://www.ibe.unesco.org › Policy_Dialogue on 14.01.2018.

Chapter 3

Privatization of the Electric Power Sector and Service Delivery in Nigeria

Ifeanyichukwu Michael Abada, Nneka Ifeoma Okafor and Christopher Ewuzie Obianagwa

INTRODUCTION

The zest for increasing private sector participation in a market economy has gained much impetus within the past two decade across Africa. The rationale for the restructuring of power sector was due to abysmal state of electricity supply and revenue losses of low operational capacity, poor regulation and corruption in the sector. The reform of power sector is in line with the vision of United Nations Department of Economic and Social Affairs (UNDESA). It stated that power sector reforms can also foster development of country-level electricity markets by allowing sufficient scale to support increased competitive participation.[1]

Privatization offers a lot of opportunities. It reduces the fiscal and administrative burdens of a large public enterprise sector but also to spur private sector development, to instil greater government accountability, and to contribute to the fight against poverty; and that opportunity has been embraced by few governments, including Nigeria. Privatization of public enterprises helps the government to redirect its efforts to spending on social security and provision of essential infrastructure while eliminating the commercial functions of the government through deregulation and transfer of public enterprises to the private sector.

Nigeria was one of the earlier African countries to embark the journey en route privatization of public sector enterprises. Public sector reforms in Nigeria began immediately after independence with the National Development Plans, 1962–1985. This exercise though slow was peaked with the introduction of Structural Adjustment Program (SAP) which was recommended by the International Monetary Fund (IMF) and World Bank (WB) as a leeway to securing their loan facilities and overcoming the inefficiency and chronic meltdown characterizing the public sector dominated economy of Nigeria. To implement SAP, the Technical Committee on Privatization and Commercialization (TCPC) was established and saddled with the management of the programme between 1988 and 1993. The outcome of privatization exercise and transfer of public assets ownership and control of major economic activities, the hallmark of SAP, was defeated by poor implementation, corruption and ineptitude. This was followed by protests and industrial actions across the country in response to hardship occasioned by SAP, thereby compelling the government to relinquish all efforts aimed at building a robust private sector economy up until the eve of the Fourth Republic in 1999.

Meanwhile, Nigeria became a pariah state for almost a decade as the IMF and WB excluded it from major economic and policy concerns. These international financial institutions were disillusioned with poor implementation of SAP. However, the year 1999 marked a new beginning in the nation's stride to improving service delivery and building a strong and broad-base market economy. Hope was renewed with the WB, IMF and other international donors. They resolved to stage a comeback in the management of Nigeria's economy. Soon, privatization now frequently featured in government policy statements and in conditionality from donors while the past decade has seen the WB and other donors get increasingly involved in lending operators towards parastatal sector reforms that included privatization components.[2]

Before the Fourth Republic, government of Nigeria had not shown genuine efforts to transfer its public holdings to private sector operators. They were rather reluctant to sell the process and the privatization exercise was mundane. With few exceptions, the efforts of the governments across the developing countries and Nigeria in particular were minimal. This was followed by Public corporations increasingly occupying larger share of the nation's economy ranging from extractive industries to manufacturing, communication, power and financial sectors of the economy. This enabled the government to acquired important economic and political status, enjoying monopolies in the major sectors of the economy and becoming major sources of employment. This was evident in the nationalization of foreign interests in Nigeria in the 1970s and 1980s and pursuit of programmes and policies that undermined the building of broad-based economy and quality public service delivery with attendant inefficiencies.

The precarious state of some public enterprises, moderate growth experienced in the 1970s and 1980s, the need to maintain high employment levels and the need to generate proceeds made public sector reform a major element in the reform efforts implemented by the countries and Nigeria's policy statements on the advent of Fourth Republic.

In Nigeria, and in most countries of Africa, interest in the privatization of government-owned enterprises is motivated by the desire to correct past failures of development policies and reduce money losing trends of public corporations.[3] However, the state-owned enterprises (SOEs) in Nigeria were bedeviled by economic inefficiency in the production of goods and services, with high cost of production, inability to innovate and unnecessary delays in delivery of the goods produced; ineffectiveness in the provision of goods and services such as failure to meet intended objectives and diversions of benefits to elite groups; and rapid expansion of the bureaucracy, severely straining the public budget with huge deficit of public enterprises becoming massive drain on government resources and poor financial performance of SOE, reflecting a history of huge financial losses, over staffing and burden or excessive debt.[4]

To strengthen service delivery and build a strong market-based economy driven by intensive private sector participation, new institutional arrangements such as the Public Enterprises (Privatization and Commercialization) Act and National Council on Privatization (NCP) were inaugurated to oversee the transition to a private sector–driven economy. Significantly, the Bureau of Public Enterprises (BPE) was located in the Secretariat of the NCP saddled with the responsibilities of monitoring the implementation of the government's policies privatization.

Similarly, existing side by side with BPE were the Economic and Financial Crimes Commission (EFCC), Independent Corrupt Practices and other related offences Commission (ICPC), Budget Monitoring and Price Intelligence Unit (BMPIU), Public Procurement Commission (PPC), Nigeria Extractive Industries Transparency (NEITI), Financial Action Tax Force (FATF), and so on which were aimed at fostering good governance, transparency and accountability as well as due process and zero tolerance to corruption in public and private sectors of the economy.

Between 1999 and 2006, about eighty-one public enterprises were either privatized or 'concessioned' and the BPE raked in over ₦500 billion between 2005 and 2006 in which 61 SOEs were privatized.[5] Corroborating this view, they affirmed that privatization of some SOEs, as well as deregulation of government activities in some sectors, was therefore needed to improve the efficiency of these enterprises, to curb corruption, and also to reduce the financial costs to the federal government. They observed that between 1999 and 2006, about 116 enterprises were privatized, including various loss-making government enterprises operating in industries such as electric power sector, aluminium, telecommunications, petrochemical, insurance and hotel.[6] This exercise saw the privatization of some key public corporations such as NITEL, NEPA, Nigerian Railway Corporation, NIPOST, NICON LUXURY, Benue Cement Company (BCC), African Petroleum (AP), and National Oil and Chemical Company (NOLCHEM), among others.

Throughout the world, electricity remains the catalyst for economic growth and everyday living. While some climes are celebrating five or ten years of uninterrupted power supply, it is common knowledge that some locations in the country exist without power for weeks and months. The deplorable state of the power sector compelled President Goodluck Jonathan to recall that as at the last count the country's power generation level stood at a paltry 3800 megawatts (MW) (courtesy of hydro power generation from persistent rainfall) a far cry from the desired level of over 6000 needed to place the country on the path of near stable power supply in 2010. Conversely, South Africa with a third of Nigeria's 140 million populations in 2010 had eight times that capacity.

The study appraises the performance of the electric power sector following the government unbundling policies between 1999 and 2017.

HISTORICAL OVERVIEW OF THE ROAD TO PRIVATIZATION OF THE NIGERIAN POWER SECTOR IN THE FOURTH REPUBLIC

Power Sector under President Olusegun Obasanjo, 1999–2007

Nigeria's power sector performs tripartite functions which are power generation, distribution and transmission. For more than two decades, the Nigerian government enjoyed monopoly of the power sector through NEPA which was established by Decree No. 24 under military rule in 1972. For years, the Nigerian government was saddled with the formulation of energy policy development and regulation, as well as operation and investment in the power sector particularly before the sector's reform initiative in 2001.

In a bid to overhaul the sector and improve on the electricity generation, distribution and generation, the Federal Government of Nigeria (FGN) established the Electricity Power Sector Reform Act in 2005. Before the reforms, the Federal Ministry of Power (FMP) was responsible for the regulation of the power sector, while the National Electric Power Authority (NEPA) handled its operation.[7] He further observed that part of the responsibility of NEPA was power generation, transmission and distribution.[8] However, NEPA ran a monopoly of the system from its inception in 1972 to its defunct in 2005, with control of power generation capacity of about 94%, while transmission, system operators, distribution and their marketing sector was 100% owned by them.[9] They maintain that since 1972 till early part of 2006, electricity production and supply in Nigeria has been a monopoly of the federal-owned electric utility body known as National Electric Power Authority (NEPA).[10]

The underperformance and fiscal imprudence of NEPA resulted in the amendment of the legal basis establishing it in 1999 to lay off the monopoly enjoyed by NEPA in order to pave way for private sector participation in the

Nigeria's power sector. He stressed that the blue-print that rolled out reform agenda of NEPA was specified in the National Electric Power Policy of 2001, while the legal basis for unbundling of the sector and formulation of successor companies (including privatization) was provided in the EPSRA.[11]

Meanwhile, with unbundling of power sector by the President Olusegun Obasanjo's administration in 2005, NEPA was restructured and renamed the Power Holding Company of Nigeria (PHCN) which became the holding company of the assets of the defunct NEPA in 2007. This is aptly captured by stressing:

> The Nigerian government under President Obasanjo (1999–2007), made effort to increase private participation in the electric power sector by commissioning independent power producers (IPPs) to generate electricity and sell it to PHCN. Independent Power Plants (IPPs) under construction as of 2005 include the 276-MW Siemens station in Afam, Agip's 450-MW plant in Kwale, Exxon Mobil's 388-MW plant in Bonny, ABB's 450-MW plant in Abuja, and Eskom's 388-MW plant in Enugu. Several state governments have also commissioned oil majors to increase generation including Rivers State, which contracted Shell to expand the 700-MW Afam station. The Obasanjo's administration also approved the construction of four thermal power plants with a combined capacity of 1,234 MW to meet its generating goal of 6,500 MW by 2006.[12]

The BPE with guidance of the National Council on Privatization (NCP) successfully unbundled NEPA. It also named seven firms that would participate in the financial bids for five power generation plants. The successful companies were Phoenix Electricity; Transcorp Consortium and Ampiron Power Distribution Limited; CMEC Energy; GPN Nestoil Power Services Limited; Mainstream Energy Solution Limited; and North South Power Company Limited.[13] Notably, to oversight the activities of private operators in the power sector, the federal government bolded its efforts and established Nigerian Electricity Regulatory Commission (NERC) and the Nigerian Bulk Electricity Trading Plc. (NBET). The NERC was established by law of the federation to regulate activities of the electricity sector in March 2005, by the Electricity Power Sector Reform Bill 2005. Some of the core objectives are as follows:

- To maximize access to electricity services, by promoting and facilitating consumer connections to distribution systems in both rural and urban areas
- To ensure that regulation is fair and balanced for licensee, consumers, investors and other stakeholders

The Operators of the Nigerian Electricity Market (ONEM) was established with the responsibility of the wholesale market and settlement operator.[14] However, the power sector reform was predicated on the following objectives:

- To promote competition to facilitate more rapid provision of service throughout the country
- To create a new legal and regulatory environment for the sector that establishes a level playing field
- To encourage of private investment and expertise, and meet social goals
- To unbundle the NEPA
- To privatize the successors to NEPA and encourage them to undertake an ambitious investment programme[15]

The idea of restructuring and unbundling of the power sector was seen as positive change that would enhance power generation and distribution which will serve as a precursor for socio-economic growth and development and to meet electricity supply needs of individuals, households and varying scales of industries in a competitive world.

The Nigerian power sector operated below its capacity, even during the time in which power outages have become a frequent occurrence. This submission was reiterated by the Power Holding Company of Nigeria (PHCN), stating that power demand in February 2006 was 7600 MW, but the actual generation capability was 3600 MW. The discrepancy between power demand and actual generation is mostly due to low water levels and inadequate maintenance of plants.[16] By 29 May 2007, power generation capacity fluctuated between 2600 MW and 3600 MW (PHCN). The real state of affairs in the nation's power sector was summarized by Oladimeji Adeyemo and Salami Adeleke in assertion:

> In a recent study, it was shown that the power generation capacity in Iran and Nigeria were both at the same level in 1970, yet in 2007, Iran with a population of 70 million, had achieved a power generation capacity of 42,000 MW. Another example is that of South Africa which distributed an average of 800 watts per person in 2007, while in Nigeria distribution sat at 30 watts per person.[17]

Power Sector under President Umaru Musa Yar'Adua 2007–2009

In spite of the promising commitments and attempts to revamp the power sector, electricity supply need on the eve of 29 May 2007 was more worrisome than it were before 29th May 1999. Under Yar'Adua, the Ministry of Power and Steel was renamed as Ministry of Energy and Power in 2007 and was charged with policy formulation while the PHCN is the operator in the electricity sector.

The unbundling of NEPA and change of nomenclature from NEPA to PHCN could barely meet the electricity target of Nigeria. This deplorable condition in the power sector angered the incoming administration of President Umaru Musa Yar'Adua. This made him to declare state of emergency in the Nigeria power sector while subsequently setting up a Power Sector Reform Committee (PSRC) under the umbrella body of National Energy Council (NEC) to overhaul the sector and set the records straight. Unfortunately, the roadmap for the comprehensive privatization of power came to a stalemate due to myriads of challenges including the demise of President Umaru Musa Yar'Adua.

Power Sector under President Goodluck Jonathan, 2010–2015

In August 2010, President Goodluck Jonathan launched the Roadmap for Power Sector Reform. The Roadmap established a clear implementation plan of the Electricity Power Sector Reform Act (2005) as a reaffirmation of the commitment to resolve the power crises and setting the path for power sector improvement. Preceding the Roadmap for Power Sector Reform was the establishment of the Presidential Task Force on Power (PTFP) in June 2010 by President Goodluck Jonathan to drive the Nigeria's power sector reform. Against this backdrop[18] was observed that the PTFP efforts to date include the following:

- Conducting a nationwide wheeling capacity stress test in October 2012 to determine the actual distribution uptake capability in the country, leading to the development of a number of capacity update projects.
- Completing development of a short-to-medium-term transmission grid rehabilitation and upgrade plan in partnership with the Transmission Company of Nigeria and the Federal Ministry of Power.
- Making full and complete recovery of abandoned imported power equipment at major ports and container depots in the country.
- Coordinating the development and implementation of the Transitional Maintenance Intervention Funding Scheme (TMIFS) to provide funding to distribution companies (DISCOs) and generating companies (GENCOs) in the transition period between the purchased DISCOs and GENCOs' sale and such companies' handover to the private sector. The TMIFS was developed to address urgent maintenance issues, which would otherwise affect service delivery quality and supply reliability during this transition period due to insufficient funding.
- Designing and launching the April 2013 Presidential Power Reform Transactions Signing Summit in collaboration with the Ministry of Power, to

showcase the execution of ground-breaking contractual agreements in the power sector, such as NBET's greenfield PPA with Azura Power West Africa Limited, and the World Bank Partial Risk Guarantee supporting the Gas Supply Agreement between Chevron Nigeria Limited and Egbin Power plc.

- Engaging in ongoing interactions with the regulators and key stakeholders to maintain commercialization, reform momentum and industry preparation for entry into the Transitional Electricity Market (TEM). Nigeria's TEM, the first private power market in Africa, constitutes the second stage of the phased power sector reform for the country's electricity market. Prior to TEM, market participants operated on a best endeavour basis without recourse to the existing industry contracts. With TEM's commencement in 2015, contractual parties will now operate under the Market Rules and the Grid Code, trade on the basis of industry agreements, and remain committed to their contractual obligations. This will culminate into an efficient, competitive, transparent and reliable market for the sale and purchase of wholesale electricity and ancillary services. The introduction of TEM is also significant as it establishes the enabling environment and fiscal framework designed to help reduce the liquidity challenges in the power sector, and attract further investment.
- Improving gas and power network coordination through conferences conducted with the Transmission Company of Nigeria and the Nigerian Gas Company.

However, the Nigerian Electricity Regulatory Commission was reinstated as a regulatory body and strengthened with a new chairman and commissioners charged for the purpose of providing appropriate regulatory functions for the electricity market in Nigeria. The Jonathan administration unbundled the PHCN into eighteen successor companies for greater efficiency and effectiveness in power generation and distribution.[19]

To provide a requisite hub for private sector investment in the Nigerian power sector, the administration created the Nigerian Bulk Electricity Trading Plc (NBET) and in August 2011, the President inaugurated the chief-executive officer (CEO) and board of the Nigerian Bulk Electricity Trading Plc (also known as the Bulk Trader). NBET Plc, aimed at providing confidence to the power generating companies that they will be paid for power produced. Also, the Jonathan administration launched the Energy Efficiency and Energy Conservation Lighting Scheme (EEECLS) to promote and encourage the use of energy-efficient bulbs and lighting systems in order to create an energy conservation culture.

In order to bring the roadmap to practical reality, the federal government of Nigeria entered into a Memorandum of Understanding (MoU) with global leading investors in the power sector, General Electric. Sequel to this MoU, the General Electric was expected to invest up to 15% equity in power projects in the country summing up to 10,00 MW capacity by the year 2020. General Electric also proposed to establish local packaging facility for small aero-derivative turbines in Nigeria which will promote job creation. Furthermore, the Federal Government of Nigeria under President Goodluck Jonathan signed an MoU with the United States' Ex-Im Bank to provide an investment window of up to ₦1.5 billion for investors willing to invest in the Nigerian Electric Power Sector. Under the road map, government was expected to in due course withdraw from mainstream power generation and distribution while allowing the private sector to drive it under the supervision of the re-invigorated National Electricity Regulatory Commission (NERC).

However, on the 30th of September 2013, the unbundling of PHCN came to a full force following President Jonathan administration's resolve to enhance private sector engagement in the power sector operation. The administration's power sector roadmap came by the desire to privatize both power generation and distribution while the government rolls back power transmission. In tune with this, Adeniyi Aladejare observed that Nigerian government under President Jonathan was committed to sell off its stake in the electricity services industry while retained the transmission grid as a public entity.[20] The Power Sector Reform has led to the unbundling of the PHCN into eighteen different companies: eleven distribution companies, six generation companies and one transmission company. The GENCOs were established for power generation. Similarly, the DISCOs were responsible for power distribution and Transmission Company of Nigeria (TCN) for power transmission. The GENCOs are Afam Power Plc, Egbin Power Plc, Kainji/Jebba Hydro Electric Plc, Sapele Power Plc, Shiroro Hydro Electric Plc and Ughelli Power Plc.[21] The DISCOs include Abuja Distribution Company, Benin Distribution Company, Eko Distribution Company, Enugu Distribution Company, Ibadan Distribution Company, Ikeja Distribution Company, Jos Distribution Company, Kaduna Distribution Company, Kano Distribution Company, Port Harcourt Distribution Company and Yola Distribution Company.[22]

Granted, efforts were made to ensure a transparent and accountable reform process by sticking to the privatization guidelines throughout the privatization process. However, allegations abound of obvious obscurity, opaqueness and favouritism in the selling process. One key instance of such was the sale of the Kaduna distribution company. The preferred bidder, Northwest Power Ltd (NPL), was unilaterally granted deadline extension for the completion of the Share Purchase Agreement rather than reverting to the reserved bidder as provided for in the privatization guidelines. This was an obvious act of favouritism because Section 15 (138) of the Request for Proposals for the Privatization of PHCN Successor Companies stipulated that failure of the preferred bidder to meet its payment obligation before the stipulated deadline would require that the 25% down payment be forfeited while the right of purchase would be given to the reserve bidder.

The FGN reserved the exclusive right of TCN. The TCN is a successor company of PHCN, following the unbundling of the sector, and is currently being managed by a management contractor, Manitoba Hydro International (Canada). Manitoba is responsible for revamping TCN to achieve technical and financial adequacy in addition to providing stable transmission of power without system failure. Currently, the transmission capacity of the Nigerian Electricity Transmission system is made up of about 5523.8 km of 330 KV lines and 6801.49 km of 132 KV lines.[23]

One major achievement of this exercise was the payment by the distribution and generation successor companies to PHCN for a total amount of around $2.5 billion, which represents the total value of the share sale price of the privatized assets while a cost-reflective tariff, the Multi-Year Tariff Order (MYTO) II, has been introduced on 1st June 2012 to make the sector attractive to both local and foreign investors.[24]

Power Sector under President Muhammadu Buhari 2015–2017

Power generation is one of the 'five pillars' of President Buhari's National Economic Recovery and Growth Plan (NERGP). What the NERGP set out to achieve include the need to redress the constraints to stabilize macroeconomic environment and ensure inclusive economic growth, manufacturing and food security through agricultural development and provision of infrastructure, including railway, road and power. Buhari's administration described as false the privatization of assets, which saw the defunct PHCN broken into eleven distribution companies and nine generation companies as well as one transmission company, pointing out that false buyers of the power companies were owing more than they could pay. It further pointed out that the power sector has been privatized and that the investors are holding large portions of the shares but the privatization has not worked well, in the sense that what government sort to achieve, by way of development of the power sector, has not yet happened.

Despite the apparent failings of the privatized power sector under President Goodluck Jonathan's administration, Buhari's presidency stressed it would not cancel the privatization of the power sector explaining that privatization is a complex investment that government cannot wake up to cancel the contract, because there are consequences. Though President Buhari's administration has not done much in the power sector, it has decided to review the power sector's privatization aimed at opening up the sector for investors with the financial capacity and technical expertise to inject fresh investments to turn the sector around. The government decried that the privatized power companies have not been able to realize the objectives for which they acquired the assets and that Nigerians expectations for improved stable supply of electricity, with government targeting the generation capacity of 10,000 MW have not been met.

Justifying the aforementioned claim, the Minister of State for Budget and National Planning, Ahmed Zainab, states:

> The process of review is ongoing to re-negotiate with the existing owners to restructure the investment to determine the right level of holding to give up for another round of sales. The equities would be sold to investors with the resources and capacity to bring in the level of investment to turn around the sector. She said the restructuring would involve the government and other private operators ceding some of their holdings to new investors to inject fresh funds and expertise to help turn the sector around in a way that would serve Nigerians.[25]

KEY ACTORS IN NIGERIA'S REFORMED ELECTRIC POWER SECTOR

- The Federal Ministry of Power: It is saddled with the formulation of broad policies for the development of the power sector and coordinating activities within the sector.
- NERC: It is responsible for the promotion of the efficiency of the power sector and improving access to electricity services. Two of NERC's key regulatory functions are:
- Licensing: NERC issues licenses for on-and off-grid generation of power, as well as for distribution of electricity to end users.
- Tariff: NERC manages price regulation through the MYTO (as defined further).
- NBET: This organization is the bulk purchaser and seller of electricity from generating companies to distribution companies; enters into industry acceptable and financeable PPAs with IPPs and other generating companies (until such time as such distribution companies are able to enter into direct purchase arrangements with the generating companies on market terms).
- The Gas Aggregation Company Nigeria Limited (Gas Aggregator): It manages the FGN's domestic gas supply obligations. Its main objectives are as follows:
- To coordinate a streamlined process for wholesale gas supply from gas producers to eligible gas purchasers, including generation companies (GENCOs)
- To act as an intermediary between gas suppliers and purchasers in the Nigerian domestic gas market

- To conduct due diligence assessments on eligible gas buyers
- To allocate available gas from the domestic supply obligations to credible buyers by issuing them with gas purchase orders
- To facilitate the negotiation and execution of the gas sale and aggregation agreement, which governs the terms of domestic gas sale and purchase and currently forms the basis of negotiations between gas suppliers and purchasers
- National Power Training Institute of Nigeria: It is the provider of training for power sector personnel and coordinate training activities in the sector.
- Bureau of Public Enterprises: It is saddled with the implementation of the privatization policies of the National Council on Privatization.
- National Council on Privatization: It is the apex body charged with the overall responsibility of formulating and approving policies on privatization and commercialization.
- TCN: It is the operator of the transmission system and oversees the security and reliability of the grid system.
- Nigeria Electricity Liability Management Company: It is responsible for the management of legacy liabilities and stranded assets of the eighteen PHCN successor companies.
- Nigerian Gas Company: It is for transmission and marketing of natural gas and by-products to industrial and utility gas distribution companies.
- Operator of the Nigerian Electricity Market: It functions as the market operator of Nigeria's electricity market and is responsible for operations, settlement arrangements and administration of the metering system among generation, transmission and distribution companies.
- Nigerian Electricity Management Services Authority: It is for enforcement of technical standards and regulations, technical inspection, testing and certification of electrical installations, electricity meters and instruments.

THEORETICAL FRAMEWORK

This study adopted the theory of developmental state. Ezeibe defined developmental state as a state that is focused on economic development and takes necessary policy measures to accomplish that objective.[26] Also, Okonjo-Iweala and Kwaafo viewed developmental state as a government with sufficient organization and power to achieve developmental goals.[27] Succinctly, Ezeibe argued that developmental states are characterized by strong ambition for development. Hence, economic growth takes the pride of place in the national policy making.[28] Again, the political and bureaucratic elites maintain a well-established relationship with state to guide the activities of business and industry according to the national strategies and interest. The developmental state maintains a strong and effective central government.

Put differently, developmental states emphasize

- shared market profits,
- promotion of economic nationalism,
- encouragement of foreign technology transfer and
- maintenance of large government bureaucracy.

Ideally, the theory posits that state plays a significant role in industrialization and economic development. He identified some examples of developmental states to include South Korea, Indonesia, Singapore, India, Thailand and so on.[29] The developmental state theory was a dominant revolutionary framework in the 1980s and 1990s and agitated economic growth and development strategies among the developing nations especially in Nigeria as seen in various reforms pursued by reallocating government spending on essential social programmes such as health, electric power, education, water and social infrastructure while seeking to eliminate the commercial function of the government through deregulation, privatization and commercialization of public enterprises. In Africa, there were efforts with a view to embracing economic growth and development among African states especially in the 1980s, 1990s, and early 2000. This led to the emergence of various reform regimes especially in Nigeria, all in a bid to achieve a desired level of development.

Nigeria is a developmental state as expressed in its reforms efforts and the importance of energy to it has led to inevitable reforms in the power sector of the economy. The Nigerian power sector has been faced with several challenges leading to reform initiatives due to the nature of the Nigerian state which is characterized by a confluence of factors.[30]

Power sector reforms are one of the strides taken by successive administrations in Nigeria aimed at achieving sustainable development in the country. Recent power sector reform in Nigeria is traceable to September 1990, when partial commercialization of the then NEPA was undertaken. The first step in this direction was the appointment of a managing director/chief executive officer to oversee the affairs of the institution. The second step involved dividing the institution into four autonomous divisions headed by an executive director, namely, Generation and Transmission; Distribution and Sales; Engineering; and Finance and Administration.

A further policy push was accorded the reform with the development of the National Electric Power Policy in 2001. This policy was the fallout from the study commissioned by the federal government in 1999 aimed at understanding the challenges of the power sector and proffering policy to transform the sector. It set the following as its key objectives: provide the framework for attracting private sector local and foreign investment into the sector; heighten local capacity in power sector technology; develop an effective and transparent regulatory framework to guide the power sector; promote full liberalization of the electricity market through promotion of competitive sector engagements that will help meet the growing electricity demand; ensure divestment of government investment in power sector entities and enshrine principles of restructuring; and review with a view to updating the power sector laws that will help promote competition and private sector operations. This policy set the tone for the reform agenda and was, indeed, the birth of the modern-day power sector reform in Nigeria to achieve a broader socio-economic spectrum.

DILEMMA IN THE ELECTRICITY SECTOR: PARADOX OF ELECTRICITY SUPPLY IN NIGERIA

The transmission system is potentially the weakest link in the entire chain of the Nigeria electricity network. Inadequate transmission infrastructure has been consistently highlighted as being responsible for stranded capacity that is characteristic of the electricity grid. Consequently, significant investment is required to improve the transmission system if it is to keep pace with the expected growth in the generation capacity and consumers' expectation.

Nigeria electricity consumption per capita is amongst the lowest in the world, with long power outages, poor quality of supply and low access to electricity. At the end of January 2016, the demand for electricity in Nigeria was estimated to be 12,800 MW.[31] They argued that the historical gap between the demand for power in Nigeria and the electricity available from the grid has led to widespread self-generation of power in the commercial, industrial and residential sectors. Regrettably, many individuals and businesses own their generators to compensate for lack of access to and supply of energy. Businesses' reliance on self-generation via diesel-powered generators has resulted in not only environmental impacts that using cleaner fuels could reduce but also an increase of the price of goods and services. This is because, typically, self-generation of electricity accounts for a significant portion of most businesses' recurrent expenditure; such significant overhead costs are clearly being passed onto consumers. The historically low level of investment in Nigeria's power sector has been a significant barrier to private investment in the country.

The Nigerian electrical power sector remains in need of significant investment as its utility-scale electricity generation capacity continues to fall short of meeting domestic demands. Currently, Nigeria has an installed electricity generation capacity for supply to the national grid of 12,522 MW, with available capacity of only approximately 4500 MW, to meet the needs of Nigeria's population of more than 170 million and a country with a gross domestic product (GDP) growth rate of 7%. In comparison, South Africa has an installed electricity generation capacity for supply to the national grid of approximately 50,000 MW with a population of only about one-third the size of Nigeria's. Similarly, He noted electricity provision in Africa has been marred by low generation, poor supply and frequent power outages.[32] One of the strategies adopted by firms to cope with this poor public supply is investment in backup generators. This strategy is not without cost. Corroborating the aforementioned context, the African Development Bank (ADB) (2009) reports showed that electricity was by far the most binding constraint to doing business in Nigeria for more than 80% of the firms surveyed. Meanwhile, epileptic public power supply and household quest to obtain power from alternative sources has become a daily occurrence in Nigeria.[33] In a similar vein, Josephine Marry laments:

> The Nigerian energy industry is probably one of the most inefficient in meeting the needs of its people. The gloomy energy service provision has adversely affected living standards of the population and made worse income and energy poverty in an economy where the majority of the people live on less than 200 naira a day. Whereas Nigeria is rich in energy resources and the sixth largest exporter of crude oil in the world, Nigeria's persistent energy crisis has weakened the industrialization process, and significantly undermined the effort to achieve and sustained economic growth, increased competitiveness of domestic industries, regional and global markets, and employment generation.[34]

Also, available data have shown that the number of Nigerians that use fuel-powered generators for alternative source of electricity has continued to increase in a geometric progression. This assertion was corroborated in 2012 in the Manufacturers Association of Nigeria's reports 2012. Frank Jacobs, the Chairman of MAN, Imo and Abia branch laments:

> An estimated 60 million residents use generators of varying sizes. In the last one year, average residential expenditure in fueling power generators climbed to an all-time high of ₦1.56 trillion, about $13.35 billion per annum. He was of the view that, 'similar level of expenditure on private power generation has characterized the affairs of industrial and commercial power consumers', adding that early last year, independent investigations recorded about half the figures outlined above. He recalled with grief that the Senior Private Sector Specialist at the World Bank, Mr. Steven Dimitryer, noted that 'Nigeria experienced the worst electricity crisis among its contemporaries, which underscores the nightmarish generation, distribution and supply in the country'. Dr Jacobs insisted that 'electricity crisis is the most important infrastructure bottleneck in Nigeria today', adding that all types of firms in Nigeria experience power outages and 85 percent of them own generators as alternative source of power generation. 'The present condition of manufacturers in Nigeria does not leave much to be

cheerful. The efforts of government have continued to totter. We are speedily losing hope', Jacobs lamented.[35]

The aforementioned context points out that power generation in Nigeria fluctuates between 2000 and 3500 MW forcing the citizens to rely on generators, which gulp ₦3.5tn annually and a reported whopping ₦17.5tn in the past five years. Despite the huge government investment in the power sector in the past sixteen years, Nigeria has only succeeded in mustering an installed electricity generation capacity of 10,000 MW. Yet, the country operates at about 30% of this capacity with generation fluctuating between 2000 and 3500 MW.[36] Painfully, per capita electricity usage in the country remains 136 kilowatt/hour, Dayo argued.

The aforementioned value is one of the lowest electricity consumption on a per capita basis in the world. This is regrettably insignificant when Nigeria is compared with the average per capita electricity usage in other countries like Libya, which is 4270 KWH; India, 616 KWH; China, 2944 KWH; South Africa, 4803 KWH; Singapore, 8307 KWH; and the United States, 13,394 KWH.

It is important to note that more than half of the nation's 180 million people are not connected to the national electricity grid. The country's paltry power generation, which is shamefully low, is expectedly inadequate for those connected to the grid. As such, these Nigerians rely on generators with its attendant operational and maintenance costs for running their homes, factories, schools, universities, government offices and the entire economy.

With this development, Nigeria has become huge market for increased sale of generators while importers have turned the country into a dumping ground fleecing the citizens of their money while supplying sub-standard generators to them. This has not only fiscal consequences but also worrying environmental impact in the nation.

CORRUPTION IN THE POWER SECTOR

In spite of the electricity sector reforms and huge investment in the sector, electricity generation is still at lowest ebb per capita in Nigeria compared to what is obtainable in South Africa, Egypt and some other African countries. Also, the electricity sector of Nigeria has continued to wallow in endemic corruption. Nigeria in 2012 had one of the lowest levels of energy use in the world.[37] For them, the history of its power sector was one of inefficient monopolies, missteps and corruption. Similarly, the mismanagement of over US$16 billion investment in the power sector between 1999 and 2007 resulted in abysmal decline of its generation capacity from 2600 MW in 1999 to 2300 MW in May 2007. He who agreed with Umar but with varying statistics observed that President Olusegun Obasanjo had himself injected a whopping ₦300 billion into NEPA alone without any discernible improvement and a record of decline from generating 4500 MW to 1500 MW.[38]

This deplorable situation in the power sector was inimical to socio-economic growth and development of the country leaving most households and business owners to resort to alternative but unsustainable sources of electricity generation particularly the use of generators. Some states and townships spent days before electric power could return to them while many others especially rural communities for years could not have a feel of electricity supply.

Furthermore, Mohinder observed that the power sector of Nigeria arguably stands in closer proximity with corruption like the oil and gas sectors.[39] Not only because of the seeming overwhelming evidence of institutional improprieties in the energy sectors generally; but also more for the fact that electricity sector is the most versatile and widely used form of energy in Nigeria. Meanwhile, Aliyu, Mustaph, Adam and Yakaka argued that the nature of the electricity sector and inherent danger of the current centralized regulatory framework in Nigeria made it possible for the 'larger-than-life' image and influence of the defunct NEPA.[40]

The extent of corruption in the electricity sector as well as its manifestations varies from country to country depending on local peculiarities. In developing countries like Nigeria and its African counterparts, areas like government policies, investment and financing decisions, customer-interfacing activities and commercial operations of the utilities, procurement and human resource management are potential avenues for corruption and operational ineptitude. Nigeria would also need to avoid or direct its institutional strategies in the energy sector by attuning to the crucial need to tighten the loose ends on the above areas and those to be subsequently identified.

The much-publicized power sector reforms in Nigeria under the Electric Power Sector Reform Act of 2005 is yet to yield desired or anticipated fruits largely due to corruption and impunity of perpetrators, regulatory lapses and policy inconsistencies (Socio-Economic Right and Accountability Project (SERAP). It further stated that the country has lost more megawatts in the post-privatization era due to corruption, impunity, vandalization of gas pipelines and other acts of restiveness in the resource-bearing communities, among other social challenges as reflected in this report. Regrettably, the total estimated financial loss to Nigeria from corruption in the electricity sector starting from the return to democracy in 1999 to date is over ₦11 trillion. This represents public funds, private equity and social investment (or divestments) in the power sector. It is estimated that may reach over ₦20 trillion in the next decade given the rate of government investment and funding in the power sector amidst dwindling fortune and recurrent revenue shortfalls SARAP observed.

The effective monitoring and supervision of the power sector has been made needlessly difficult and shrouded in secrecy through over-centralization of the administration and governance of the sector. This often gives room for institutionalized, carefully structured corruption in the power sector of Nigeria. The top-down model of electricity governance in Nigeria encourages corruption and other illegal dealings. Despite the reforms, the electricity sector in Nigeria has continued to wallow in endemic corruption and impunity.

Several corruption allegations have been checklisted in the Nigerian power sector. Some of which include an allegation of Mr Goodknows Ighali on the diversion of funds of deceased PHCN workers, allegation of Elemelu on the Rural Electrification scandal, allegations of the National Assembly over the manipulation of the award of electricity contracts or cite projects in their constituencies under the guise of 'Constituency Project'. Corruption in the electricity sector ranges from petty corruption at the level of meter reading/readers to grand larceny by the executives who award lucrative contracts and give concessions in the Power Purchase Agreement (PPAs). Power or electricity theft is rampant among the citizens. This is a form of corruption by end users who consume power and circumvent billing or tap into electricity from a DISCO illegally without paying bills for such electricity consumption. This form of corruption is rampant among low-income electricity consumers in Nigeria. Available data reveal that more than one-tenth (12%) of Nigerian households and companies pay one form of bribes or another for electricity services. The DISCOs have been unable to adequately bill or collect minimum amount of revenue required for their operations for varied reasons, and have resorted to difference means of survival ranging from borrowing, taking advantage of government subsidies, deferring payments, over-billing paying customers, reluctance to install pre-paid meters and other corrupt means.

CONCLUSION

In spite of the huge government investment in the power sector in the past sixteen years and series of reforms, Nigeria has only succeeded in mustering an installed electricity generation capacity of 10,000 MW. The country has continued to operate at about 30% of this capacity with generation fluctuating between 2000 and 3500 MW. This deplorable condition has not only got its own fare share in the meagre economy of Nigeria with increasing unemployment and high cost of running businesses but also shaped every strata of the Nigerian society namely, education, household and so forth. Investors' morale is also low with Nigeria becoming a third-class destination for investment. The country's once booming industries are collapsing under the weight of abysmally poor power supply. Many factories, which used to be thriving hubs of production activities, have either closed their workshops, throwing the workers into the labour market or relocated to better investment destinations. Many multinationals equally relocated to Ghana to reduce the huge cost of production caused by Nigeria's woeful power situation. The Nigerian power sector is characterized by myriad of problems such as limited access to infrastructure, low connection rates, inadequate generation and usage of power capacity, ineffective regulation, high technical losses and vandalism, insufficient transmission and distribution facilities, unclear delineation of roles and responsibilities between the government and the holding companies, over-billing of electricity consumers and systemic corruption, among others.

RECOMMENDATIONS

The study recommends the following:

- That the government should improve on the state of electric power infrastructure to ensure unlimited access and optimum performance of the sector.
- That the government in collaboration with other relevant stakeholders should improve the protection of electric power facilities in order to minimize the rate of vandalism.
- That effort should be made to step up the capacity of power generation, distribution and transmission facilities to meet the increasing need for electricity consumption in Nigeria.
- That NERC and other regulatory bodies should wake up to their duties even beyond minimum expectation to eliminate weak operational capacity in the sector.
- That the operation of the sector should be more transparent to eliminate endemic corruption in the sector.
- That significant investment is required to improve the transmission system if it is to keep pace with the expected growth in the generation capacity and consumers' expectation.

NOTES

1. Trask, Bahira. *The Role of Families and Family Policies in Achieving Inclusive Societies. Focus on Sustainable Development Goals 16 & 11.* Geneva: United Nations Department of Economic and Social Affairs (UNDESA), 2005.

2. Onyewuchi Ikechukwu, 'Nigerian Electricity Debacle', *Guardian*, 10 April 2016, 18.

3. Idris Aliyu, Kura Mustaph, Ahmed Adam and Abba Yakaka, 'An Assessment of the Power Sector Reform in Nigeria', *International Journal of Advancements in Research and Technology* no. 2 (2013): 87.

4. Omoleke Ife and Adeopo Adejumo, 'Privatization of Nigerian Public Enterprises: Its Practical Challenges as a Reformulated Policy of the Fourth Republic', *AJPAM* no. 16 (2005): 65.

5. Jonah Onuoha, *The State and Economic Reforms in Nigeria: An Explanatory Note on the Capture Theory of Politics* (Nsukka: Great AP Express Publishers, 2008), 17.

6. Ngozi Okonjo-Iweala and Philip Kwaafo, *Nigeria's Economic Reforms Progress and Challenges* (Washington, DC: Brookings Institution, 2007), 12.

7. Ernest Aniche, *World Bank and sectoral reforms in Nigeria, 1999–2007* (Saarbrucken: Lambert Academic Publishing, 2015).

8. Ibid., 28.

9. Bureau of Public Enterprises (BPE), *Guidelines for Commercialization and Privatization of Public Sector in Nigeria* (Abuja: BPE, 2006).

10. Aliyu, Mustaph, Adam and Yakaka, 'An Assessment of the Power Sector Reform', 88.

11. Ibid., 28

12. Ibid., 89

13. Ibid., 90

14. Ibid., 29

15. Ibid., 90

16. Dino Maleye, Corruption in Electricity Reports, *Vanguard*, 16 February 2017, 8.

17. Oladimeji Adeyemo and Salami Adeleke, 'A Review of Privatization and Public Enterprises Reforms in Nigeria', *Journal of Contemporary Management Research* 4 (2008): 401–18.

18. Latham and Watkins, Reports, 2016, 2.

19. Simeon Mienpamo, 'Mid-Term Reports of President Goodluck Jonathan', *Vanguard*, 18 March 2013, 9.

20. Adeniyi Aladejare, 'Energy, Growth and Economic Development: A Case Study of the Nigerian Electricity Sector', *American Journal of Business, Economics and Management* 2 (2014): 41–54.

21. National Electricity Regulatory Commission (NERC), *Electricity Regulation in Nigeria* (Abuja: NERC, 2014).

22. National Electricity Regulatory Commission (NERC), *Multi Year Tariff Order (MYTO)*, (Abuja: NERC, 2013).

23. Ibid., 3.

24. African Development Fund, ADF Reports, 2013, 1.

25. Ahmed Zainab, Nigeria: Why We Cannot Cancel Privatization of PHCN, This Day, February 16, 2017; 11.

26. Christian Ezeibe, *ABC of Political Economy: A Beginners Guide* (Nsukka: University of Nigeria Press, 2015), 23.

27. Okonjo-Iweala and Kwaafo, *Nigeria's Economic Reforms Progress and Challenges*.

28. Ezeibe, *ABC of Political Economy*.

29. Ibid., 29.

30. Socio-economic Rights and Accountability Projects (SERAP), *From Darkness to Darkness: How Nigerians Are Paying the Price of Corruption in the Electricity Sector* (Enugu: University of Nigeria Press, 2017), 23.
31. Latham and Watkins, Reports, 1.
32. Aliyu et al., 'An Assessment of the Power Sector Reform', 90.
33. Mieonpamo, 'Mid-Term Reports of President Goodluck Jonathan', 8.
34. Josephine Marry, 'Analysis of Energy Crisis and how it Affects Production Sector and Economic Growth of Nigeria', *WCECS* no. 1 (2014): 261–5.
35. Oketola Dayo, 'Power Failure: Nigerians Burn #17.5 trillion Po Generators in Five Years', *Punch*, May 20, 2015, 7.
36. Ibid., 7.
37. Werker Eric, Ezekwueche Onyebuchi, Igun Olatomiwa and Wei Alice, 'Privatization of the Power Sector in Nigeria', *Harvard Business School* no. 3 (2014): 713–43.
38. Tijani Haruna, 'The Dynamics of Corruption', *Vanguard*, February 23, 2005, 4.
39. R.A.O. Mohinder, 'Corruption in the Electricity Sector: A Pervasive Scourge', in *Many Faces of Corruption-Tracking Vulnerabilities at the Sector Level*, eds. Edgardo Campos and Sanjay Pradhan (Washington, DC: The World Bank Press, 2007), 1.
40. Aliyu et al., 'An Assessment of the Power Sector Reform', 87.

BIBLIOGRAPHY

Adeyemo, Oladimeji and Salami Adeleke. 'A Review of Privatization and Public Enterprises Reforms in Nigeria'. *Journal of Contemporary Management Research* no. 4 (2008): 401–18.

Aladejare, Adeniyi. 'Energy, Growth and Economic Development: A Case Study of the Nigerian Electricity Sector'. *American Journal of Business, Economics and Management* 2 (2014): 41–54.

Aliyu, Idris, Kura Mustaph, Ahmed Adam and Abba Yakaka. 'An Assessment of the Power Sector Reform in Nigeria'. *International Journal of Advancements in Research and Technology* 2 (2013). ISSN 2278-7763.

Dayo, Oketola. 'Power Failure: Nigerians Burn #17.5 trillion Po Generators in Five Years'. *Punch*, 20 May 2015.

Eric, Werker, Ezekwueche Onyebuchi, Igun Olatomiwa and Wei Alice. 'Privatization of the Power Sector in Nigeria'. *Harvard Business School* 3 (2014): 713–43.

Ezeibe, Christian. *ABC of Political Economy: A Beginners Guide*. Nsukka: University of Nigeria Press, 2015.

Haruna, Tijani. 'The Dynamics of Corruption'. *Vanguard*, February 23, 2005.

Ife, Omoleke and Adeopo Adejumo. 'Privatization of Nigerian Public Enterprises: Its Practical Challenges as a Reformulated policy of the Fourth Republic'. *AJPAM* 16 (2005).

Ikechukwu, Onyewuchi. 'Nigerian Electricity Debacle'. *Guardian*, 10 April 2016.

Maleye, Dino. 'Corruption in Electricity Reports', *Vanguard*, 16 February 2017.

Marry, Josephine. 'Analysis of Energy Crisis and how it Affects Production Sector and Economic Growth of Nigeria'. *WCECS* 1 (2014): 261–5.

Mienpamo, Simeon. 'Mid-Term Reports of President Goodluck Jonathan'. *Vanguard*, 18 March 2013.

Mohinder, R.A.O. 'Corruption in the Electricity Sector: A Pervasive Scourge'. In *Many Faces of Corruption-Tracking Vulnerabilities at the Sector Level*, edited by Edgardo Campos and Sanjay Pradhan. Washington, DC: The World Bank Press, 2007.

Okonjo-Iweala, Ngozi, and Philip Kwaafo. *Nigeria's Economic Reforms Progress and Challenges*. Washington, DC: Brookings Institution, 2007.

Onuoha, Jonah. *The State and Economic Reforms in Nigeria: An Explanatory Note on the Capture Theory of Politics*. Nsukka: Great AP Express Publishers, 2008.

Socio-Economic Rights and Accountability Projects (SERAP). *From Darkness to Darkness: How Nigerians Are Paying the Price of Corruption in the Electricity Sector*. Enugu: University of Nigeria Press, 2017.

Trask, Bahira. *The Role of Families and Family Policies in Achieving Inclusive Societies. Focus on Sustainable Development Goals 16 & 11*. Geneva: United Nations Department of Economic and Social Affairs (UNDESA), 2005.

Zainab, Ahmed. 'Nigeria: Why We Cannot Cancel Privatization of PHCN'. *This Day*, 16 February 2017.

Chapter 4

The Relevance of Creativity Economics of Contemporary Nigerian Diaspora Art for Political Socialization

Timothy Olusola Ogunfuwa

INTRODUCTION

A few phrases have been brought into play in this chapter, although they have been preempted by choice of their relevance to this study. These phrases also create different disciplinal parallels if interrogated from some particular angles. If interrogated from some other viewpoints, again, these phrases can create possible harmonic literary concords in their usages. The phrases are creativity economics, political socialization and art, the economics of art and political socialization and creativity. They have come into topical construction in this chapter. The reason is that the researcher has explored an area of artistic discourse that needs scholarly consideration. This validates the discourse angle that focuses on the responsibility, role, usage, and effectiveness of arts in a citizenry's political socialization. Invariably, a researcher's perception can be on the political, sociological, historical, archaeological and economical points of reference.

This chapter, however, engages this discourse from the economics perspective of creativity actualization, manipulation and evaluation. Addressing the political socialization of artists through their agents of political culture is still scholastically new in art study in Nigeria, but for the Kalilu[1] which is likely to be first. It is, therefore, necessary to highlight Kalilu's viewpoint. His study emphasizes that 'there hs not been broad based art historical analysis of economic themes in modern Nigerian art. There have also not been such studies on the impact of policies and economic experiences on the Nigerian art'.[2] His work focuses on the value of art as a corrective, economic, educational and historical object that creatively and positively correct the mentality of a nation when the content and context of the art are thematically articulated.[3] Though Kalilu's study's approach of understanding Nigerian economics through vocational education is enlightening and a forerunner in this regard, it would be then foolhardy to say that the approach of methodology, emphasis and typology of this political socialization study is sacrosanct. Essentially, this study starts with an explanation of a few basic definitions and applications of those topical phrases earlier mentioned and then systematically proceeds to expatiate on their subject relevance and implications. Overall, in the study's submissions, it would be observed that the analytical considerations are sizably actualized and justifiably achieved. Nonetheless, submissions and recommendations are not considered conclusive or all-solving in their approaches, for the simple fact that this aspect of art and political economics research is just evolving.

Political socialization usually discusses two broad sociological, systemic, conceptions. One is the political system, while the second is the psychological/educational system. The process of evaluating the former is called macro, in form; while that of evaluating the latter is called micro. When considering a macro examination, the larger society is favoured in perception and evaluation. But when considering a micro examination, the individual is favoured in perception and evaluation.[4] Significantly, therefore, the political socialization of the people is shaped by and dependent on the activities of a society. Generally, this is discussed as the political culture. Political culture is cultivated from political socialization. Dekker quotes Dawson et al. as defining political socialization as 'the process through which citizens acquire political views that become aggregated in ways that have consequences for the political life of the nation'.[5] This definition is from a political point of view. He also provides a definition from the individual's point of view: 'The process through which an individual acquires his particular political orientations, his knowledge, feelings, and evaluations regarding his political world'.[6] But Weisberg[7] defines political socialization as the systemic transfer of political values of a society, through the agents of political socialization,[8] whether formal or not, regular or otherwise, from the present generation to succeeding generations with the aim of maintaining political stability and continuity.[9] What is paramount in this situation is the political culture, which is actively transmitted, processed, and used by the citizenry. The agents classified as assisting the process of political socialization are the institutions, organizations and individuals.

Next is economics. The notion that economics operates on the principle of demand and supply of goods and services at the micro and macro levels of human engagements has become a piece of general knowledge. In order nations sustain the wellbeing of their people, organizations and governments, they have evolved and experimented on economics and economic theories. They have also propounded ideas and means of executing them. Since micro and macro economists also abound, Markusen[10] has called for a rise in the number of mezzo-economists. This, he says, would create a direction for the arts and artists to navigate around in the society's economic structure. Reiterating the significance of the artists in a society's development, she emphasizes that 'as human capital investment targets, artists are also worthy, because their creativity drives cultural industries – media, publishing, advertising, music, and tourism – that are among the most important US exports'.[11]

But in Nigeria, at least, it is a general knowledge that music and dance have projected cultural and contemporary values. Invariably, Markusen is soliciting more leverages than the functions of the art economists, who, most of the time, concentrate on the socio-cultural demand, management, and creation of art itself. Markusen is particularly interested, through her studies, in the importance of the political economy of art and of art management and propagation,[12] which emphasizes an all-inclusiveness of artists, public and private institutions, government and the public sphere participation.

CONCEPTION OF CREATIVITY ECONOMICS AND POLITICAL SOCIALIZATION

It is, however, important to note that the history of the economic study of art and artists has been traced back to the mid-1960s with the work of William J. Baumol and William G. Bowen. The publication is titled, *Performing Art: The Economic Dilemma,* and it was published in 1966.[13] When in the 1970s the Association of Cultural Economics was founded, and it began to publish the *Journal of Cultural Economics*, art-economics study blossomed.[14] Two issues have been relatively discussed. The first one is on the economics of arts and artists, the necessity for politics and socio-political integration in the broader understanding of arts and artists' expressivities and capabilities. The second is on the understanding of the meanings of political socialization. It is now necessary to direct our attention to this study's focus, so as harmonize the divergent disciplinal meanings into a plausible discourse framework.

Every citizen of a country goes through a process of political socialization. The artist is no exception – at least primarily as a citizen, and secondarily as a stakeholder in the several agencies of the political socialization process. Art institution develops its artist's initial interest through its verifiable learning culture, curriculum and philosophy. This peculiar orientation is regularly passed on through succeeding generations. However, this sustained orientation influences the political socialization standpoints of the artist to a great extent. Again, while an institution can characteristically formulate its postures as a style or as a movement, its graduates sometimes, unconsciously, display their institution's tendencies. These practice tendencies are commonplace. But the artist's socialization and interaction with other artists from other institutions, with the public sphere, and coupled with the artist's economic and socio-political interest, the artist's posture is likely to start shifting. As this shift coincides and interlaces with other personal interests and motives, and that of other people, it alters again. But if artists' postures are strong enough, they can gradually alter the political socialization posture of people who are close to them.

A conflict process, though sometimes healthy, thus arises. It is this process of articulating an eventually decisive posture that this study conceived as creativity economics, on the one hand. On the other hand, the process that the artist also takes in achieving his or her artistic product to become noticeable in its style, material and method, also it is in the packaging of its appeal to the potential buyer and art critics through the artist's personality packaging. It is the creativity process of creating demand and supply by the artist and the sustenance of this through various agents and elements of political socialization. Thus, while the involvement of mezzo-economists can assist, in part, the process, it can also be fully actualized by the artists and the artists' community.

From the standpoint of economics, creativity template has been addressed equally from the same perspective of the artist, art critic and aesthetician. Furthermore, the creativity economists agree that the ascertainment of value placement and measurement is achievable of the object and the individual of creative substance. But for these economists, again, evaluating ideas remains problematic.[15] This fact reiterates the point that frameworks for economic evaluations are frequently structured along quantitative methodology. The precept explored in studying creativity dimensions in this chapter is qualitative. As such, this provides another leverage for evaluating creativity dimensions utilized in artistic works. It equally identifies and characterizes a complex, possible typology structure, which would also expand interrogation the frontiers of style, theme and material/medium development in areas of the arts.

Foremost, this researcher holds two fundamental positions. One, he believes that political socialization extends beyond the value circumstance of people, from one generation to another. And two, that political socialization also extends beyond the peculiarities of its application to the political atmosphere of the immediate and extended cultural and environmental boundaries. Advancing from this standpoint, therefore, political socialization is conceptualized to also extend, in its structural scholastic framework and definition possibility, to one, the harmonization of artistic and spiritual properties of the person or a class of persons; and two, its placement in the larger socio-cultural and political society. Art has played an important role in positioning and re-positioning political socialization in all cultures of the world. This role is particularly emphasized in some contents of social realism in the arts and crafts, and it further tilts towards addressing the circumstances of specific socialization exercises within a cultural and spatial boundary.

This chapter discusses contemporary Nigerian artists (particularly exemplifying with those in the diaspora) within the purview of political socialization processes through a conception of the economics of artistic creativity. The works of two Nigerian painters in diaspora, who have been used to illustrate this chapter's conception, have been classified in this study as the *Inside-outsiders*. They are classified as such because, though many diaspora artists have re-oriented themselves in space and socio-culture dimensions, some are still deeply involved in the processes of political socialization of their motherland. As progressive agents of an uncommon, political socialization medium that is considered as the critical arts in this study, the Inside-outsiders constantly interrogate, literally and visually, the standards of the economic and socio-political values of their mother nations. By this understanding, the Inside-outsiders must always be a diaspora – an emigrant. The Inside-outsiders used as a case study are two Nigerian painters. They are Dele Jegede and Moyo Okediji. They both emigrated to the United States over three decades ago. Notwithstanding, they found it necessary to constantly socio-politically, critically and visually examine, question and recommend plausible solutions to many of the problems that stagnate Nigeria through their arts.

THEORETICAL CONCEPTION

Inglehart's theory of post-materialism[16] is adopted for the theoretical framework for this study. The theory's conceptual paradigm is set on the principle values of materialism/post-materialism. The principal denominating factor for materialism is individual-intended, while that for the post-materialism is collective-intended. Inglehart's theoretical conception is, however, developed from a Western living style's point of view. He points out that, before World War II, the concern of the individual was basically security and survival. After the war, however, and with the growing advancement of technology and nations' stability, there grew a general awareness and demand in the quality of life, self-esteem, wellbeing of the populace, freedom of speech, sustenance of democracy, environment, gender rights and equality, liberty and so on.[17] He further sees the process as a seamless integration in the socio-political and economic systems that become a generational, sequential transfer from which has gradually emerged permanent behavioural tendencies in values acquisition process of Western nations. It is a political socialization process and agents' development, which logically seemed tied to the growth of political socialization paradigms that earlier developed in 1959 by Herbert Hyman, and whose words got cultivated in the 1960s and beyond.[18]

The post-materialism theory provides a possible dimension to interrogate both the creativity economics and the political socialization angles of the sample illustrating this study. This is because the sample shifted from a geo-political zone of the African continent, a continent still enmeshed in materialism values, to North America, a continent that is fast entrenched in post-materialism values. The creative process of transferring values, which they have gradually accustomed themselves, which influenced their interrogatory acumen, and some of which are appositional to current Nigerian values, but which they have creatively addressed and extended to some privileged sector of the Nigerian economy, is the crux of this chapter.

THE ARTISTS' PRE-DIASPORIC POLITICAL SOCIALIZATION STAGES

The two painters discussed are of Yoruba descent. Dele Jegede was born in Ikere Ekiti, in Ekiti State; and Moyo Okediji was born in Lagos State. Yoruba socio-cultural values and mores were much instilled into the hearts of children those days. If on the average these painters left secondary school education on or before the age of seventeen years, it shows that education was the primary responsibility of families among the Yoruba people of south-western Nigeria. Education largely became a source of measurement of a family's wealth and social respect. In order to follow up this educational responsibility, it took courage and understanding for a family to willingly agree that a child studies professionally any course in the field of creative arts because it was considered a lowly profession. Doubts on complimentary societal achievement through this assumed lowly profession became commonplace among many people in the Yoruba community. As the arts were usually considered vocational professions,[19] their immediate and extended relevance in the society as a means of assessing or determining several societal activities, in their various dimensions, was only comprehensible to an elitist few.[20] In this regard, the institution of the visual arts itself became a political socialization agent that is not accorded much relevance in the community.[21] Further still, based on this art institution's assessment thus far, it would not be said that it has achieved as much as it should when compared to many others in its category in the Western world.[22] It is from this laidback socio-geographic background that these two painters (and several others) grew, worked and relatively excelled. Because the level of value assessment and appreciation was (and still essentially is) materialistically defined, virtually all experiences were captioned under the umbrella of insecurity. This was common knowledge of almost all of the Nigerian post-colonial values.

In the current circumstance of our socio-geographic and political economy, particularly from the late twentieth century, a good number of Nigerian contemporary artists achieved prominence. Individually, they also tried to fight against personal insecurity and promote individual relevance. Interestingly, this position was not peculiar to the arts alone: it was a general attitude and value that permeated through the veins of almost all Nigerians. This attitudinal posture of insecurity was passed down from generation to generation.

When the elitist class in the society became visibly stratified through an economic superiority, they became thirsty for creative genres. While this period began with the nation's democratic republic, there grew a thirst, too, among the creative personnel to explore other spatio-geographical and political environments to exhibit their talent. From the late 1980s to the 1990s that followed, the urge for creative was at its noticeable height, even across several other disciplines in Nigeria. At this period, the contributions towards creativity by Jegede and Okediji, were in different moods and mediums, but both virtually treat some similar thematic conceptions: socio-political commentaries, even before they left the shores of Nigeria (figures 4.1 to 4.4). Figures 4.1 and 4.2 are imageries that resonate the state of distress in the society. Jegede's representations become iconographical of his illustrative and cartoon-like prowess. They are emblematical of his satirical, poetic and metaphorical pronouncements of the economic state of the Nigerian nation. The expanse of his creativity manoeuvrability could be attested to by some

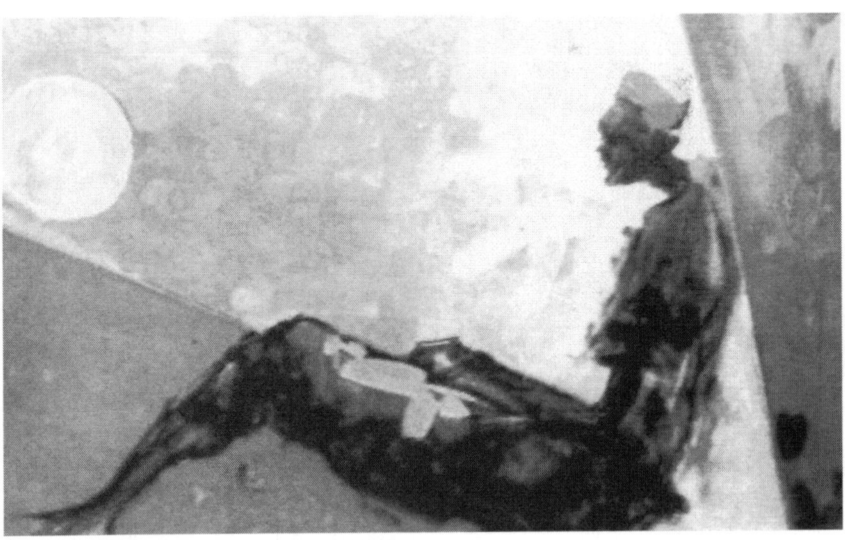

Figure 4.1. ***Hope*: Dele Jegede (1991), Oil on board.**
***Source*: Jegede20.**

Figure 4.2. *Eko re e*: Dele Jegede (1991), Oil on canvas. *Source*: Jegede21.

Figure 4.3. *Sokoyokoto*: Moyo Okediji (1990), Plasticography. *Source*: Ona 222.

people outside the established elitist class of the 1980s and 1990s. His visually constructed political socialization instrument greatly assisted by his curiosity, cartooning skill, and coloured canvases employed to interrogate the socio-politics of those periods.

In the case of Okediji, he started to display his unique attitudinal posture that could be classified as reactionary or anti-regularly social when he restricted his daily wears to Yoruba and Hausa fashion traditions. This period was before he became a diaspora. His social resolution and cultural

Figure 4.4. ***Essentaye*: Moyo Okediji (1991), Natural pigments on baked clay. *Source*: Courtesy of the artist.**

attributions, nonetheless, have their flavours and expressionistic dimensions. He directs his economics and creative postures, inwardly: the soil, local dye, thread, discarded plastic, metal, fabric and so on, transcending the materials' ordinary day-to-day usages, thus becoming his artistic mediums and creative directions (figures 4.3 and 4.4). The items, in their contextual extensions, later serve as his searchlight to original storytelling and traditional lore of Nigerian cultural, economic and political theatrical tools, mediums and surface-scape in creativity economics manoeuvrings and political socialization exploration devices in the diaspora. But *Sokoyokoto* (figure 4.3) is re-enlivening the aquatic magnificence of south-west Nigeria, and a part of the area's economic source. *Essentaye* (figure 4.4) creates a visual drama in an abstract configuration that laces with fear, relationship and mythological presence, which, again, is a value projected in the materialism theory. All this has been creatively harmonized to actualize a socio-cultural synthesis of the few people who are knowledgeable in African philosophy and aesthetics.

THE PAINTERS' CREATIVITY ECONOMICS AND THE ADVANCEMENT OF NIGERIAN POLITICAL SOCIALIZATION

In all of this, one would still acknowledge the fact that Nigerian contemporary artists and historians have gone a long way in literally and visually documenting cultural values, even before the post-independence era. Sofola[23] is devoted to the values of African cultures. He emphasizes that 'the non-material aspects of it [that is, our culture], the ideas, the beliefs and world-view of our people' must be shared and 'socially transmitted . . . from one generation to another'.[24] Many of these aspects have been explored by the Nigerian painters to create political awareness in the society.[25] In most cases, it is the contextualization of such works that usually turns their visual imagery into objects worth ruminating.[26] But how successful are their contextual interpretations and apprehensions by the politically-aware public? This particular question is important. But a successful approach to an easy answer and equally valuable determination can only be quantitative.

When we consider the wide range of political socialization agents that abound, that is functional, and that is easily accessible today, then it becomes relatively noticeable that the configuration of the political socialization of the 1990s and before was not qualitatively dignifying. Most likely, the level of creativity economic system available in Nigeria would be responsible. But one major, noticeable agent, which tremendously increases the possibilities of creativity economics and has also improved political socialization in Nigeria in the past fifteen years, is the mass media, particularly, the information technology. How has this affected the works of these Nigerian diaspora painters in the effectiveness of the political socialization of Nigerians? The rest of the discourse will concentrate on this question.

Focusing on this aspect of the discourse, two diasporic works of each painter are used as illustrations. The political socialization awareness of the painters has also built positively, with consistent diasporic exposures and with time. In the past five to ten years, some visual works of many Nigerian diaspora artists have exceedingly dignified the repertoire of contemporary Nigerian art, making the local and international art periscope rich and colourful. In an attempt to answer some pressing societal issues in Nigeria, many of these diaspora artists engage in serialization of topical events and concepts. In order that such strong socio-political, economic and cultural issues are explored extensively in visually and literally formats, these painters employ both critical, scholastic theorization, and stylistic and thematic serializations. This instructive and intuitive attitude is a sign of the positive global influence that activates the artists' critical thinking and their informed spatial environments. Artists that naturally bow to such influence interest themselves in the goings-on of their country. Such a dedicated position becomes a psychologically and patriotically driven motive. The artist that maintains close attachment to his or her premier creativity source – in their physical, mental and environmental forms – can be considered a creative patriot. Technically from this discourse dimension so far, this set of artists can also be logically construed as the *Outside-insiders*. They continually participate and contribute to the knowledge development of both the countries that they emigrated from and which they currently live. Again, the preceding sentences preempt a further classification of another set of artists and other professionals. These are immigrants (diasporas) who do not participate in the development of any sector of their mother country. They just would not phantom any plausible reason so to do. Or other pressing avocations and circumstances may not afford them such a sacrifice. These are the *Outside-Outsiders*: they have no trace of political socialization influence on their native country.

In furtherance of the painters' contribution in some measures to the political socialization of Nigerians, two interesting serials by Jegede should easily catch the attention of any critical mind. These serials are the Delta avengers and oil pollution series (see figure 4.5), and the Boko Haram–abducted Chibok girls of the 'Bring Back Our Girls' fame series (see figure 4.6). These thematic concerns, which are internally generated pathetic environmental and security situations, have become global discourse. They have also received considerable literary attention. Visual interpretations on them are also gradually gaining art consideration from within Nigeria and outside. The Delta avengers and oil pollution series interrogate the desecrated state of south-eastern Nigeria commonly referred to as the Niger Delta and the ignoble scale that the oil regions have been pitiably conditioned. The questions usually prompted from these sad scenarios several. One, is the so-called Delta avengers truly avenging for the common good of the Delta people? Are they not increasing their blotted greed and self-aggrandizement? Is the whole exercise not in praise of a few selected sponsors? Are the people in power of authority in Nigeria not seeing the vast aquatic destruction and degradation that have turned the whole Delta environmental landscape into a sickening

Figure 4.5. ***Niger Delta: Shell-shocked*****: Dele Jegede (2010), Mixed media on canvas.** ***Source*****: Jegede25.**

sight? These are recurring questions that trigger some artistic works, which are post-materialistic in the form and intention, and which sometimes visually parody, satirize, allegorize and philosophize on this negative issue.

Again, Jegede's serial on the Chibok girls also addresses fundamental issues from two diametrically opposing contexts. While discourse on some of these paintings can be deliberated from the position of gender, insecurity, liberty and oppression glaringly point of view, there is equally a suggestion

Figure 4.6. ***African, Europe and America Suite 1*****: Moyo Okediji (Year not indicated), Pen and ink. *Source*: Courtesy of the artist.**

that mocks the physical and spiritual being of the Nigerian youths, while their future burns in the veiled time and form, and in the spiritual terms. The female representation of the Nigerian child (see figure 4.7), in its sad visual metaphor assessment in colours and imagery, reiterates a fertile continuum in oppression – generational damnation – and bleak is the view of its horizon. The intentional usage of 'its' is to characterize the poetic normative in the figure, which the Nigerian child/youth has gradually conditioned its physical and spiritual bodies to seek and hunt, attain and sadly retain. This whole scenario, then, is a test of conscience, which Jegede supplants in the sub-consciousness of some well-meaning Nigerians, who, by the hierarchical social class of their political socialization and economic status, should be able to influence some positive change along the line of his serialized works. Invariably in both serialized themes, Jegede is calling our attention to the level of injustice perpetrated in Nigeria. He and a few others in this conceptual category gravitate towards post-materialist economic ideology, while creditably discharging their political socialization means through creatively underscoring an easy process of public understanding, but which deeper contextual parameters are continually revealed to the highly creatively conscious individual.

Moyo Okediji's notable attempt at advancing the frontiers of political socialization is through the networks of artists, and art and culture lovers through a virtual school on the internet. The website, University of African

Figure 4.7. ***Aisha*****: Dele Jegede (2015), Acrylic on canvas.**
Source**: The News26.**

Art, has become a melting pot for literary and visual artists, and art critics of various cultural backgrounds. This domain promotes arts and culture of the continent of Africa, and from creative people of African descent all over the world. The conception of this forum and the kind of internet surfers that participate, that also controls, indicates and the same time validates high-level creativity economics that Okediji has brought into play. Raising the level of awareness of all facets of the African, and African-American cultural lives using the advantage of the information technology and its availability across socio-economic strata of many nations in the black world is particularly congratulatory.

But this being as it may, Okediji has used this medium to accelerate idea and knowledge dissemination among many of the internet literate public that is interested in the arts of the black race. Because of Okediji's artistic versatility, information technology has also been creatively used by him to further his art propagating interest. Since he also encourages artistic collaborations, creative outputs through such process have yielded highly contextual, critical and playful artistic works, which have many times ended up in art installations. *Egungun* (figure 4.8), which is generally known as masquerade among the Yoruba, has been conceptualized by Okediji (with Wole Lagunju) as a 'Masque-Raiding' form.[27] Egungun, known as *Ara orun* (the one who is from heaven, or the spirit from the land of ghosts), has played the double-imaged persona, the one in whose meaning is rested in the meaning of its opposite or otherness. Okediji encapsulates egungun's qualification and personification in 'deathlessness'. What is unique in the *Egungun* series is the vibrancy of their costumes, which adumbrates the richness of the Yoruba culture: its transformation, and its deathlessness ('aiku') in the face of other cultures' threats and globalization tyranny.

Okediji's propagation of the African culture is through an elevated scholastic repertoire of visual and literary commentaries that is expanded in the classical representation of symbolism of life, continent, surrogating and justice in a serial. *Africa, Europe, and America Suite* serial (see figure 4.6) addresses the socio-political and economic imbalance that perpetuates through colonialism by the Western powers. The serial is a continuous reminder of the mystery might of mother Black Africa, while she provides life and succour for the whites. But a message that is even richer in its historical, economic and mythical re-presentation is Africa feeding the West with life, which can ultimately be likened to knowledge, and which is the bosom of man's existence. The set of drawings particularly directs our minds to the consequences of the slave trade and how mother Africa was forcefully made to feed the West. Allegorically, one would decipher in these drawings the mythical symbolism of the Greek She-Wolf breastfeeding Romulus and Remus, who were both acknowledged as the founding fathers of the city of Rome.[28] The work draws our attention to the mythical philosophy behind the lives of these gods, which sometimes involved miraculous survival and painful death. Such was the myth of Romulus and Remus. In the personification of Africa, Europe and America, Okediji has tacitly explicated the continents' colonial history. Africa actually symbolizes the protective She-Wolf. After concluding its

Figure 4.8. ***Egungun*** **(two installations in view): Moyo Okediji (with Wole Lagunju), (2008), Mixed media.** ***Source*****: Okediji29.**

duty, though probably done reluctantly, Africa is left with its remains of poverty to manage and to also ceaselessly wander in the wilderness like a worn wolf. It would not be out of order, however, to submit that Okediji would fervently pray for the circumstance of these Greek gods equally re-presents itself, but on the continents of Europe and North America.[29]

CONCLUSION

Primarily, it is important to note that all these contemporary Nigerian diaspora artists are the first set of generations of such people to be labelled as such. There are over forty of them.[30] This number of artists is significant when the contributions of these artists to the theory and practice of art generally are considered. For the fact many of them left Nigeria during the brain drain era of the late 1980s to the early period of 2000s,[31] some of them are equally among the respected few during the period while still in Nigeria. A few of them still maintain that enviable status, a few others have changed focus, and a few others have fizzled out. In all of this, there are some undisputable levels of practice conflicts and resolutions. And in whichever direction these artists had turned, it was an experience towards creativity economics. The overall experience must have been, undoubtedly, aided by the change in the geographical environment. The experience would have also led the artists to find means of solving some of these unavoidable diasporic issues. Logically, this ever-present diasporic circumstance would have obvious alterations in artistic form, style, material and theme in varying degrees. Whatever that was eventual arrived at created the dimension to each diaspora artist's political socialization.

From the foregoing, therefore, it follows that there would be several other Nigerian diasporas who, by the nature of their profession and their unreserved patriotism, are bonded with Nigeria. These people find all ways of contributing to Nigerian's development. They are the *Inside-outsiders*. Invariably, there are those who no longer feel any obligation to Nigeria. They are considered the *Double-outsiders*. These people have socio-culturally, politically and economically severed root relationships. But it is important to also note that not all Inside-outsiders participate in the political socialization of their country through their art. In the case of some contemporary Nigerian diaspora artists like Nnenna Okore, for example, she could find difficulty in integrating activities of Nigerian political socialization with her intense material exploration. This is because her thematic concerns are continuously restricted to highly abstracted, philosophical contexts that could be far removed from the understanding of many in the Nigerian elitist class. Nevertheless, artists of her mental and cultural stature still regularly identify with their native roots in creativity, economic-wise. However, they artistically and creatively integrated into the community they domicile.

Overall, this study has shown that a researcher can identify an artist's level of political socialization, whether as an *inside-outsider* or as an *inside-insider* (a patriot stationed within the nation of his or her birth), through the artist's skilful manipulation of the economics of creativity. While this study has further directed our mind to political socialization perspective as a scholastic angle that could enrich art critical thinking and writing, it has shown that analysis of several elements of the artist's creativity economics from this perspective would likely add positively to aesthetic and typological evaluation of some artistic productions, and which will significantly raise the importance, and financial value of art and artists. Particularly in the African art scholasticism, when this typological framework for art assessment is adequately explored in the propagation of art's intrinsic ingredients as a tool for political socialization (primarily, for the enlightenment and enhancement of the masses and social order), a noticeable growth in economic and creative value of art itself will be felt in all strata of a nation's citizenry. This, ultimately, will influence positive acknowledgments from government and non-government quarters alike, which would help equate art and culture benefits of a nation to that of its science and technology. Although Nigerian diaspora art and artists are used as the case studies, some vocations can also be studied through their economic ingredients to determine the levels of their affectations on the political socialization in some immediate and extended cultures.

NOTES

1. Rasaq Olatunde Rom Kalilu, *Vocational Education and the Challenges of Nigerian Economy* (Milton Keynes: AuthorHouse, 2010).
2. Ibid., 4.
3. Ibid., 6–10, 32–73.
4. Henk Dekker, 'Political Socialization Theory and Research', In *Politics and the European Younger Generation; Political Socialization in Eastern, Central and Western Europe* (Oldenburg: BIS, 1991), 15–58, quoted Richard E. Dawson, Kenneth Prewitt and Katherine S. Dawson, *Political Socialization* (Boston, Toronto: Little, Brown & Company, 1977).
5. Ibid., 16.
6. Ibid., 16–17.
7. Robert Wiesberg, *Political Learning, Political Choice and Democratic Citizenship* (New Jersey: Prentice Hall, 1974), 13.
8. Kenneth P. Langton, *Political Socialization* (New York: Oxford University Press, 1969), 15.
9. Laxman Singh Rathore, *Political Sociology* (Meenakshi Prakashana, Delhi, 1981), 203.
10. Ann Markusen, *The Economics of Art, Artists, and Culture: Making a Better Case* (2009), http://www.giarts.org/article/economics-arts-artists-and-culture.
11. Ibid.

12. Charles M. Gray and J. Heilburn, *The Economics of Art and Culture* (Cambridge: Cambridge University Press, 2001).

13. William J. Baumol and William G. Bowen, *Performing Art: The Economic Dilemma: A Study of Problems Common to Theater, Opera, Music, and Dance* (New York: Twentieth Century Fund, 1966).

14. Markusen, *Economics of Art.*

15. Roland F. Inglehart, *The Silent Revolution: Changing Values and Political Styles among Western Publics* (Princeton: Princeton University Press, 1977).

16. Inglehart, *Silent Revolution.*

17. Samir Dasgupta, *Political Sociology* (New Delhi: Pearson Publication, 2011), 38.

18. Stephen Fisher, 'Social Attitudes and Value Change', http://users.ox.ac.uk /~nuff0084/polsoc.

19. Ademola Azeez, 'Art and Craft', in *Culture and Customs of the Yoruba*, eds. Toyin Falola and Akintunde Akinyemi (Austin: Pan-African University Press, 2017), 203–10.

20. Dele Jegede, *Eko re e (This Is Lagos)* (Lagos: Center for Cultural Studies, University of Lagos, 1991), 29.

21. Jegede, *Eko re e*, 8.

22. Ona 2, *Ona: Radiance of Rhythms* (Lagos: National Museum, 1990): 9.

23. J.A. Sofola, *African Culture and the African Personality* (Ibadan: African Resources, 1978).

24. Sofola, *African Culture*, ix.

25. Dele Jegede, *Peregrinations: A Solo Exhibition of Drawings and Paintings* (Spenta Multimedia, 2011), 29.

26. Segun Ojewuyi, 'Dele Jegede's Art', *TheNews*, 27 March 2016, http://s16745.pcdn.co/wp-content/uploads/2016/03/Dele-Jegedes-work e1458339494412.jpg.

27. Moyo Okediji, 'On Egungun', (2008). http://okedijiuniverse.blogspot.com.ng/2009/ 04/egungun.html.

28. Horst De La Croix, Richard G. Tansey and Diane Kirkpatrick, *Gardner's Art through the Ages* (Orlando: Harcourt Brace, 1991): 194. Robert Wolverton, *An Outline of Classical Mythology* (Littlefield, Adams, 1975), 76–7.

29. Okediji, 'Egungun'.

30. Timothy Olusola Ogunfuwa, 'Morphology of Practice Conflict in Nigerian Painters in Diaspora', (PhD thesis, Ladoke Akintola University of Technology, Ogbomoso, Nigeria, 2015).

31. Akanmu Adebayo, 'Brain Drain – Brain Gain: Leveraging the Nigerian Diaspora for the Revitalization of Nigeria Higher Education', (lecture, 25th Conference of the Association of Vice Chancellors of Nigerian Universities, Akure, Nigeria, 14 April 2010).

BIBLIOGRAPHY

Adebayo, Akanmu. 'Brain Drain – Brain Gain: Leveraging the Nigerian Diaspora for the Revitalization of Nigeria Higher Education'. Lecture, 25th Conference of the

Association of Vice Chancellors of Nigerian Universities, Akure, Nigeria, 14 April 2010.

Azeez, Ademola. 'Art and Craft'. In *Culture and Customs of the Yoruba*, edited by Toyin Falola and Akintunde Akinyemi, 203–210. Austin: Pan-African University Press, 2017.

Baumol, William J. and William G. Bowen. *Performing Art: The Economic Dilemma: A Study of Problems Common to Theater, Opera, Music, and Dance*. New York: Twentieth Century Fund, 1966.

Croix, Horst De La, R.G. Tansey and D. Kirkpatrick. *Gardner's Art through the Ages*. Orlando: Harcourt Brace, 1991.

Dasgupta, Samir. *Political Sociology*. New Delhi: Pearson Publication, 2011.

Dekker, Henk. 'Political Socialization Theory and Research'. In *Politics and the European Younger Generation; Political Socialization in Eastern, Central and Western Europe,* edited by Henk Dekker, 15–58. Oldenburg: BIS, 1991.

Fisher, Stephen. 'Social Attitudes and Value Change'. http://users.ox.ac.uk/~nuff0084/polsoc.

Gray, Charles M. and J. Heilburn. *The Economics of Art and Culture*. Cambridge: Cambridge University Press, 2001.

Inglehart, Roland F. *The Silent Revolution: Changing Values and Political Styles among Western Publics*. Princeton: Princeton University Press, 1977.

Jegede, Dele. *Peregrinations: A Solo Exhibition of Drawings and Paintings*. Mumbai: Spenta Multimedia, 2011.

Jegede, Dele. *Eko re e (This Is Lagos)*. Lagos: Center for Cultural Studies, University of Lagos, 1991.

Langton, Kenneth P. *Political Socialization*. New York: Oxford University Press, 1969.

Markusen, Ann. 'The Economics of Art, Artists, and Culture: Making a Better Case'. 2009. http://www.giarts.org/article/economics-arts-artists-and-culture.

Ogunfuwa, Timothy Olusola. 'Morphology of Practice Conflict in Nigerian Painters in Diaspora'. PhD thesis, Ladoke Akintola University of Technology, Ogbomoso, Nigeria, 2015.

Ojewuyi, Segun. 'Dele Jegede's Art'. *The News*, March 27, 2016. http://s16745.pcdn.co/wp-content/uploads/2016/03/Dele-Jegedes-work e1458339494412.

Okediji, M. 'On Egungun'. 2008. http://okedijiuniverse.blogspot.com.ng/2009/04/egungun.html.

Ona 2. *Ona: Radiance of Rhythms*. Lagos: National Museum, 1990.

Rathore, Laxman Singh. *Political Sociology*. Delhi: Meenakshi Prakashana, 1981.

Sofola, J.A. *African Culture and the African Personality*. Ibadan: African Resources, 1978.

Wiesberg, Robert. *Political Learning, Political Choice and Democratic Citizenship*. New Jersey: Prentice Hall, 1974.

Part II

INSTITUTIONS AND DEVELOPMENT CHALLENGES IN AFRICA

Chapter 5

Emerging Democratic Institutions and Culture in Africa: Challenges and Prospects

Toyin Falola

This chapter highlights the problems of government and governance in Africa. For example, the expectations are clear as to what the Nigeria as a country wants, having been defined as far back as the 1970s. Nigeria's Second National Development Plan spelled out the country's objectives, a list which has since been repeated and has actually become part of the daily conversation and media narrative: (a) a united, strong and self-reliant nation; (b) a great and dynamic economy; (c) a just and egalitarian society; (d) a land of bright and full opportunities for all citizens; and (e) a free and democratic society.[1]

Although democracy was listed last among the five objectives, by the 1990s, the belief was widely held that without an end to military regimes and without the enthronement of civilian democratic government, none of the other objectives would ever be attained. Nigerians strongly link democracy with good governance and development while equating military rule with authoritarianism and disasters. There are established democratic traditions, as in some past societies that governed on the basis of consensus, as well as the full awareness of a democratic system, which the people have been struggling to attain.

In the second half of the twentieth century, when African countries became independent of European powers, many were ushered into so-called democratic governments but they did not last. Political parties were formed and they contested power, but election-rigging, various electoral frauds and violence characterized the contests. The rewards of power were too attractive, and power was sought at all costs. The desired outcome could not be left to the electoral process, since one party was not sure of what the other would do. The police and the judiciary were compromised. The army struck, and the country entered a long period of military rule. Even in other parts of Africa, where there were no coups or military rule, a one-party state was the rule, as in Kenya, Tanzania, and Cote d'Ivoire, to mention but a few examples. The leadership and institutional crises of the post-independence years were deeply troublesome: institutions of state exercised punitive and coercive powers without much regard for human rights. The judiciary, subordinated to dictatorship, dispensed justice not always with equity and fairness. Paradoxically, misgovernance and a slow rate of development instigated the demand for democracy everywhere, a rather long process, lasting almost four decades in many countries.

Although the desire for democracy and the struggles to attain it have a long history, it should be borne in mind that its contemporary history is less than thirty years old. What scholars like Samuel Huntington call the 'third wave of democratization' is recent, dating to the mid-1990s.[2] The wave coincided with global changes in politics, with the dissolution of the Soviet Union, the collapse of communism, the fall of the Berlin Wall, and the end of the Cold War. Democracy entered its triumphalist moment, and was described as the best political system, which, together with capitalism, was said to signal 'the end of history'.[3] In this 'third wave of democratization', there are notable key developments, which some even call achievements: the number of countries under military dictatorship has been significantly reduced; apartheid collapsed in South Africa and four successful elections have followed; whereas the number of electoral democracies were four in 1985, the number increased to ten in 1993, eighteen in 1995, and twenty-four in 2006; between 2000 and 2002, forty-two countries in sub-Saharan Africa conducted multi-party elections; during that same period, ruling parties in Mali, Ghana, Mauritius and Senegal conceded defeat and yielded power to the opposition parties; by 2003, only 39% of African countries were described as unfree; and Nigeria's current Fourth Republic entered its sixteenth year in 2015, a real achievement in longevity bearing in mind that the First Republic lasted less than six years; the Second for four years; the Third was aborted. Today, a number of African countries are now members of the Community of Democracies, an international inter-governmental coalition of states committed to the promotion of democratic values.[4]

In 1999, a civilian democracy was installed in Nigeria, but it became an elite exercise, and the governance experience has been grossly disappointing, to say the least. There have been cycles of violence, ethnic and religious conflicts, rising poverty and brazen looting of public treasuries by the very people entrusted to spend public funds for development. This chapter takes state pathology as the hidden text, the critique of governance regarded as being similar to the critique of democracy. Despite the propaganda about its benefits and the near-global consensus around these values, democracy is riddled with a lot of contradictions that limit its utilitarian value to the majority of the citizens. The expectation is that political modernity would involve the evolution of a political culture and the emergence of viable resilient institutions that would generate stable politics.

Former President Goodluck Jonathan of Nigeria, a beneficiary of anti-military struggles, defines democracy as a 'system to comprise interdependent and mutually enforcing rights, systems, norms, and intuitions aggregated into what can be referred to as an essential elements of democracy'.[5] He goes further to spell out the essential elements:

1. Respect for human rights – including freedom of expression, freedom of the press, freedom of religion and conscience
2. The Rule of Law, and due process
3. Holding of clearly defined, periodic, free and fair elections based on secret balloting and universal suffrage, and monitored by independent election watchers
4. Freedom of association, including the right to form independent political parties
5. Transparent and impartial administration of elections by an independent body
6. Separation of powers, with an independent judiciary
7. Constitutional subordination of all state institutions, including the military, to the legally constituted civilian authority[6]

He seems to be very well aware of the intricacies, both in terms of electoral democracy which put him in power and of the tenets of liberal democracy which his people desire. The rule of law is fundamental to a liberal democracy, assuming of course that the police and judges are not corrupt. So also is the right to own property and the duty of the state to protect this ownership. Freedom of speech is ensured. It is deliberate that I have cited Goodluck Jonathan, as a practitioner at the highest level of government, instead of using the words of a scholar or of a person who can be called a non-African voice, who can be dismissed as peddling a Western idea. His definition, and the scope of its constituent elements, leaves out issues of development and governance, which are the real source of problems in Africa. Neither is there a correlation between the definitions on paper and the reality in practice, as his administration made abundantly clear.

DISTURBING TRENDS AND DANGEROUS SIGNALS

What we are witnessing in most parts of Africa are the current problems of governance in a democratic framework. The problems are legion, the hopes are constrained and the expectations are large. Be it in Nigeria, Tunisia or Kenya, the problems tend to be similar: violence, election malpractices and blatant fraud, corruption, judicial manipulation, ethnic rivalries, humongous theft of public money and many more.[7] Sometimes, the problems become impediments, such that these impediments are in turn converted to negative ideas, some of which will be discussed later on.

What are these problems? The legacies of European control in the first half of the twentieth century continued to affect institutions and governance. Prominent are issues around identities that have become consolidated in ethnicities whose members permanently fight for power. Some are minority ethnicities, defined in such a manner that they can be excluded from power. Religious identities remain stronger and they continue to create serious pressures of their own. Sudan has had to be divided into two countries, with the Muslims in their own country to the North, and Christians and a myriad of ethnicities in South Sudan where, soon after independence in 2011, they succumbed to power rivalries and a civil war.

In liberal theory, the assumption is that democracy is a cure to political fragmentation. To the contrary, democratic political communities are very much divided. Regional, ethnic and religious cleavages shape the emergence and orientation of political parties. The electoral process is marked by bloc voting, which reflects regions and ethnicities. Indeed, arguments based on ethnicity compromise those of merit, and it does happen that emphasis on selecting leaders rests on where they come from and not about building inclusive institutions to enable all individuals to have a sense of belonging, to exercise their rights and ingenuity, and to contribute to nation-building. As stated further, the democratic process is also tied to violence, and there have been cases of bloody conflict.

Postcolonial economic development issues have overwhelmed the democratic processes and democratic institutions. In the 1980s and 1990s, economic crises destabilized many countries. Africa had the highest number of poor countries in the world, a circumstance that produced conditions of violence. While economic growth has been recorded in a number of places, poverty remains endemic. Democracy and governance, in the case of poor countries, cannot be delinked from poverty. To the poor, the ballot box must change their lives; to the rich and powerful, it provides them with access to higher levels of accumulation, influence, and power.

The problems keep repeating themselves. Electoral malpractice is very much widespread. Campaigns are always about promises not about challenges concerning insecurity, corruption, unemployment, energy, health, education and so on. Programmes are promised without considering the cost. Even when there is a cost, already inflated, kleptocracy makes a nuisance of it. The toleration of corruption and ugly environment (ugly buildings, bad landscaping) is tied to declining civic cultures and degradation of traditional ethos. An observer of Nigeria politics, writing in pain and disappointment, remarks on the problem of corruption:

> There is no other time in the political history of Nigeria that corruption has thrived so amazingly and alarmingly than since 1999 when the current democratic structure became operational. The extent, nature, trend and content of corruption in Nigeria have altogether assumed sophisticated dimensions. Is it among governors, law-makers, public office holders, or within governors, law-makers, public office holders, or within government establishments? Corruption is pervasive. Apparently, democracy seems to have become the guise under which corruption thrives in the public sector. Those who are officially responsible to operate government machinery in Nigeria use the opportunity to exploit the state thereby using the democratic structure to personal advantage.[8]

He echoes the voices of others as the most common topic in the Nigerian media is about missing funds, public corruption and abuse of power. The behaviour is not limited to the politicians, but extends to judges, police, civil servants and others. Office holders do not have any regard for accountability. The cost of democracy is too high, its dividends to the people too little.

Poor leadership is a common narrative topic. The crises of institutions are visible all over. That of leadership is always obvious for everyone to see. No doubt, to fix institutional problems and promote the rule of law will persuade leaders to behave. However, the leaders have to create those institutions. Corruption is a stumbling block to producing great leaders. The civil society has to work hard, first reforming the mindset of citizens to promote values of respect and honesty, to seek the collective public good to work for. It is not uncommon to ask God for good and 'godly' leaders, perhaps because politics is infused with faith or perhaps as a reflection of people's frustration. The Mo Ibrahim Prize has diverted attention to a crisis, offering the largest prize in the world ($5 million over ten years, and $200,000 each year for a lifetime) for a democratically elected leader who governed well and who reduced poverty and generated sustainable development.[9] Whether you regard the Mo Ibrahim Prize as pragmatic or silly, the point is to induce the emergence of good leadership, and for long only the former presidents of Mozambique (Joaquim Alberto Chissano, 2007), Botswana (Festus Gontebanye Mogae, 2008) and Cape Verde (Pedro de Verona Rodrigues Pires, 2011) had won it. In March 2015, the name of President Hifikepunye Pohamba of Namibia was added to the list of winners. It is not only difficult to get winners but also presidents from such a rich country as Nigeria would not care for amounts that represent peanuts when compared to their wanton greed and insatiable appetite for stealing from their nation's treasuries. What a drop of water to a mighty sea!

PROBLEMS IN CONTEXT

Democracy in Africa remains unsettled both at the practical and theoretical levels. At the theoretical level, its critical definitions have yet to be clarified in many countries, and in some cases clearly less understood in different applications. On the one hand, some claim that democracy has a universal application and it should defy race, ethnicity, nationality, religion and culture. On the other hand is a wide range of arguments on the need to make it fit for different cultural milieus, adapt it to different cultures; but leaders, motivated by personal interests, also alter its meaning in practice.

The stress, thus far, has been on electoral democracy, that is, the country is democratic by virtue of elections held and ballots counted. Voting and counting ballots are not the same, as in many cases, numbers are just declared – sometimes more than the number of registered voters. Elections are hardly free and fair, and it is only the winners who accept the outcome. The cheated losers and their followers have no respect or regard for those in power. Indeed, election periods reveal the fragility of the state, and fear is ubiquitous about the collapse of the entire nation. The person in power sees power as a game. The voters, the so-called electorate, relate democracy to a host of problems. Over the years, especially against the background of the failures of authoritarian military regimes, the expectation is that democracy will cure ethnic problems and bring about development. Indeed, most see democracy as a solution to problems of human rights, unemployment, environmental degradation and many other persistent issues.

Corruption and neo-patrimonialism damage democratic institutions and prevent the emergence of credible leadership. By various accounts such as those from Transparency International (a global watchdog on anti-corruption), Nigeria is one of the most corrupt countries in the world. The purpose of political participation for a majority of its leaders is not public service but access to state money. Politics is very lucrative. Thus, the differences between a democratic and a non-democratic government are minimal when it comes to the use of power for private ends. The salaries and benefits of Nigerian politicians are among the highest in the world, with the total pay package of a senator at ₦354 million a year, the equivalent of over $2 million.[10] House members make just slightly less. The chairman of a local government council that hardly generates any significant revenues but is dependent on federal allocation collects ₦1 million (about $5,000) a month, ₦5 million as security vote, 100% of annual salary for accommodation, 400% of annual salary for car loan, 300% of annual salary for furniture, 30% of annual salary for utility bills and 75% of annual salary for domestic staff. When the terms of politicians and civil servants are over, they continue to draw significant pensions.

The Nigerian political class has developed an immoral entitlement attitude. The system, in general, rewards those who go into public service not to do the critical work of contributing to national development and collective transformation but to reward personal ambitions. There are now firmly in place structures of accumulation that disregard the poor and the aspirations of the majority of the country's population. The political philosophy seems to suggest that members of the political class want to convert the majority of the population into beggars as a form of control, using democracy as a ruse. Nigeria has a democracy that works for a few, using almost 85% of its resources to maintain a small percentage of its population. An ex-governor of the Central Bank of Nigeria once alleged that it cost Nigeria more than 25% of the government's recurrent expenditure to service the National Assembly!

A SERIES OF CONTRADICTIONS

Liberal democracy has to be evaluated on the basis of governance, institutions of governance, leadership, policies and their outcomes. Democracy is a rational system of governance with a matrix of evaluation. Some analysts push the evaluative yardstick to include civil and political rights, economic freedom and even the cultural freedom to give room to women's rights and the right to same-sex marriage. People must be allowed to live the way they choose and to express their desires and grievances.[11]

In the case of Nigeria, the most critical matrices are those of economic development and political stability. Is there overall security? With respect to the economy, what is the gross domestic product (GDP) growth rate? Are prices stable to check inflation? What about the unemployment rate and poverty rate? The prerequisites for democracy and governance to function are in the process of creation. A presidential system was copied, without considering the cost and the cultural and historical context that shaped its development in the United States. The appearance has been created that so-called democratic freedom translates to the consolidation of religious and ethnic lines instead of creating cross-cutting national institutions and citizenship. To win elections, political aspirants divide the society, and are quick to suggest the use of violence.

The intellectual origins of Western liberal democracy do not reside in Africa. The intellectualization of the political process by such famous names as Aristotle, Plato and others were grounded in lived experiences of their own societies and cultures. In the case of Africa, democracy is treated is an imported form sometimes divorced from the cultures and philosophy of the West that sold the idea to, or forced it on, Africa. The West is much economically richer, with the capacity to sustain its form of liberal democracy. With

Nigeria, democracy drains its resources; the elections do not necessarily lead to major changes; victories to a new set of leadership only add to the number of those eligible to steal.

That a country calls itself a democracy does not mean that it is not repressive. Democracy and repressive regimes can go together. A state can constitute a threat to itself by repressing its own people, tearing human rights to pieces, and torturing and detaining innocent citizens.

Democracy does not translate to the creation of democratic institutions to manage the lives of people. Thus, there could be elections of presidents and governors, but it does not mean that they govern democratically. It does not mean that state agencies, universities and so on run as democratic institutions. Indeed, the heads of those places behave exactly like emperors, and democracy becomes no more than a mask.

Democracy does not necessarily promote meritocracy, that is, the search for the most competent to govern. Indeed, democracy may become a tool to advance prebendalism. It privileges mediocrities in power, appointed because of loyalty to the party and party leaders, not because of any other qualifications. Democracy has not meant that the rights of marginalized people are protected. One case in point is the treatment of minorities, a way of undermining the rights of citizens.

Constitutionalism defies the boundaries of democracy. A constitution may reveal the shortcomings of human nature. Its interpretations and practices may reflect elite interests that may override, in some cases, the interests of the majority of the population. Those with money constitute the minority that controls power. As members of the political class, they circulate themselves in power, reproducing themselves as they add their children, wives and core friends to the network. There is a lust for power in order to benefit from a rentier state. This minority becomes the 'constituent power', to use a term of Hardt and Negri, governing the majority, the constitutive masses.[12] The boundary between both seems locked.

As part of the attempts to make a constitution work, political parties may devise mechanisms that can actually disenfranchise. For instance, the zoning of political offices, in the attempt to balance the interest of political identities, may disenfranchise qualified people.

As the administration of President Olusegun Obasanjo clearly demonstrated, while a constitution was in place and the system was democratic, practices showed individual whims and caprices, ambition and political intrigues. From the personal testimonies of those who served in the administration, there was incongruence in the balance of rights and obligations. Even Obasanjo schemed very hard to amend the constitution to have a third term in office. El-Rufai, a core insider to President Obasanjo's government, made a confessional statement in his long memoir:

> But we all remain disappointed at the blemish our administration got by the pursuit of the tenure extension, and the consequences of what has turned out to be poor outcomes resulting from his personal choice of successors. The very notion of thinking that no third term means the end of Nigeria seems to suggest that he considered himself more important than Nigeria. It was a breath-taking realization: all his decisions and actions since that fateful evening [that is, May 16, 2006 when the Senate voted to reject a constitutional amendment to elongate the presidential term] indicated to me that he believed that Nigeria was a creation of nature for him to use at will, that wherever and whenever the narrow interest of Obasanjo and the broad interests of Nigeria conflicted, Obasanjo's preferences must trump Nigeria's interest. One still does not know how he arrived at that conclusion, but it was quite clear to me that this was what he had come to believe, and perhaps what he still thinks.[13]

To be clear, the statement is not referring to a military general heading a dictatorship but to a civilian in a so-called democracy. Various narrations in the book do indeed show that the people counted for less in various calculations and schemes. Obasanjo handpicked his successor, Umaru Yar'Adua, who was known to have complicated health problems and who, after a flawed election, spent more time in the hospital than in his office. That Obasanjo was able to handpick his successor shows one of the weaknesses in a democracy. While on the one hand, political parties claim to be agents and faces of democracy, it does not mean that they run on a democratic model. As Robert Michels remarks in the example of political parties in Europe, their internal workings may not be just or egalitarian.[14] Various testimonies and accounts of those who served in civilian democratic regimes are consistent about the excesses and abuse of power, the disregard for the people. The institutions in place do not give voice to the majority of the population. Politicians have no commitment to programmes but to pacts among themselves to distribute largess. The pacts function because they create institutional, social and political barriers to developing a credible system. Politicians manufacture chaos and they benefit from it. Underdeveloped infrastructures disempower the population from engaging in pursuits that would liberate them.

Obasanjo would be the first to deny that his actions were authoritarian and fell outside the scope of a democratic system. For it must be underscored as yet another contradiction: democracy does not mean that there will be no patriarchy. This is where African theorists have a lot of work to do, for from private homes to the very apex of power, patriarchy is the norm of governance. For centuries, kings, chiefs, men have crafted recognizable authority systems that marginalize women and disempower youth. Authority has a centre in patriarchal power even at the most basic household level where the head is a man. Patriarchy as a cultural model of authority either has to collapse or be accepted as one of those cultural parameters of the African domestication of democracy. Can patriarchy be aligned with liberal democracy? This is one aspect that theorists have to think about more carefully and come up with new ideas or, at the minimum, a new kind of explanation. That Nigerians called Obasanjo 'Baba' (Father) instead of President suggests how even the vernacular of communication captures the reality of patriarchy and the grammar of authority.

Of course, there are places far worse than Nigeria, as in The Gambia under the mercurial figure Yahya Jammeh, a man who could pronounce his citizens as witches and sorcerers, and cure HIV/AIDS, Ebola and other diseases. Thus, while official documents in The Gambia frame the country as a liberal democracy, Jammeh's governance institutions are not. In many so-called democracies in Africa, the person in power manipulates the constitution to stay in power (e.g. Paul Biya of Cameroon and Robert Mugabe in Zimbabwe have devised means not to leave power). Elections can be annulled if the result does not favour those who want to control the state. The executive can disregard the legislative branch and the judiciary. Extra-judicial actions can be taken against those championing opposition like the assassination of politicians. Democracy becomes a way to stay in power, which a person like Jammeh has done for twenty-seven years while daily management is autocratic. Gerard Roland seems to be advancing this argument when he makes the point that:

> A democracy and an autocracy also often differ in a number of other critical aspects related to economic development. In autocratic countries, a small group of elites usually controls a large part of the country's wealth and productive assets. The elite will tend to use the political regime to perpetuate its economic control and privileges by discouraging both the entry of new firms into the economy and market competition, favoring instead to erect barriers to market entry via laws and regulations. In contrast, in a democracy, while special interests and political lobbies generally favor established firms, there are also countervailing tendencies as consumers favor market competition and low prices, and small medium enterprises favor low costs of entry into the economy.[15]

Jammeh, for example, controls the economy; The Gambia's resources are used to maintain his loyalists. The rule of law operates at the pleasure of one person, whose official title is His Excellency Sheikh Alhaji Dr Professor Yahya Jammeh, who controls the monopoly of power and of violence. He could invade anyone's house, confiscate his or her assets, extort and take over the lucrative business of a citizen. So-called democratic leaders in such places as Equatorial Guinea behave in the same manner: Teodore Obiang Nguema Mbasoto has been in power since 1979, and his son is the country's vice president. Zimbabwe's leader Robert Gabriel Mugabe, the oldest head of state in Africa, has been in power since 1980. In Angola, President Jose Eduardo Dos Santos has been in power since 1979, and Paul Biya has governed Cameroon for over thirty years.

Democracy does not solve the income inequality divide. Where the majority of the population is poor, participation can become limited. There are indeed theorists who think that liberal democracy functions poorly in poor societies: the argument is that the poor have no leverage over the rich who are able to manipulate the system in their favour and control electoral politics.[16] Party politics can become gentrified, and the outcome be such that the poor have limited benefits.

CRITICAL CHALLENGES

Islam

Islam has entered into the critical discourse on democracy. The arguments concerning Islam's relationship to democracy are many, and can sometimes contradict one another. First, the argument that predominantly Islamic populations, like those of the Middle East, are undemocratic. Some are much older civilizations, as in the case of Egypt, but they have been grappling with the tensions between authoritarianism and democracy. Second, there are those who see the religion itself, and the culture it promotes, as undemocratic. Third, there are those who argue that Islam is being misread and that while it is true that there is a fear of democracy and fear on other issues (of the West, of its past, of its present, of individualism, and of freedom of thought), Fatema Mernissi argues that some of these issues sometimes misplace blame. With respect to Islam and democracy, she opines:

> Arabs do not so much have a fear of democracy as suffer from a lack of access to the most important advances of recent centuries, especially tolerance as principle and practice. By this I mean the secular humanism that has allowed the flowering of civil society in the West. Humanistic ideas – freedom of thought, the sovereignty of the individual, the right to freedom of action, tolerance – were propagated in the West through secular schools. With a few rare exceptions (notably Turkey), the modern Muslim state has never called itself secular, and has never committed to teaching individual initiative. On the contrary, individualism always held a rather ambiguous place among the 'reformers' of the nineteenth-century nationalist movement. This movement, focused on the struggle against colonization and therefore viscerally anti-Western, was obliged to root itself more deeply than ever in Islam. Facing the militaristic, imperialistic West, Muslim nationalists were forced to take shelter in their past and erect it as a rampart – cultural *hudud* to exorcise colonial violence. The Muslim past they reactivated did not anchor modern identity in the rationalist tradition. In fact, the nationalists were prisoners of a historical situation that inevitably made

> modernity a no-win choice. Either they might construct modernity by claiming the humanistic heritage of the Western colonizer at the risk of losing unity (for when we speak about the rationalist tradition, we are talking about *ra'y*, 'individual opinion', and '*aql*', 'reason', and therefore about the possibility of divergence of opinion); or they could carefully safeguard a sense of unity in the face of the colonizer by clinging to the past, favoring the tradition of *ta'a*, 'obedience', and foreclosing all Western innovation.[17]

To Mernisi, Arab leaders chose the option that would ensure the unity of their people with consequences on freedom of thought and the freedom to differ.

Fourth, as in the case of Nigeria, violence associated with Islamic radicalism has been seen to constitute a danger to democracy. In particular is the case of Boko Haram (BH), which has caused serious havoc in the country since 2009. The inability of the state to deal with the BH crisis has impacted negatively on democracy and undermined the credibility of those in power. Boko Haram has demonstrated that the Nigerian army and federal police forces are impotent. It has consequently destroyed villages and towns, captured some places effortlessly, and engaged in brutal killings and in extortions as terrorists. So-called caliphate flags have been raised in some areas to proclaim them as territories independent of Nigeria. Massacres and bombings have occurred at Abuja, Kano, Kaduna, and Borno, to cite but a few examples. As of the time of writing in 2016, the kidnapped Chibok girls, more than two hundred, have not been recovered. BH has made Nigeria insecure, and is responsible for killing an estimated 13,000 people, displacing millions more, and controlling a large part of the country's northeast, the size of which is equivalent to that of Belgium.

Violence

The route to power may be through violence. This takes various forms. Power can be captured by violence, as in military coups. Existing power structures may collapse and supplanted by an alternative leadership, as in the overthrow of Muammar Gaddafi in Libya, Ben Ali in Tunisia, Blaise Compaoré in Burkina Faso, and some other examples. Violence may be used to retain power, in combination with the fraudulent adjustments to the constitutions, as in Paul Biya's Cameroon and Robert Mugabe's Zimbabwe, where both leaders have refused to leave power. Political crises may lead to civil war, always long-lasting and difficult to resolve, as in Liberia, Sierra Leone, Somalia and Sudan.

The most serious is in relation to transfer of power when a new leader has to be produced or an incumbent retained through an electoral process. Elections are seen as the means to decide on choice, succession and legitimacy. The rules and regulations guiding the conduct of elections and the electoral laws are simple on paper; they can even be copied from other countries. But in practice, they are very difficult to implement, and their failure can ultimately lead to political instability and violence that impact upon not just the political process but on the society as a whole. A country can move from the conduct of an election to conditions of civil war, as it happened in Nigeria following the 12 June 1993 election that produced victory for late Chief M.K.O. Abiola, but whose results were annulled by the military government of retired general Ibrahim Babangida. All the major elections in Nigeria (1964, 1979, 1983, 1993, 1999, 2003, 2007 and 2011) produced violence. The 2015 election was complicated because of the expectation that the country could transition from being dominated by one party to a more open and competitive electoral system.

The desire for power creates a breeding-ground for violence. As power seekers manipulate religion and ethnicity, the political narratives become those of verbal violence and of physically creating ethno-religious militias. Thugs are hired, and vigilante groups are created. Rival gangs extort money. Thugs take to kidnapping to demand huge ransoms. The Boko Haram terrorists are not the only ones with access to guns. Firearms of all types are now everywhere, purchased by criminals, party thugs and even principal politicians. In villages, rival political parties can fight with knives, machetes, spears, clubs and bows and arrows, as it has happened many times around Jos. But where the rewards of power are more substantial, thugs use AK-47 assault rifles, bazookas, sub-machine guns, double-barrelled shotguns and Beretta pistols.

Violence is now an integral part of the democratic culture. A former inspector general of police, Mike Mbama Okiro, identifies three reasons:

> Whenever there is political competition, there is always an element of electoral violence.
>
> Violence has been used by groups holding power and by groups in the process of losing power.
>
> Violence has been pursued in the defiance of order, by the privileged; in the name of justice, by the oppressed; and in fear of displacement, by the threatened.[18]

The linkages between politics and violence are strong, and Okiro's cogent points can be cited again:

(i) Democratic governance here in Nigeria has not instituted sufficient policies and programmes to alter the structures of imbalance and inequity entrenched by colonialism and prolonged authoritarian military arrogant rule.

(ii) As a result of the multi-ethnic character of the country and the inability of the nationalistic project to evolve a true nation and a corresponding national identity, ethnic, religious and other primordial points of reference assumed added importance in democratic processes.

(iii) The desperation for political office, and by extension, for unrestrained access to state resources heightens the feeling of insecurity in the people. This was why the premium on power is exceptionally high, and as the system lacks the institutional arrangements to moderate political competitions, political campaigns in Nigeria tend to assume the character of warfare.

(iv) The serious level of affinity between the militants who were hitherto political foot soldiers to the politicians makes counter-insurgency efforts or directives against them difficult to effect. These militants can still be mobilized for violence against the opposition during future elections by the political class in the region/states of militancy.

Paul Collier describes political violence as a curse and an obstacle: 'It is a curse because the process of violent struggle is hugely destructive. It is an obstacle because where power rests on violence, it invites an arrogant assumption that government is there to rule rather than to serve'.[19] He devotes his book, *Wars, Guns, and Votes*, to explaining why political violence is endemic, made possible by the three things in the book's title, which he characterizes as the 'technologies' of violence. The three, he argues, 'have destroyed societies that were confidently expected to develop'.[20] He sees democracy as universal but troubled by the promotion of its wrong features, by which he means electoral politics, instead of its infrastructure. The façade is incapable of promoting democratic accountability:

> When political power is won through violence, the results are usually awful. The political strongman in a divided society is seldom a visionary leader, he is more likely to be self-serving, or in thrall to the interests of a narrow support group.[21]

In cases where violence is endemic, it means that democracy is dangerous and destructive, and its outcome is actually fake. If democracy lacks the capacity to reduce or minimize violence, its fundamentals are flawed.

Globalization

The forces that created the African countries as an imperialist project continue to manifest themselves in new dimensions of globalization with implications for democracy. The international system is structured on political and economic inequalities. The West preaches democracy, but the global structures of power are not based on democracy. International power and global financial institutions are exploitative.

Failed states have serious global consequences. A failed state can destabilize an entire region: it produces internally displaced refugees, it instigates migrations within and outside the region, and it encourages the rise of terrorist cells. Nigeria may not be a failed state but it appears dysfunctional. Perhaps democracy will prevent a slide down the political scope, but on the condition that good governance delivers development.

Globalization has varied impacts on various countries and their politics. Some impacts are direct, as those on immigration, the environment, and nationalism. Some may be indirect, as those on citizenship, religion, education, and health. In a recent book, *Africanizing Democracies*,[22] the authors list as challenges issues around health and healing, women, gender and sexuality, as part of the challenges of democracy. Also, they discuss how the thinking on these issues become part of the conversation on modernity and democracy in Africa. To Claude Ake, democracy is imperilled by globalization: global financial institutions, he argues, can disempower national ones.[23] To Benjamin Barber, globalization has destructive impact on local cultures, and can undermine how states control the use and consumption of their own cultures.[24]

A silver lining is for Africans to connect with people in other parts of the world to create larger a social movement for justice, the empowered 'multitude' that Michael Hardt and Antonio Negri optimistically think can emerge to redress the imbalances in global power.[25]

Anti-democratic Impulses

Where the leadership is corrupt and the pace of development has been slow, people have wondered about the need for democracy. Various voices have emerged questioning the necessity and relevance of civilian governments. Some have even called for the return of military regimes. The link between democracy and development has been questioned, as various people call attention to how an authoritarian government in Japan after the Meiji Restoration generated changes, and how the same model changed the development of Singapore, South Korea, Taiwan and China under authoritarian regimes. To develop good governance and functioning, institutions may not always require democracy, and it is even argued that authoritarian regimes may actually govern better. Shocked by the data of the salaries and remunerations of politicians, members of the public often wonder whether the cost of democracy is worth it. If a country claims to be a liberal democracy, critics wonder why its government cannot supply electricity and drinking water, why the quality of education has become degraded, and why human capital is poorly developed, and why most people make less than $2 a day.

CORRECTIVES AND FUTURE POSSIBILITIES

A most common phrase in African politics is the 'roadmap to democracy', as one analyst after another offers ideas on how to make democracy a possibility. It is a 'spirit', declared Larry Diamond, which is global in outreach.[26] It is also complementary, I think, to talk about a roadmap to authoritarianism, as democracy does not always work while the efficacy of the system is being questioned. Indeed, the number of electoral democracies declined from twenty-four in 2008 to nineteen in 2012, and the number of countries described by Freedom House as 'unfree' increased from 35% in 2003 to 41% in 2013.[27] Some countries had also witnessed political turmoil and reversals: Burkina Faso, Central African Republic, Cote d'Ivoire, Guinea, Guinea-Bissau, Lesotho, Madagascar, Mali, Mauritania and Togo.

Thus far, democracy has not enhanced accountability or good governance, or brought about a higher standard of living to the poor. It is a process, many analysts would admit, and it can be a long one. President Jonathan of Nigeria spoke the mind of leaders and scholars when he remarked:

> The establishment of a functional democratic system in any society is a long and complex process with ups and downs because it requires full understanding of the cultural, and social and political environment in which this democratization process is taking place. But since political systems are also cultural systems, the makers and actors of the democratic order have to deliberately undertake a creative application of the political, social and cultural heritage with the formal tenets of democracy for it to take root and become truly national.[28]

President Goodluck Jonathan was right about seeing democratization as a 'process', and he recognized the need to think about its 'creative application'. General Muhammadu Buhari, a former military dictator who became a democracy convert and Nigeria's president, worried about the quality of elections and warned that 'mere elections do not democracy make'.[29] Democracy should be treated 'not [as] an event but a journey . . . to attain democratic consolidation'

> With this important destination in mind, it is clear that though many African countries now hold regular elections, very few of them have consolidated the practice of democracy. It is important to also state at this point that just as with elections, a consolidated democracy cannot be an end by itself. I will argue that it is not enough to hold a series of elections or even to peacefully alternate power among parties. It is much more important that the promise of democracy goes beyond just allowing people to freely choose their leaders. It is much more important that democracy should deliver on the promise of choice, of freedoms, of security of lives and property, of transparency and accountability, of rule of law, of good governance and of shared prosperity.[30]

Africa needs to question its current practices of democracy, as they are not serving the people, it can be characterized as a failure, and it is certainly a drawback to collective progress. The search is not for a perfect democratic system or a governance model without problems. Rather, it is to rethink the borrowed ideas and see how democracy and governance can deliver the expectations of the population, ensure accountability, produce credible leadership and secure legitimacy to political leadership. Even in the West, where liberal democracy took root and whose constitutions shaped those of Africa, democracy underwent various phases arising from criticism, modification of practices and responses by the people to misgovernance, wars, power of religious institutions and secularization. These adjustments and rethinking explain the long list of thinkers of the subject, notable among them being Niccolò Machiavelli, author of *The Prince* and the idea of realism and force; Thomas Hobbes, whose 'Leviathan State' called for a strong government that must ensure peace so that life did not become 'solitary, poor, nasty, brutish, and short'; and Edmund Burke, advocate of the place of tradition in stabilizing institutions. John Stuart Mill, observing democracy in the nineteenth century, regarded it as a way of protecting the private interest of a few, while the majority voted just to give them a feeling that they were part of the system. Liberal democracy could have legitimacy, argued Max Weber, but it does not mean that it is ethical. Similarly, there have been debates about the role of government, the use of money in the electoral process, which allows the rich and the powerful to control power, and the manipulation of democracy to use public resources for private purposes.[31] It is not unusual even to lament the fact that citizens no longer bother to vote, and that the process of understanding the intricacies of democracy may be time consuming, and fighting for one's rights may be too costly to afford. The outcome of apathy has led to the formation of a theory of 'rational ignorance', which is that people choose not to know.[32]

Politics is central to the solution of the country's problems. The country has to produce first-rate theoreticians of democracy. The citizens have to combine to create powerful pressure groups, using the civil society to reform governance. Political demands must be totally aggressive and combative to remove corrupt people from power, to institutionalize accountability, to be less afraid of state violence. Citizens must see politics as the agency that will allow them to function, that is, politics must safeguard their freedom of association, and freedom to participate in the marketplace. Professor Samuel Zalanga, a critical voice in the search for a new alternative to the current system, has been so extremely disturbed that he has lost respect for the Nigerian variant of democracy: 'there are non-liberal democratic societies today that are run by authoritarian regimes but are functioning very well, and the countries are well-governed'. He sees the demands by the people as one of the key solutions to what he perceives as a crisis of the failure of democracy:

> I will argue without hesitation that the Nigerian elites and the political system have not only prevented but have made it a major concern of theirs to not allow the ordinary Nigerian [to] develop the capability to function to the point he or she can hold his leaders accountable and live as a human being with dignity. It is not enough for the Nigerian government to adopt a presidential system of government or write a new constitution without sincerely asking: what are the conditions that will truly ensure the true functioning of the political system, in order to uplift the lives of the least advantage[d] people. We should measure our development not by the number of expensive cars driven by rich Nigerians, the skyscrapers or the money people have to buy the conscience of others. Rather it is the human development and the capability to function of the least advantage[d] people that matters. We should be able to achieve that while allowing others who have great talents to excel [and] function as well. This requires working hard to balance equality and liberty. But this is not a simple question of getting a constitution written or even having a process adopted.[33]

Zalanga is looking for an alternative political system that delivers development, like in the case of Singapore or China. Certainly he is not alone in this critical interrogation of the failure of democracy and its weak linkage to good governance. In other words, as he and others tend to suggest, democracy is not the only route to good governance. In his endorsement of the non-democratic model of Asia, he invokes the statement by Deng Xiaoping of China that 'it does not matter whether a cat is black or white, as long as it catches mice'.[34] Private and media accounts tend to say that the differences between military and democratic regimes are limited, that liberal democracy is not suited to places that have urgent needs to build infrastructures and create jobs.

As bad as democratic practices might be, a return to military rule cannot be an option. A military regime installs a dictator who is difficult to remove. A military regime can unleash violence on the people. Even in its most benign form, past experience suggests that a military regime will take away civil liberties and the rule of law, and curtail the freedom of the press and free speech in general. It is true that the cost of running the government is reduced, but the motivation of power 'for profit' remains. The military's tenure in government, as the overall records show, did not generate impressive economic development and progress. Nigeria has endured military regimes before, and the record of the dictator, General Sani Abacha, should frighten everyone from even proposing the return of the military: a regime of tyranny, his government had no respect for freedom of speech and human rights and lacked the vision to build a nation. While democracy is not a guarantee of immediate development, it offers the most effective ways of resolving political conflicts in a country as plural as Nigeria.

It is better to engage in dialogue and struggles to reform democracy than to look for a benevolent military dictator. A conversation has become necessary to see how democracy can serve the people, be less expensive, and be grafted to local cultures. Democracy cannot be an abstract subject taught in schools, but must emerge from applied governance experienced on street corners. Among the serious questions to be answered: Can the cost of running a democratic government be reduced in order to have money for development purposes? Are there elements in past cultures better suited to our conditions that can be worked into modern practices? Are there emerging positive democratic cultures that can be used to redefine current practices? How can the obligations between the leaders and the citizens be respected?

It is true that constitutional panels have been formed, and a National Conference convened that has produced significant documents. Many of the constitutions have been imposed, both by the departing British colonial government and by the military. Members of the political class interested in power sharing and revenue allocations have tinkered with such constitutions. It is now common to hear people talk about 'grassroots democracy' to suggest a non-elitist orientation, but there is no suggestion on how to organize dialogue around it. Can there be an African democracy? The 'contents' of such a democracy must deal less and less with received political models and more and more with what bothers Africans: mismanagement, corruption, accountability, human development, conflicts, peace, hunger and so on.

The contextual imperatives must be clearly defined. The empirical reality must link governance with the ability of people to pursue their aspirations and liberate themselves from poverty. Borrowed liberal democracy must be scrutinized. The oft-quoted statement by John Dewey, 'The foundation of democracy is faith in the capacities of human nature; faith in human intelligence and in the power of pooled and cooperative experience',[35] must be questioned if there is no faith in leadership, if the agencies of governance are not necessarily governed by the logic of rationality and if communities are in a state of conflict. In fairness to Dewey, he sees democracy as 'much broader than a special political form, a method of conducting government, of making laws and carrying on governmental administration by means of popular suffrage and elected officers'.[36] He continues: 'Universal suffrage, recurring elections, responsibility of those who are in political power to the voters, and the other factors of democratic government are means that have been found expedient for realizing democracy as the truly human way of living. They are not a final end and a final value. They are to be judged on the basis of their contributions to an end'.[37]

There must be a peaceful and developed future, and this must be the minimum that democracy must ensure. Democracy has not produced a land without serious ethnic politics, social and political conflicts, and fragmented citizenship. Democracy has not eliminated our fears: fears of neighbours, of communities, of people of other faiths. Democracy has not solved the problems of intolerance. Democracy has produced a model of authoritarian leadership. There are even cases of dictatorship, as in some of the management styles of President Olusegun Obasanjo already alluded to.

Pluralism is the country's common fate. Democracy must enhance the capacity to dialogue, to respect diversity and differences. Development is the ultimate goal; thus democracy must deliver development. Both are linked, and either intellectually or in practice, cannot be separated. Leadership has not figured out how to deliver development. The state itself has not been an efficient agent of development. There are pressures to reconstitute the space, sometimes extreme suggestions of secession and the creation of smaller and manageable states.

Perhaps, to reform democracy, attention can shift to the means to develop a much stronger civil society. People know what they want, and they have developed the grammar to express dissent. However, the values to reject corruption and oppose corruption are still weak as many continue to think in terms of aristocratic values, and it is not unusual to see wealthy citizens, including corrupt politicians, as the role model. In this regard, the culture of discourse must be decisively hostile to corruption. The citizens, too, have been implicated as willing collaborators, to say nothing of nursing a desire to have power in order to participate in looting and stealing.

CONCLUSION

A democratic culture and system will ultimately emerge over time. Sure, there will be moments when some will call for benevolent dictatorship, but forces in support of democracy will continue to remain strong. The transfer of power remains a problem and will continue to create conditions for political violence. For as long as corruption is tied to power, so too will the competition for power and the ambition for lucrative position be the main driving force. Those in power through the democratic system grapple with campaigns in different methods and styles, and, in some cases, recognize that they may lose power. As those in power realize that incumbents can lose, this may reduce the recourse to violence to settle scores.

Disappointments with those in power will instigate pressures to reform practices, and even demand for radical democracy, or the use of the revolutionary possibilities that democracy offers. A small positive sign is that a number of politicians in power now speak about change and a 'transformation agenda', thus displaying an awareness that the exercise of power must not always be linked to their pockets but to the delivery of public goods. Indeed, in the speeches of political leaders, they now use the language of democracy and of governance, pointing to what it means. To return to the example of President Jonathan, he said there is a 'collective conviction and commitment' towards:

1. Ensuring the sustainability of democratic government in Nigeria
2. Regional and international assistance in restoring and sustaining democratic systems in our sub-regions and beyond
3. Timely delivery of democratic dividends to our people in these critical and sensitive areas:

   (i) Rule of Law, respect for human rights and due process
   (ii) Electoral reforms, and free and fair elections
   (iii) Women's empowerment and equality in all spheres of Nigerian life
   (iv) Freedom of information
   (v) Job creation and poverty reduction
   (vi) Education
   (vii) Infrastructural development and upgrade
   (viii) War against terrorism.[38]

His list shows that governance is key, and change is needed. It is instructive that he leaves out corruption. The overall quality of debate around governance must be enhanced.

Good leadership is critical, but not enough. What is needed are the reconstruction and reconstitution of institutions of governance and democracy. Strong and effective institutions are more likely to bring forward good leadership, whereas leadership on its own may lack the capacity to produce good institutions and promote the rule of law. Beyond institutions are the issues of values and ethics. Due to the commodification of life that global forces of neoliberalism foster, values of integrity, hard work, diligence, and delayed gratification have been sacrificed on the altar of immediacy and instant self-gratification. Due to lack of commitment to punishing corruption, this cankerworm has become endemic at both micro and macro levels. Thus, in order for democracy to deliver development, there is need for value re-orientation both by the citizens and the leaders. In particular, integrity and delayed gratification should be promoted through the agents of socialization such as religious institutions like churches, mosques and shrines. Elementary and high schools should also remake civic studies that emphasize the importance of enduring values to development.

To be clear, democracy, in its recent incarnations, is a Western-derived idea, copied as a label and practice. As an assumption that it is the government of the people, its theoretical premise derives from whether 'the people' are seeking freedom or security or both. There are normative and cultural issues that must be part of the definition and understanding of the behaviour of politicians or even the application of democratic principles.

Social engineering is needed to address the issues of ethnic identity, religious differences, Islamic radicalism and violence. Without jobs and social services, it is easier to build a coalition of the aggrieved to destabilize the polity. The case of the notorious BH, for instance, demonstrates how an insurgency by misguided citizens can wreck the progress of others and attack the fundamental rights of the majority of the population to freedom of religion and opinion, even to carry out their day-to-day activities. BH claims the right to special privileges, to political exclusivism that is not possible in a democracy.

Constitutions must be revisited to restore confidence in political pluralism, to provide strong ways to live together, to destroy all tendencies towards dictatorship, to create conditions for reform and development and to condemn corrupt practices. Strengthening democratic institutions will involve the creation of an independent judiciary, an electoral commission that can conduct free and fair elections, respect for all citizens, a free and independent media, an educated and enlightened citizenry, a committed civil society, promotion of human rights, the right by citizens to choose the leaders of their choice, equality before the law and respect for the rule of law, honest political communication between the leaders and the citizens, and decentralization of authority and political power. The most urgent condition, without which democracy itself will lose its meaning and create cynicism, is the promotion of accountability.

The next fight, an urgent one, must be over accountability. The account books of all levels of government must be open, budget discussions must be public, leakages must be prevented, and corruption severely checked. There must be overall increase in efficiency per naira or dollar spent. Without winning the battle over accountability, the dividends of democracy will continue to be disappointing.

For accountability to occur, for a genuine people-oriented constitution to emerge, for social engineering to work, the civil society and media have to become stronger and entrenched, with the capacity to tap into their freedom to circulate information, criticize the government and organize protest. The mission of the civil society is to police the activities of politicians, curb excesses, prevent abuses and insist on an economic management that focuses on job creation.

A coalition of Nigerians, instead of a coalition of politicians or a coalition of ethnic nationalities, will be a better way to manage an emergent democracy. This coalition will wage a total war against corruption, will lead the country towards genuine development, will have organizations in place to intervene in policies, and will not yield space to the myrmidons of politics who could not care less about people's lives and welfare as long they have protected comforts and secure bunkers. Indeed, the civil society has to create the knowledge and skills to create production systems so that the majority of the people can be mobilized to minimize poverty. People who want to defend their jobs and earnings, health and education can be better organized politically, and work for social welfare programmes.

For democracy to work in Nigeria, it is best to place less hope in politicians who have a vested narrow interest in wealth accumulation rather than in service, less hope in leadership that has shown itself to be selfish and uncaring, less hope in the military that is arrogant, self-serving and corrupt; but more hope and desire in institutions of nation building that can endure and function, more hope and expectation in the power of the people to struggle for their own liberation and even far more hope and commitment in institutional strategies that can uplift the poor. The common interests by the majority of the population can be organized around democracy, economic development and the creation of a unified identity that will transcend ethnic and religious divides and sustain the existence of a viable nation state.

NOTES

1. Nigeria. *Second National Development Plan 1970–8* (Lagos: Federal Ministry of Information, 1970), preamble.
2. Samuel Huntington, *The Third Wave: Democratization the Late Twentieth Century* (Norman: University of Oklahoma Press, 1991).
3. Francis Fukuyama, *The End of History and the Last Man* (Washington, DC: Free Press, 1992).
4. On this organization, see http://www.community-democracies.org/
5. Goodluck Jonathan, 'Consolidating Our Democratic System', in *Strengthening Democratic Traditions and Institutions in Nigeria*, eds. Martin Uhomoibhi and Ehiedu Iweriebor (Abuja, Nigeria: Ministry of Foreign Affairs, 2014), xviii.
6. Ibid.
7. For instance, see Olufemi O. Ajayi, *Crises of Democracy* (Lagos: Self-published, 2012); and Saliba Sarsar and Julius O. Adekunle, eds. *Democracy in Africa: Political Changes and Challenges* (Durham, NC: Carolina Academic Press, 2012).
8. Zimako O. Zimako, *Face of a Nation: Democracy in Nigeria, Foreign Relations and National Image* (Lagos: Modern Approach, 2009).
9. http://www.moibrahimfoundation.org/prize/
10. http://www.agendang.com/index.php/news/item/655-special-report-salary-of-nigerian-senators

11. An expansive definition is offered in Shireen Hassim, 'Democratization: A View from Africa', *Signs: Journal of Women in Culture and Society* 31, no. 4 (2006): 928–32.

12. Michael Hardt and Antonio Negri, *Multitude: War and Democracy in the Age of Empire* (New York: Penguin, 2004).

13. Nasir Ahmad El-Rufai, *The Accidental Public Servant* (Ibadan: Safari Books, 2013), lvii–lviii.

14. Robert Michels, *Political Parties: A Sociological Study of the Oligarchical Tendencies of Modern Democracy* (Kitchener, Ontario: Batoche Books, 2001).

15. Ronald Gerard, *Development Economics* (Boston: Pearson Publishers, 2014), 241.

16. See, for instance, Del Dickson, *The People's Government: An Introduction to Democracy* (New York: Cambridge University Press, 2014), chapter 11.

17. Fatema Mernissi (translated by Mary Jo Lakeland), *Islam and Democracy: Fear of the Modern World* (New York: Basic Books, 1992, 2nd edition, 2002), 42–3.

18. Mike Mbama Okiro, 'Law Enforcement, the Electoral Process and Democracy in Nigeria', in *Strengthening Democratic Traditions and Institutions in Nigeria*, eds. Martin Uhomoibhi and Ehiedu Iweriebor (Abuja, Nigeria: Ministry of Foreign Affairs, 2014).

19. Paul Collier, *Wars, Guns, and Votes: Democracy in Dangerous Places* (New York: Harper Perennial, 2009), 2.

20. Ibid., 8.

21. Ibid., 9.

22. Alicia C. Decker and Andrea L. Arrington, *Africanizing Democracies, 1980–Present* (New York: Oxford University Press, 2015).

23. Claude Ake, 'Dangerous Liaisons: The Interface of Globalization and Democracy', in *Democracy's Victory and Crisis*, ed. Alex Hadenius (Cambridge: Cambridge University Press, 1997), 282–96.

24. Benjamin Barber, *Strong Democracy: Participatory Politics for a New Age* (Berkeley: University of California Press, 1984).

25. Hardt and Negri, *Multitude.*

26. Larry Diamond, *The Spirit of Democracy: The Struggle to Build Free Societies throughout the World* (New York: Henry Holt and Company, 2008).

27. Reports on 'free' and 'unfree' can be found in annual reviews by the Freedom House based in New York. https://freedomhouse.org.

28. Goodluck, 'Consolidating Our Democratic System'.

29. General Muhammadu Buhari, 'Prospects for Democratic Consolidation in Africa: Nigeria's Transition', Lecture, Chatham House, London, 26 February 2015. http://www.vanguardngr.com/2015/02/chatham-house-buharis-speech-on-nigerias-transition/

30. Ibid.

31. See, for instance, extensive writings on public choice theory: Dennis C. Mueller, *Public Choice III* (Cambridge: Cambridge University Press, 2003). See also the argument that democracy can undermine public interest, by Michael J. Crozier, Samuel P. Huntington and Joii Watanuki, *Democracy: Report on the Governability of Democracies to the Trilateral Commission* (New York: New York University Press, 1975).

32. Olson Mancur, *The Logic of Collective Action: Public Goods and the Theory of Groups* (Cambridge, MA: Harvard University Press, 1971); Olson Mancur, *The*

Rise and Decline of Nations: Economic Growth, Stagflation and Social Rigidities (New Haven, CT: Yale University Press, 1984).

33. https://groups.google.com/forum/#!searchin/usaafricadialogue/$20Zalanga$20on$20democracy/usaafricadialogue/uOtAPnx6ugY/dixNz0k-tkoJ

34. Ibid.

35. John Dewey, 'Democracy and Educational Administration', *School and Society* 45 (3 April 1937): 457–67.

36. Ibid., 457.

37. Ibid.

38. Goodluck, 'Consolidating Our Democratic System', xxi.

BIBLIOGRAPHY

Ake, Claude. 'Dangerous Liaisons: The Interface of Globalization and Democracy'. In *Democracy's Victory and Crisis*, edited by Alex Hadenius Cambridge: Cambridge University Press, 1997.

Ajayi, Olufemi O. *Crises of Democracy*. Lagos: Self-Published, 2012.

Barber, Benjamin. *Strong Democracy: Participatory Politics for a New Age*. Berkeley: University of California Press, 1984.

Buhari, Muhammadu. 'Prospects for Democratic Consolidation in Africa: Nigeria's Transition', Lecture, Chatham House, London, 26 February 2015. http://www.vanguardngr.com/2015/02/chatham-house-buharis-speech-on-nigerias-transition.

Collier, Paul. *Wars, Guns, and Votes: Democracy in Dangerous Places*. New York: Harper Perennial, 2009.

Crozier, Michael J., Samuel P. Huntington and Joii Watanuki. *Democracy: Report on the Governability of Democracies to the Trilateral Commission*. New York: New York University Press, 1975.

Decker, Alicia C. and Andrea L. Arrington. *Africanizing Democracies, 1980–Present*. New York: Oxford University Press, 2015.

Dewey, John. 'Democracy and Educational Administration'. *School and Society* 45 (1937): 457–67.

Diamond, Larry. *The Spirit of Democracy: The Struggle to Build Free Societies throughout the World*. New York: Henry Holt and Company, 2008.

Dickson, Del. *The People's Government: An Introduction to Democracy*. New York: Cambridge University Press, 2014.

El-Rufai, Nasir Ahmad. *The Accidental Public Servant*. Ibadan: Safari Books, 2013.

Fukuyama, Francis. *The End of History and the Last Man*. Washington, DC: Free Press, 1992.

Gerard, Ronald. *Development Economics*. Boston: Pearson Publishers, 2014.

Hardt, Michael and Antonio Negri. *Multitude: War and Democracy in the Age of Empire*. New York: Penguin, 2004.

Hassim, Shireen. 'Democratization: A View from Africa'. *Signs: Journal of Women in Culture and Society* 31, no. 4 (2006): 928–32.

Huntington, Samuel. *The Third Wave: Democratization the Late Twentieth Century*. Norman: University of Oklahoma Press, 1991.

Jonathan, Goodluck. 'Consolidating Our Democratic System'. In *Strengthening Democratic Traditions and Institutions in Nigeria*, edited by Martin Uhomoibhi and Ehiedu Iweriebor. Abuja, Nigeria: Ministry of Foreign Affairs, 2014.

Mancur, Olson. *The Logic of Collective Action: Public Goods and the Theory of Groups*. Cambridge, MA: Harvard University Press, 1971.

Mancur, Olson. *The Rise and Decline of Nations: Economic Growth, Stagflation and Social Rigidities*. New Haven, CT: Yale University Press, 1984.

Mernissi, Fatema. *Islam and Democracy: Fear of the Modern World* (translated by Mary Jo Lakeland). New York: Basic Books, 2002.

Michels, Robert. *Political Parties: A Sociological Study of the Oligarchical Tendencies of Modern Democracy*. Kitchener, Ontario: Batoche Books, 2001.

Mueller, Dennis C. *Public Choice III*. Cambridge: Cambridge University Press, 2003.

Nigeria. *Second National Development Plan 1970–8*. Lagos: Federal Ministry of Information, 1970.

Okiro, Mike Mbama. 'Law Enforcement, the Electoral Process and Democracy in Nigeria'. In *Strengthening Democratic Traditions and Institutions in Nigeria*, edited by Martin Uhomoibhi and Ehiedu Iweriebor. Abuja, Nigeria: Ministry of Foreign Affairs, 2014.

Sarsar, Saliba and Julius O. Adekunle. *Democracy in Africa: Political Changes and Challenges* Durham, NC: Carolina Academic Press, 2012.

Zimako, Zimako O. *Face of a Nation: Democracy in Nigeria, Foreign Relations and National Image*. Lagos: Modern Approach, 2009.

Chapter 6

Historicizing Development and the Dilemma of Adopting Western Models in Nigeria

Cinderella Temitope Ochu

INTRODUCTION

Since independence, West African states have maintained close political and economic ties with their former colonial powers. During the colonial era, the administrators successfully imposed and impressed their alien pattern and orientation in the socio-political and economic affairs of their colonies. West African economic affairs were distorted to an extent that two decades after independence, all the countries are helplessly dependent and volatile. Post-colonial African economies are replete with the scars of the uneven and exploitative nature of colonialism, and are largely a function of their colonial past. The current economic structures of these states are directly linked to the economics of their previous respective metropolitan powers through an array of policies ranging from control of currency, trade policies and infrastructure. As a result, despite the abundant resources of Africa, African countries are among the least developed and industrialized nations in the world.

Consequently, in recent time, one of the problems of the new independent states is the struggle to break the colonial economic system inherited at independence. The systems in Nigeria, for instance, discouraged indigenous industrialization, but promoted export crop and mineral production to feed the British factories. Also, the imported and exported trades were dominated by the multinational companies of the colonial powers.

These big trading companies lay a smooth ground for economic exploitation even in modern time. As Boateng rightly observed:

> Owing to the greatly superior economic and technological advantages which the developed nations enjoy, they are still in a position to determine or even to dictate to a large extent, the economic fortunes of the developing nations which

> depend on them for the very things, such as capital goods, technical know-how and entrepreneurial skills, which they need in order to modernize and upgrade their fragile economies.[1]

However, Nigeria and other West African states are very much aware of the problems arising from the modern-day imperialism and have devised various strategies since independence to deal with this menace. The determination is reflected in the various development plans that have been drawn up over time. In the light of this, the chapter examines the various development plans put in place, their objectives and factors that played against them.

DEVELOPMENT PLANNING: A CONCEPTUAL DISCOURSE

Development planning can be better comprehended by explaining the concepts of development and planning separately. Development however is not an easy term to define as it is relative. This lends credence to Chilivumbo's argument that development as a concept is amorphous and rather difficult to articulate.[2] Development according to Todaro involves not only economic growth but also conditions in which the people of a country have adequate security of job and income inequality among the people is considerably reduced.[3] The concept is widely perceived as a product of human efforts. This is because human beings manipulate the resources available and ensure they serve the goal of increasing the living standard of the people. This assertion is emphasized by Mobogunje when he defined development as essentially a human issue, a concern with the capacity of individuals to realize their inherent potentials and effectively to cope with the changing circumstances of their lives.[4]

It is instructive to note that development transcends this; it is a multidimensional process involving changes in structures, attitudes and institutions as well as the acceleration of economic growth, the reduction of inequality and eradication of absolute poverty. This view is seconded by Rodney who tends to draw a distinction between the perceptions of development as it relates to the individual, and as it relates to the larger society. He explains that development, at the level of the individual, implies increased skill and capacity, greater freedom, creativity, self-discipline, responsibility and material wellbeing. However, Rodney goes on to state that the achievement of any of those aspects of human development is very much tied in with the state of the society as a whole. What this means is that any society that intends to develop would naturally hinge the success of its development on meeting these basic needs of those within its confines. Explicitly, development here is seen as an aspect of desirable and planned change influenced by governmental action.[5]

Planning on the other hand is deciding what actions to be taken in future for the purpose of achieving organizational goals, it involves thinking ahead, initiating and taking a predetermined course of action and deciding in advance what should be done, how, when and by whom. Without planning, the activities of organizations, institutions, societies and nations may well become a series of random actions with meaningless objectives.[6] As corroborated by Cole, planning is an activity which involves decisions about ends as well as means and about conduct as well as result. Nwachukwu observes that planning entails determination of control, direction and methods of accomplishing the overall organization or national objective. Plans must be directed and controlled towards achieving desired objectives.

For the purpose of this chapter, development and planning is looked at within the context of the nation state and its adopted development paradigms. Scholars like Jhingan and Conveys have noted that the term *national development plan* connotes the preparation of a process through which set goals for development are intended to be achieved. The development of any nation is multi-purposed and the process towards achieving it involves different criteria. The contents of every nation varies and this difference is due not only to the initial level of development but also the characteristics of each nation, its industrial structure, geographical location, production specialization and many other factors.[7]

The need for development planning among nations is stressed by the need to eradicate widespread unemployment and ensuring human capital development. In the absence of sufficient enterprise and initiative, a centralized planning authority is the only institution for planning the development of the economy. Suffice it to say that development planning is necessary because development is neither accidental nor does it take place naturally; it is expedient to plan it deliberately.

Thus, Todaro conceptualizes development planning as the conscious governmental effort to influence, direct and in some cases, even control changes in the principal economic variables of a country over the course of time in order to achieve predetermined set of objectives. Development planning as opined by Datta involves processes which ensure that national policies and strategies are realized and development concerns at all levels are fully integrated into the overall national development thrust.[8] Obviously, no meaningful development can take place in any system or society without adequate planning.

ANTECEDENT OF DEVELOPMENT PLANNING IN NIGERIA

After the Second World War in 1945, with the emergence of the United States and the Union of Soviet Socialist Republics (USSR) as the new superpowers, and a new world order that fostered the principle of national self-determinism and racial equality, Britain faced virulent criticism.[9] This situation, however, stimulated considerable political awakening among the colonized people and they began to question the imperial powers. These tensions within and outside of Britain evoked a response from the British government which led to the transformation of the existing Colonial Development and Welfare Act of 1940. This plan was expanded in 1945 after the war and the Ten-Year Plan (1946–1956) was created. The Ten-Year plan was intended to focus on promotion of exports through marketing boards, improving road networks especially in rural areas to facilitate evacuation of agricultural products, improvement in health and sanitary condition especially in rural areas, town and country planning and the establishment of a university in Nigeria.

In 1951, the plan was revised as a result of the rapid structural changes occurring in the country at the time, to cover the period 1951–1956. This revision was not essentially different from the initial plan of 1946. The introduction of federalism in 1954 scuttled the plan leading to the formulation of a new plan based on a World Bank report to cover the period 1955–1960. This plan was slightly modified to give colonial authorities a more active role in the Directly Productive Activities (DPA) sector which had hitherto been left to the whims of private investors. Although this plan served as a launch pad to subsequent development plans in Nigeria, it has been criticized with several flaws.

According to Iheanacho, the Ten-Year Plan of Development and Welfare for Nigeria cannot be termed a plan in the real sense because it contained mainly a list of uncoordinated projects in various regions.[10] To Egonmwan and Ibodje, the plan focused on meeting the perceived needs of the colonial government rather than influencing the overall performance of the Nigerian economy.[11] No attempt was made to articulate and incorporate the needs and interest of the Nigerian people into the objectives and priorities of the plan. Ayo stated rather vehemently that the plan suffered from non-specialized colonial administrator's approach to development planning, the inadequacy of planning machinery and absence of clearly defined national objectives.[12]

POST-INDEPENDENCE DEVELOPMENT PLANNING IN NIGERIA

Since 1962, Nigeria has embarked on series of national development plans and visions in its endless efforts to search for appropriate development strategy. This provides a succinct but concrete analysis of the various development plans undertaken in Nigeria. The first plan of 1962–1968 which marked the first attempt towards national planning became redundant due to political upheaval which resulted in the fratricidal war lasting for thirty months. After the war, another plan was put in the place primarily for the purpose of restructuring, rehabilitating and restoring victims of the war. As envisioned, the second plan was launched as not just a child of necessity but also prosperity because the period coincided with the era of the oil-boom. Egonmwan and Ibodje reported that this plan involved a capital expenditure of ₦3.2 billion and an anticipated overall growth rate of 7% per annum. Resulting from the profligacy that characterized the oil-boom period, the initial plan budget of ₦3.2 billion was revised upwards to ₦5.3 billion. It can therefore be persuasively argued that the Nigerian governing elite started the march towards economic regression from this period as a result of fiscal and financial indiscipline. This trajectory became the norm even in subsequent development plans in Nigeria.

As revealed in the chart, in the third plan, the initial total expenditure was put at ₦30 billion over five years. Further adjustments put the total at ₦60 billion in 1980. Osifo reinstated that the plan represented ten times that of the second plan and about fifteen times that of the first plan. Thus, the plan was seen as the largest plan ever launched as compared to the ones that preceded it. Regardless of the huge capital allocated to the plan, Adeniji affirmed that its implementation was abysmal as the change of government in July 1975, barely three months after the plan was launched, adversely affected its actualization.[13] The fourth plan would seem appealing as it was the first plan prepared by the civilian government since the intervention of the military in Nigerian politics in 1966. The plan being the first to be drawn under presidential democracy was unique because it elicited the participation of local governments. The uniqueness of the plan was, however, instrumental to the economic misfortune that has bewildered the country to date. The projected capital investment of the plan was put at ₦82 billion. Out of this figure, the public sector investment was ₦70.5 billion, while the private sector was expected to invest ₦11.7 billion. From all indications, the plan was the largest and most ambitious programme of investment ever launched in Nigeria.[14] As a result, the plan was characterized by huge debt servicing which resulted from various foreign loans obtained in the previous years and increased import bills amidst a drastic fall in crude oil export revenue. These factors no doubt limited the scope of the objectives and laid a foundation for another plan which resulted in the fifth plan. Instead of the launch of the plan, there were several Integrated Development Initiatives which Okoli and Onah referred to as rural development strategies such as the Agricultural Development Scheme; National Accelerated Food Production Program (NAFPP); and Directorate for Food, Road and Rural Infrastructure (DFRRI).[15] The Structural Adjustment Program (SAP) was, however, articulated under the Fifth Development Plan on 26 September 1986. The need for SAP came as a result of the poor state of the economy that witnessed the decline in oil prices in the first half of the 1980s. To reverse the worsening economic crisis in terms of declining growth, increasing unemployment, galloping inflation, high incidence of poverty, deteriorating balance of payment, debilitating debt burden and increasing unsustainable fiscal deficits,[16] among others, government embarked on austerity measures in 1982, which was a brainchild of SAP in 1986.

After the SAP initiative, several other approaches were employed mostly short-term instruments for socio-economic management. These are: the Perspective plan, Rolling plans (1990–1999) and Vision 2010. The main report of Vision 2010 submitted to Abacha's government in September 1997 among other things recommended that the vision should provide the focus of all plans including long (perspective), medium (rolling) and annual plans (budgets). The vision of the plan was to transform the Nigerian nation by 2010 into what Ukwu explained as a united, industrious, caring and God-fearing democratic society, committed to making the basic needs of life affordable for everyone, and creating Africa's leading economy.[17,18] The inconsistencies of these plans led to the establishment of the National Economic Empowerment and Development Strategy (NEEDS). It availed the country the prospect to experiment with medium-term economic development plan from 2003 to 2007.

Regrettably, most of the objectives of NEEDS were not realized as the country's annual budget dewed into billions, then trillions of naira at the period. A major initiative undertaken as a long-term or perspective plan is Vision 2020. The vision came as a far cry to the burning issues of economic instability and poverty dampening the image of the nation. This programme, reinstated by the Yar'Adua's administration, was previously embarked upon during Obasanjo's regime but not effectuated. It is said to be based on a proactive reaction to a 2001 Jim O'Neil's prediction that if Nigeria and some other developing countries can mobilize their resources effectively, it is anticipated that by 2025, Nigeria and countries like Egypt would have joined the top-twenty economies (Canada, Austria, Belgium, France, Greece, Italy, the Netherlands, Spain, Denmark, Norway, Poland, Russia, Sweden, Switzerland, Turkey, Australia, India, Indonesia, Malaysia and Brazil[19]) in the world. Instructively, the foundation of this plan appeared fluid *abinitio*. How can a National Development Master Plan be based on an 'untested thesis' or at best the hypothesis of a foreign economist? Out of the twenty countries listed that Nigeria would purportedly compete with, which among them appear 'planless' to enable Nigeria displace it by 2020? The hypothesis of Neil is based on the assumption of prudent economic management which has been lacking in Nigeria for a long time.

Another programme put in place by Yar'Adua's was his Seven-Point Agenda. The programme was intended to tackle the problems of power and energy, food security, wealth creation, transport sector, land reforms, security and education.[20] These were to run in tandem with the Nigerian version of the 2015 United Nations Millennium Development Goals (MDGs) of eradicating extreme poverty and hunger, ensuring Universal Primary Education (UPE), reducing child mortality by two-thirds, improving maternal health, combating HIV/AIDs, malaria and other diseases, ensuring environmental sustainability between 2015 and 2020; and developing a global partnership for development by 2015. The Yar'Adua's Seven-Point agenda failed due to incoordination and clumsiness.

REASONS FOR DEVELOPMENT PLANNING FAILURES IN NIGERIA

It is worrisome that the various development planning initiatives put in place to salvage the development crisis in Nigeria has been a mirage. Several reasons have therefore been adduced for its failures.

The Western Model Syndrome

Development plans in Nigeria since 1962 appear compatible with Western notion of development. On this note, Ake and Onah argued that the national development plans and development initiatives did not encourage the disengagement of Nigerian economy from the exploitative structural links with Western capitalist economies.[21] This argument of disengaging from Western notion of development was corroborated by Munroe thus: 'this standard of measuring success is the source of much Third World frustration as nations. . . . This success trap will not bring true fulfilment or freedom, but greater bondage'.

Since independence, African leaders have accepted and absorbed a number of mythical notions and models about development and planning which were to influence thinking in post-colonial era. These are:

- Planning had to be elitist in initiation and implementation; there was no need to involve the masses whose lives and future were being planned.
- For a plan to be successful, it must involve huge capital expenditure on all sorts of projects whether coordinated or not was a secondary matter and
- Planners must rely on foreign aid capital, technology and manpower.[22]

These notions which are replete of the colonial plan carry its own flaws from inception and this was replicated in post-independence era. The post-colonial development plans have remained largely dependent on external trade, foreign technology, foreign enterprise and other stimuli.

The dependent nature of West African economies is further expounded by *dependency theory*. The theory is predicated on the notion that resources flow from a 'periphery' of the poor and underdeveloped states to the 'core' or 'centre' of the wealthy states, enriching the latter at the expense of the former.[23] This definition is exemplified by the analyses of Obikeze and Obi on the objectives of Nigerian colonial development plan. The plan, they asserted, was focused more on transport, communication and cultivation of selected cash crops. With the aim of evacuating agricultural resources, the plans paid little attention to the development of the productive base including the manufacturing and service sectors of the country. This is evident in the fact that of the £55 million (or ₦110 million) budgeted for the Ten-Year plan (1946–1956) a significant proportion was set aside for social services and transport and communication. Water supply and health services were allocated up to 25% while the directly productive sectors of agriculture and industry got as little as 6.4% of the total budget. Similarly, of the £330 million slated for the 1955–1960 period, industrial and agricultural development were allocated a paltry 9.0% while the transport sector alone received 38.7%. Coleman averred that the colonial state was all interventionist, repressive and exploitative.

According to Imoh, whether from laudatory or derogatory perspective, colonialism has been a major impeding factor to the development of most periphery societies such as Nigeria. The plan was scarcely aimed at the development of the colonies either economically or otherwise. It did not show any intention of establishing popular and democratic institutions or a preparedness to involve the majority of the people in the planning of their lives and society. Its conceptualization and implementation were highly static, elitist, discriminatory and undisciplined.[24] The projects had no linkages with one another and rather than improve the living standards of the people, the plan had an opposite effect. The plan have created among several others, poverty, mass unemployment and social inequalities. Unfortunately, this is the plan that Nigerian leaders have adopted after independence in their quest for economic stability.

From the fore given analyses, any claim that the British colonial government developed West Africa either in terms of laying the foundation or achieving concrete development on behalf of the people must be illusory. It is crystal clear that the peripheral role and location of West Africa formation today in the international division of labour, the existence of a weak and largely unproductive bourgeoisie, the co-existence of production (capitalist models), the existence of an unstable state and the generally low standards of living were the direct consequences of the colonial planning and policies which are being reproduced in contemporary time. The outward orientation of the West African economy, the absence of a technological base, the neo-colonial content of the educational system, the viciousness of the armed and security forces and the existence of inefficient and ineffective institutions are also products of colonial rule which deliberately emphasized the interest of the metropolis at the expense of the colonized people.[25] Thus, it is not misleading to say that Nigeria has been following a wrong path towards the realization of its development goals.

The Big Push Strategy

Another factor is the idea of conceiving development planning as a 'big push strategy' which attempts to do everything in one plan. Development plans in Nigeria are overambitious, trying to achieve many objectives at the same time without considering the conflicting and competing priorities. In most cases, policy objectives are contradictory. Also, plans are often grandiose in design but vague on specific policies needed to achieve stated objectives. This hampers development efforts as resources are overstretched and little or nothing is achieved in the process. As a result, the technical expert of the second development plan, W.F. Stolper, described the plan as 'planning without facts'.[26]

Corruption

Corruption in Nigeria has become epidemic. Ejumudo termed this 'System Corruption'. The term according to him is a situation where corruption has been institutionalized and raised to the level of a structural parameter. Thus, it has become part of the value-system of a society, that is, a condition par excellence.[27] Corruption in Nigerian political system has so far hampered development plans and programmes. More disheartening is the fact that the purported development plans are to a large extent corruption avenues to some Nigerian politicians and bureaucrats. Illicit misappropriation of privileges and opportunities in public and private sectors for personal aggrandizement, particularly those in positions of authority, is sine qua non to Nigeria. This behaviour brings about inefficiency, bitterness and frustration which have an unsettling effect upon focused minded citizens.

Lack of Plan Discipline

The failure of Nigerian political leaders and bureaucrats to abide by the plan objectives has frustrated development plans in Nigeria. Though plan projects acquired priorities since 1962, these are invariably ignored by the bureaucratic bourgeoisie in a blatant demonstration of the superiority of its selfish-class interests over avowed national objectives. Typical examples could be found in the FESTAC project which cost millions of naira, yet not stipulated in the plan document. Another was the Universal Primary Education (UPE) programme which was not in the second plan, yet its implementation began in the period and its critical phase commenced during the third plan.[28] In fact, the plans of the various governments could be described as competitive in character and aberration in plan execution as well as under spending on directly productive projects and overspending on prestigious or white elephant projects. Although plans are made to accommodate little variations, the various plans in Nigeria in the past were so much altered during the implementation stages to the extent of distorting the overall objectives of the plans.

Lack of Continuity of Government Programmes

This is a corollary of the aforementioned problem. Governments are scored high on promises, but lacking in delivery. Often time, successive regimes do not feel obligated to continue the national plans and other developmental projects of their predecessors as they introduce new projects and litter the nation with uncompleted projects. Most of these projects like the Ajaokuta Steel Complex that ought to play catalyst roles in the country's industrialization drive are still comatose. Arguably, sustainable development is not genuinely on the agenda of successive Nigerian governments and the absence of a true development agenda has not placed the country on the right sustainable development path.[29] It has been stressed that the existence of a good plan is not enough as the basis for achieving development. There must be, in addition, a political leadership that has the vision, will, credibility and capacity to manage the process of change.

Lack of Commitment

Development plans are often prepared without consulting the people, hence public apathy towards its implementation. Obi reiterated that since the plan is meant for the people, but they are not even aware of its existence or objectives, they do not feel duty bound to contribute to its success. This lackadaisical attitude of the people is a contributing factor to the stagnation of the economy. For instance, the second plan was criticized as the type of plan whose document were produced largely by an expatriate team without much local involvement and therefore less effective as a means of mobilizing domestic efforts. People are both the means and ends of development, and for a nation to develop, both the people and leaders must work towards it. A new nationalism, civil society emancipation and novel brand of nation building and patriotism are not to be seen as an option but a necessity.

Absence of Relevant Data

Development planning depends basically on the availability of data. Accurate data is a very scarce commodity in Nigeria due to problems arising from the inadequacies of the federal office of statistics, the unwillingness of Nigerians to reveal information and the outright manipulation of data for pecuniary or other gains. A striking example of this problem is the fact that the demography of the country is still unknown. A country that does not know its population would definitely not be in position to determine the other vital statistics necessary for planning life, birth rate, death rate, number of those of school age and other demographic changes which are essential for planning.[30] The absence of reliable background data has made the use of social indicators difficult and inadequate for plan preparation, implementation and monitoring of national progress.

Public Service Inefficiency

Public service is an institution that is saddled with the responsibility of executing development plans. The Nigerian public service is beset with many problems which militate against its efforts in the implementation of development plans. Although, the public service reforms, which among other things, attempted to increase the level of professionalization in the service, it has only achieved minimal results. The service is still plagued with a plethora of problems such as management malady, poor conditions of remunerations, overstaffing, inadequate working materials, poor communication system and lack of a clear-cut job description.

Public and Private Sector Partnership

There is a poor collaboration between the public and private sectors in development planning process in Nigeria. In fact, development planning has largely followed bureaucratic process with little private sector participation so much so that such efforts can be appropriately described as lacking in synergy. Ordinarily, development planning is supposed to incorporate broad policy frameworks that will have elements of public and private sector initiatives.

Misplacement of Priorities

Similar to the colonial plans, the subsequent plans also exhibited a basic lack of urgency. A typical example is the iron and steel industry that was in the first and second plans and was initiated for projected completion during the fourth plan. This represented a lag of twenty years; yet this project was repeatedly acclaimed the cornerstone of Nigeria's industrialization. Similar examples include petrochemicals, fertilizers, the petroleum refinery, liquefied petroleum gas and other heavy industries. While this leisurely pace persisted, the country completed such counter-productive projects like the National Stadium and Trade Fair Complex in Lagos, the FESTAC Durbar Hotel at Kaduna and staged the multi-million naira FESTAC in 1977.

Inadequate Executive Capacity

This is one of the greatest problems of development planning in Nigeria. In fact, it is frustrating to plan the execution of programmes which require the availability of organization, institutions and skills which the economy does not possess and cannot normally be expected to generate during the plan period. Executive capacity also involves the existence of competent contracting firms and basic socio-economic infrastructure including competent hands to run the civil service and allied government machinery.

Domestic-Foreign Resource Generation Ratio

There is the tendency to have oversized or massive plans because of the high expectations from foreign resources. This situation became obvious during the fourth plan when the original capital outlay of ₦70.5 billion for the public sector became unrealistic as a result of the disturbances in the oil market. The plan's resource allocation was based on the assumption that oil production would remain at over two million barrels a day at a price of at least $40 per barrel. Unfortunately, by February, 1983, Nigeria was producing less than one million barrels per day at about $30 per barrel. Also, the first plan could be considered oversized because of the total planned investment of ₦1,307.8 million, domestic resource availability amounted to ₦526 million with the expectation of 50% of the capital budget from foreign sources. Worse still, Nigeria's economy is mono-product and not technology-driven in a domestic sense.

Other factors adduced for the failure of development plans are technology transfer syndrome, paucity of funds due to misappropriation for personal gain, lack of project monitoring and revision of plans.

CONCLUSION

It can be concluded that it is apparent that planning towards national development is a burning issue globally, and as such been a core motive of academic discourse. It is imperative to note that the plethora of development plans, beginning from the first post-independence plan in 1962 down to the fifth, and other integrated development initiatives and visions have been channelled towards achieving similar objectives with emphasis on economic growth. As laudable as the plans appeared, none achieved desired results. The adoption of western models in the plans is adduced as a major setback. As a corollary, poor leadership, political culture and recruitment processes have manifested in very tragic results for development planning initiatives in Nigeria. Other impediments are lack of continuity of programmes, misplaced priorities, technology transfer syndrome, public service inefficiency, corruption, lack of relevant data, lack of commitment and indiscipline, amongst others.

As a consequence of development failures, all economic and social indicators have shown that the economy is in doldrums. Acute unemployment, widespread poverty, illiteracy, decayed social and physical infrastructure, technological backwardness, urban congestion, excessive debt burden, poor growth of agricultural production and high incidence of diseases are common features of Nigerian economy. Given this situation, development in Nigeria has become elusive.

RECOMMENDATIONS

To make headway in any human endeavour, there must be the will and genuine interest to make such endeavour materialize. The failure of the political elite to genuinely respond to the development needs of the people, through home grown strategies and make rational policy decisions will continue to foster economic and political insecurity. For the purpose of a realistic plan and progressive nation, Nigerian leaders must be honest and enthusiastic about development policies and ensure its actual implementation. Leaders must lead by example in every way. Discipline, morals, ethics and commitment must be showed not only in words but in deeds. As pointed out earlier, the lack of commitment by successive leaders has led to the discontinuation of government plans and the littering of uncompleted projects all over the nation, this has made development unsustainable. On this note, the paper suggests that Nigerian leaders go through training, orientation and re-orientation. This will make them imbibe the requisite skills and traits in effective governance, and also has the potential of arresting the phenomenon of poor leadership that has been confronting the country for decades. In addition, the recruitment agencies should be enhanced and fortified to produce true leaders.

Furthermore, planners should come up with realistic plans that are internally oriented and suits their peculiar situation rather than adopt models which are counterproductive. Plausible alternative strategies that are non-dependent should be espoused. Nigeria cannot perpetually remain twisted with the ugly memory and sad commemoration of colonial plunder. The country should rise beyond the woes of colonialism and confront the exploitative international capitalist system. It should develop its sectors and concentrate on efforts that would turn its economic situation around. The rural areas should be developed for the purpose of agriculture and diversification of the economy. Inclusive-development is integral to economic growth, to achieve this, economic diversification and a shift from the failed oil economy are recommended. The country needs to revamp not only its agricultural sector but also all other sectors. This will help to provide alternative revenue for project funding.

Also, the machineries/institutions for gathering data for planning require strengthening or total overhaul. A weak database presents an unrealistic plan, as such, efforts should be made to enhance data accuracy and reliability through effective instruments and personnel.

Development plans should also embrace a multi-sector approach to planning and implementation of public sector programmes and policies. Through this, the disconnection between planners and beneficiaries can be bridged. Harmonization of development programmes and initiatives is also strongly advocated to enable plans operate as a whole rather than isolated and scattered ideas which make implementation a herculean task.

The objectives of development plans can be achieved if the governments, the private sector, civil society organizations and multi-national corporations work as a team to ensure tangible results that will meet globally recognized and acceptable benchmarks of true development. The efficacy of such plans will therefore require, as a matter of exigency, getting the basics right and that includes instituting sound development policies, ensuring good economic management, promoting private investment, developing human resource capacity, fostering synergistic public/private sector partnership and collaboration as well as providing good physical and institutional infrastructure.

NOTES

1. Daniel Neumark, *Foreign Trade and Economic Development in Africa: A Historical Perspective* (Standford: Standford University Press Food Research Institute, 1964), 741–3.
2. Olusegun Adeyeri and David Adejuwon, 'The Implications of British Colonial Economic Policies on Nigeria's Development', *International Journal of Advanced Research in Management and Social Sciences* 1, no. 2 (2012): 5.
3. Kelly Ejumudo, 'The Problematic of Development Planning in Nigeria: A Critical Discourse', *Developing Country Studies* 3, no. 4 (2013): 69.

4. Akin Mabogunge, *The Development Process: A Spatial Perspective* (London: Hudtchinson, 1980), 45.

5. Walter Rodney, *How Europe Underdeveloped Africa* (Abuja: Panaf Publishing, 2005).

6. Kelly Ejumudo, 'The Problematic of Development', 70.

7. Michael Todaro, *Economics for Developing World* (London: Longman, 1979), 90.

8. Michael Crowder, *West Africa under Colonial Rule* (Benin: Ethiope Publishing, 1976), 167.

9. Bekeh Utietiang, 'Historicizing Development: Nigeria's 1945 Colonial Plan', *The Journal of Pan African Studies* 8, no. 9 (2015): 5.

10. Tamuno Tekena, 'British Colonial Administration in Nigeria in the 20th Century', in *Groundwork of Nigerian History*, ed. Obaro Ikime (Nigeria: Heinemann Educational Books, 1980), 524.

11. Kelly Ejumudo, 'The Problematic of Development', 70–5.

12. Emmanuel Iheanacho, 'National Development Planning in Nigeria: An Endless Search for Appropriate Development Strategy', *International Journal of Economic Development Research and Investment* 5, no. 2 (2014): 51–2.

13. Imoh Imoh-Itah, Luke Amadi and Roger Akpan, 'Colonialism and the Postcolonial Nigeria: Complexities and Contradictions 1960–2015: A Post-Development Perspective', *International Journal of Political Science* 2, no. 3 (2016): 15, http://dx.doi.org/10.20431/2454-9452.0203002.

14. Imoh-Itah, 'Colonialism and Post-colonial', 17.

15. Iheanacho, 'National Development Planning in Nigeria', 55.

16. Chukwuma Ogbonna. 'Structural Adjustment Program (SAP) in Nigeria: An Empirical Assessment', *Journal of Banking* 6, no. 1 (2012):17.

17. Adeyeri, 'The Implications of British Colonial', 6.

18. National Planning Commission, *National Economic Empowerment and Development Strategy (NEEDS) (Abridged)* (Abuja: NPC, 2005).

19. Julius Ihonvbere and Toyin, Falola, 'The Illusions of Economic Development', in *Britain and Nigeria: Exploitation or Development*, ed. Toyin Falola (London: Zed Books, 1987), 200.

20. Julius Ihonvbere, 'The Illusions of Economic Development', 205.

21. Claude Ake, *A Political Economy of Africa* (Lagos: Longman, 2008), 35.

22. Daniel Neumark, 'Foreign Trade and Economic', 738.

23. James Paul, 'Post-Dependency: The Third World in an Era of Globalism and Late Capitalism', *Alternatives: Social Transformation and Human Governance* 22, no. 2 (1997): 205.

24. Ihonvbere, 'The Illusions of Economic', 208.

25. Ejumudo, 'The Problematic of Development', 77.

26. Neumark, 'Foreign Trade and Economic', 755.

27. Jide Ibietan and Oghator Ekhosuehi, 'Trends in Development Planning in Nigeria: 1962–2012', *Journal of Sustainable Development in Africa* 15, no. 4 (2013): 301.

28. Ibietan, 'Trends in Development Planning', 305.

29. Mabogunge, 'The Development Process', 54.

30. Ibid., 60.

BIBLIOGRAPHY

Adeniji, Adepoju, Oluwayemisi Ajoke and Amos Kolawole, 'Development Planning in Nigeria: A Road to Sustainable Development'. *International Journal of Innovative Research in Education, Technology & Social Strategies* 3, no. 1 (2016): 79–84.

Adeyeri, Olusegun and Adejuwon David, 'The Implications of British Colonial Economic Policies on Nigeria's Development', *International Journal of Advanced Research in Management and Social Sciences* 1, no. 2 (2012): 5–6.

Claude, Ake, *A political Economy of Africa*. Lagos: Longman, 2008.

Crowder, Michael. *West Africa under Colonial Rule*. Benin City: Ethiope Publishing, 1976.

Ejumudo, Kelly. 'The Problematic of Development Planning in Nigeria: A Critical Discourse'. *Developing Country Studies* 3, no. 4 (2013): 69–77.

Ibietan, Jide and Ekhosuehi Oghator. 'Trends in Development Planning in Nigeria: 1962–2012'. *Journal of Sustainable Development in Africa* 15, no. 4 (2013): 301–5.

Iheanacho, Emmanuel. 'National Development Planning in Nigeria: An Endless Search for Appropriate Development Strategy'. *International Journal of Economic Development Research and Investment* 5, no. 2 (2014): 51–5.

Ihonvbere, Julius and Toyin Falola. 'The Illusions of Economic Development'. In *Britain and Nigeria: Exploitation or Development*, edited by Toyin Falola. London: Zed Books, 1987.

Imoh, Imoh-Itah, Luke Amadi and Roger Akpan. 'Colonialism and the Post-Colonial Nigeria: Complexities and Contradictions 1960–2015: A Post-Development Perspective'. *International Journal of Political Science (IJPS)* 2, no. 3 (2016): 15–7, http://dx.doi.org/10.20431/2454-9452.0203002.

James, Paul. 'Post-Dependency: The Third World in an Era of Globalism and Late Capitalism'. *Alternatives: Social Transformation and Human Governance* 22, no. 2 (1997): 205–8.

Mabogunge, Akin. *The Development Process: A Spatial Perspective*. London: Hudtchinson & Co, 1980.

National Planning Commission. *National Economic Empowerment and Development Strategy (NEEDS) (Abridged)*. Abuja: NPC, 2005.

Neumark, Daniel. *Foreign Trade and Economic Development in Africa: A Historical Perspective*. Stanford: Standford University Food Research Institute, 1964.

Obikeze, Sunday and Emeka Obi. *Public Administration in Nigeria: A Development Approach*. Onitsha: Book Point, 2004.

Ogbonna, Chukwuma. 'Structural Adjustment Program (SAP) in Nigeria: An Empirical Assessment'. *Journal of Banking* 6, no. 1 (2012): 17.

Rodney, Walter. *How Europe Underdeveloped Africa*. Abuja: Panaf Publishing, 2005.

Tamuno, Tekena. 'British Colonial Administration in Nigeria in the 20th Century'. In *Groundwork of Nigerian History*, edited by Obaro Ikime, 524. Ibadan: Heinemann Educational Books, 1980.

Todaro, Michael. *Economics for Developing World*. London: Longman, 1979.

Utietiang, Bekeh. 'Historicizing Development: Nigeria's 1945 Colonial Plan'. *The Journal of Pan African Studies* 8, no. 9 (2015): 5.

Chapter 7

Local Government-State Joint Account and Crisis of Grassroots Development in Nigeria

Nneka Ifeoma Okafor, Ifeanyichukwu Michael Abada and Paul Hezekiah Omeh

INTRODUCTION

The local government as a unit of governance at the grassroots level with primary role of development, and transformation of lives of the people has in the recent times faced with myriads developmental challenges. Conventionally, the law establishing the existence of local government carved for it, specific functions expected of it to deliver grassroots development. But the reverse is the case because of the operation of joint account with the state governments. The joint account exercise between the tiers of government has conscripted local government and made it a mere appendage to the state government. The lack of financial autonomy of local government is a swift design to make the institution of third tier government impracticable. According to Nwabueze:

> That if the state government has the locus standi and constitutional power to establish local government and to define its structure and functions, it clearly and necessarily imply that local government is a mere agency of a creation of the state government.[1]

The aforementioned text depicts that local government has become a myth rather than a reality. The appreciation of the complex nature and character of local government creation in post-colonial entities had shown how the constitution of the Federal Republic of Nigeria has conferred power on both the national and state governments over the local government councils. According to the 1999 Constitution, Section 7(1) confers adequate responsibilities on every state of the federation to essentially ensure the existence of democratically elected local government councils, under a law which provides for the establishment, structure, composition, finance and functions of such councils.

It has been noted that the fall-outs in the achievements of the local councils' needs are due to financial matters repose on state government over the local councils within the state. The constitution of the Federal Republic of Nigeria as amended states:

> The National Assembly shall make provisions for statutory allocations of public revenue to local government councils in the federation and the house of Assembly of a state shall make provisions for statutory allocation of public revenue to local government councils within the state.[2]

This implies that if the statutory allocations cease to come as when due, local government will find it extremely difficult in addressing its fundamental objectives and roles to localness. The third-tier government which has the needs and aspirations of its citizens is supposed to be relieved from such an entanglement, made autonomous like other two-tiers. It is based on this general backdrop that the study is divided into the following headings.

THE NATURE AND CHARACTER OF LOCAL GOVERNMENT IN NIGERIA

Extant literature in the field of local government and local administration abounds. This is due to apparent lack in the level of precision in the use of the construct. According to the Guidelines for Reform of Local Government in Nigeria, it conceives local government as:

> Government at the local level exercised though representative council established by law to exercise specific powers within defined areas. These powers should give the councils substantial control over local affairs as well as the staff and institutional and financial powers to initiate and direct the provision of services and to determine and implement projects so as to complete the activities of the state and federal government in the areas and to ensure through active participation of the people and their traditional institutions that local initiatives and responses to the needs are maximized.[3]

This excerpt shows that local government has a legal existence and enjoys certain degree of autonomy. The nature of local government in Nigeria can be seen as an essential instrument of national or state government for the performance of certain basic services, which can best be decided upon and administered locally in the intimate knowledge of the needs, conditions and peculiarities of areas concerned.[4] It unites the people in a defined area in a common organization whose functions are essentially complicate to those of the central government in the interest of the local residents of satisfaction of common community needs. Consequently, its effectiveness is judged through the developments it generates, social amenities it provides, and to what extent it has catered satisfactorily for the happiness and general wellbeing of the communities it has established to serve.

From the aforementioned context, one can easily deduce the facts that local government as an essential and veritable instrument for provision of certain services and effectiveness is strictly judged through the available indicators of development and transformation indices. But, despite the available opportunities for the local council to deliver on the needful expectations and aspirations of its people, it has been crippled and made incapable through the institutionalization of State Joint Local Government Account.

INTER-GOVERNMENTALISM AND POLITICS OF 'AUTONOMIZATION' OF LOCAL GOVERNMENT IN NIGERIA

The concept of inter-governmentalism or better still inter-governmental relations refers to all the complex and inter dependent relations among various spheres of government as well as the coordination of public polices among national, provincial and local government through programme reporting requirements, grants-in-aid, the planning and budgeting process and information communication among officials.[5] Implicit here is that every tier of government has been identified and their financial relation is clearly noted. This is because finance is very pertinent to combat the developing challenges affecting all the tiers of government and local government in particular.

Inter-governmental relations as interaction that take place among the different levels of government exist within a state.[6] Also, it comprises all the permutation and combinations of relations among the units of government in a federal system.[7] On the financial relations to local government, the position and functions of an auditor-general for the local government of a state is detrimental to the struggle for granting autonomy to local government by state and the federal governments, and distort thorough active participation of the people and their traditional institutions in local initiatives.

In Nigeria, the practice of inter-governmental relations is streamlined into central-state-local, central-state, state-local and inter local relations; and fiscal relation is central. According to the Constitution of the Federal Republic of Nigeria, Section 7(7b) as amended. the House of Assembly of a state shall make provisions for statutory allocation of public revenue to local government councils within the state.[8] Also, the state wields greater level of control over the financial resources of the local government. The office of auditor-general who is answerable to the state governor is responsible to the control of the monies accruable to the local governments within the state. This depicts that the attainment for the autonomy of local governments is a serious issue to be granted on a platter of gold.

THE ESSENCE OF THE INSTITUTION OF LOCAL GOVERNMENT AND SERVICE DELIVERY

The position of local government in both prismatic and developed societies cannot be really over emphasized. As a unit of governance and a veritable instrument, local government in Nigeria had continued to discharge its functions to realization of its fundamental philosophy and objectives despite odds. The essence of the third-tier government has been viewed from different perspectives. One of the school thoughts on the essence of local government associated with it the functions of local government as were contained in the (documents) establishing it; while the other schools of thought argued that the essence of local government can only be presumed on the academic standard theories.

However, the understanding and appreciation of the essence of local government will be evaluated through the schools of thought. The function or essence of local government which is premised on the schools of thought include the democratic participatory school, the efficiency services and the holistic integrationist school.[9] The democratic participatory school of thought was propounded by scholars like J.S. Mills, Roberts Dahl and Jeremy Bentham et al. According to the theorists, they maintained and argued vehemently that local government functions to bring about democracy and to afford opportunities for political participation to the citizens as well as to educate and socialize him politically.[10] They succinctly supported their stands by arguing that the institution of third-tier government is superior to the other levels of government since it is only at level of the local self-government that individual can really participate in his own government and so government is truly democratic.[11] Appreciating the indicators of the democratic participatory school, the institutions of local government function as political educator and breeder of better societies.

Furthermore, the efficiency service delivery theory is instrumentation to essence of local government. According to its proponents, local government is a veritable instrument for efficient service delivery at the grassroots. It strongly believes in a high-level performance and holds that the essential function of local government is not to bring about political participation or some other form of political education, but to provide services and must be judged by its success in providing the services.[12] It is argued that because of its closeness to an area, local government can provide certain services more efficiently than the central government.

Moreover, on the holistic integrationist approach, local government in the contemporary millennium has continued to exist to make and contribute its own quota, thereby helping to achieve national integration, national evolution and national consciousness. Theorizing on the essence of local government Gabriel Almond and Bingham Powell adopted capabilities approach as the essential functions of local government.

DEVELOPMENTAL CHALLENGES AND STATE PERSISTENCE INTERVENTION IN LOCAL GOVERNMENT AFFAIRS

Following the ratification of the 1999 Constitution of the federal republic of Nigeria; the position and functions of the third-tier government has been clearly spelt to reflect the local government reforms of 1976. Critics had observed the abysmal space occupied by local government in Nigeria. Accordingly, the 1999 Constitution was systematically designed and bequeathed to the people by the then military oligarchy. This implies that the 1999 Constitution is not a true reflection of the demands, yearnings and aspirations of the people.

This is not only restricted to the needs of people but extend to the position of local government in discharging its numerous functions as were contained in the constitution.

However, with the gap created by the constitution on local government in Nigeria has been construed as a mere appendage of former at the mercies of the state government and national government. Many state governments had in the recent past reduced the tenure of the local council to suit their selfish aggrandizement. This is not limited to total sack of council chairmen as witness in Ondo State, Nigeria under the watch of the then governor, Chief Olusegun Mimiko. The deliberate hand-picking and installation of caretaker and transitional council chairmen had worsened the situation. Based on this, the later becomes and an Automated Teller Vending machine for siphoning the treasure of the local government. It is no longer making news that the state government has continued unabated to divert the monies needed for the development of the council areas with the state. The swift diversion and deduction of funds and other statutory allocations to local government by the state through the instrumentality of state-local government joint account has been a serious hurdle that continued to thwart the efforts of local government in addressing its challenges in developing its jurisdiction.

Furthermore, many state governments in connivance with the state chief of staff, chief accountant and commissioner of finance had double their planned repetition in deducting the monthly allocations to the local government within the state. For instance, in Enugu State, during the political regimes of the former governor, Chimaroke Nnamani, local government councils were made to smell hell in delivering developmental services as a result of the holy alliance between the governor and the seventeen council chairmen. The chairmen of the councils were mandate, and forcefully made to sign prepared claims and documents that some amount of money meant for their respective local governments were adequately collected by the later. But the fact remains that the council chairmen were denied to collect in full the statutory allocation due to them from the state government.

Addressing the developmental challenges and institutional transformation through the local government is the inability of the local councils' ineffectiveness to bring about development as a result of the joint account operation with the state government.[13] He noted that in Ondo state under the then governor Olusegun Agagu, there was perceived holy alliance between the state government and the local councils in the state where the former constituted Joint Action Committee (JAC), which made the federal allocations to local government first deposited in to a particular account before calling for committee meeting. This was a systematic design by the state to clear ways to hijack local councils' allocation and a times releases instrumentally at its will.

Table 7.1 and figure 7.1 show the total statutory allocations during 1999–2005. These showed that 92.9% of revenue accrued to the North-east region within the period. The North-west and North-central got 185.7% and 110.2%, respectively. On the other hand, South-east got 81% while, South-west and South-south got 121% and 110%, respectively. But, available empirical indictors on ground had shown that despite huge statutory allocations accruable to local governments from both governments at centre and state, the local councils had continued to witness perpetual challenges in development which could be linked to joint account operation with state government.[14]

Summarily, table 7.2 shows the deductions of funds by the Government of Enugu State on three selected local council between April 2002 and September 2007 indicate that in April 2002, the net allocations made available

Table 7.1. Statutory allocation to Local Government Areas according to the six geopolitical zones (1999–2005) percentages

Geopolitical Zones	*1999*	*2000*	*2001*	*2002*	*2003*	*2004*	*2005*	*Total*
North-East	12.7	14.6	14.6	13.2	12.6	12.6	12.6	92.9
North-West	24.3	28.3	30.3	26.6	25.1	25.4	25.5	185.7
North-Central	15.9	14.7	15.0	15.4	16.4	16.0	16.8	110.2
South-East	12.0	10.7	10.2	11.8	12.1	12.1	12.1	81
South-West	18.6	16.0	14.9	17.2	18.1	18.1	18.1	121
South-South	16.4	15.8	14.7	15.7	15.7	15.8	15.9	110

Source: Eboh and Igboke.[15]

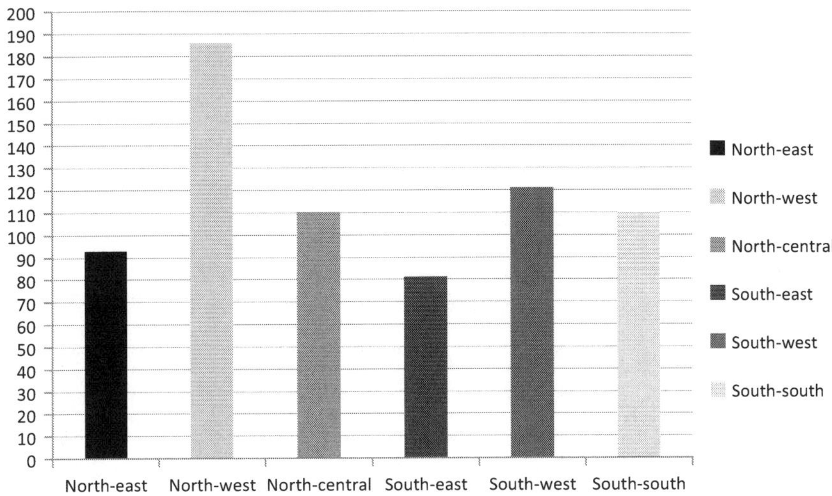

Figure 7.1. Bar chart showing the statutory allocation to the six geo-political zones, 1999–2005

to them was ₦326,971,121.63, while total amount received as net allocation after the deductions on ₦74,935,042 amounting to 253% was ₦12, 869,076.21 which represented 47%. Also, in May 2002, the total amount of ₦157,603,635.67 was supposed to be made available but through the instrumentation of joint account, the thee local governments were able to receive as their net allocation of ₦13,740,460.39 after the deduction of 233.4% representing ₦143,863.101.11.

Furthermore, it is pertinent to recall that, between the months of April, 2003, December 2003 and August 2004, the whopping sum of ₦144,644,975.14, ₦177,285,954.41 and ₦167,246,226.25, respectively, were supposed to be accrued to the three council areas, but after placing deductions of 42.3%, 54.7% and 67.6%, the leftover amounts to the three local government as their net allocation were ₦42,328,582.21, ₦94,699,250.98 and ₦75,745,782.48, respectively.

In addition, between October 2004, January 2005 and April 2006, the three local government received as their net amount the sum of ₦77,664,133.48 (163.7%), ₦86,231,392.26 (127.6%) and ₦84,901,395.26 (11.4%) after deduction, respectively, while in the actual sense, their respective net allocations amount to ₦175,672,046.85, ₦208,415,289.57 and ₦231,305, 094.73. Also, looking at the allocations on the months of September 2006, January 2007 and April 2007, the three local governments were supposed to get ₦443,514,651.01, ₦219,103,464.08 and ₦245,051,575.52, respectively, on the identified months. But, the issue remains that after the

Table 7.2. Deduction of funds by Government of Enugu State on selected local councils, April 2002–September 2007

S.No.	*L.G.*	*Month*	*Net Allocation (Million Naira)*	*Total Deduction at Source (Million Naira)*	*Net amount Received by Local Government (Million Naira)*
1	Aninri	April, 2002	265,741,156.86	17,143,484.8 (65%)	9,430.36 (35%)
2	Enugu North	April, 2002	27,870,959.44	24,432,553.59(88%)	3.438,403.88(12%)
3	Nsukka	April, 2002	33,359,005.33	33,359,005.33(100%)	0.00(0%)
			326,971,121.63	74,953,043.42(253%)	12.869,076.21(47%)
1	Aninri	May, 2002	47,636,395.88	37,930,815.03(79.6%)	9,705,508.85(20.4%)
2	Enugu North	May, 2002	49,990,512.67	46,192,034.59(54.7%)	3,778,403.55(12%)
3	Nsukka	May,2002	59,976,727.12	59,740,251.49(99.1%)	236,475.69(0.4%)
			157,603,635.67	143,863,101.11(233.4%)	13,740,460.39(32.8%)
1	Aninri	April, 2003	42,563,411.82	20,971,204.74(42.3%)	21,592,207.08(7.6%)
2	Enugu North	April, 2003	48,557,799.86	26,554,763.59(54.7%)	19,003,036.27(39.1%)
3	Nsukka	April, 2003	53,523,763.46	36,190,424.6(67.6%)	17,33,338.86(32.1%)
			144,644,975.14	83,716,392.93(164.6%)	12,328,582.21(78.8%)
1	Aninri	Dec. 2003	46,155,568.48	16,153,504.56(55%)	30,0031,055.92(65%)
2	Enugu North	Dec. 2003	59,660,428.33	27,708,233.88(46.4%)	31,952,194.45(53.6%)
3	Nsukka	Dec. 2003	71,469,961.60	38,725,960.99(54.2%)	32,744,00.61(45%)
			177,285,958.41	82,587,699.43(155.6%)	64,699,250.98(163.6%)
1	Aninri	Aug. 2004	51,398,552.33	24,784,053.8(48.2%)	26,611,298.53(51.8%)
2	Enugu North	Aug. 2004	52,188,601.52	32,172,620.43(61.6%)	29,115,786.76(39.4%)
3	Nsukka	Aug. 2004	63,659,072.40	43,640,375.21(68.6%)	20,018,697.19(31.4%)
			167,246,226.25	100,597,049.44(178.48%)	75,745,782.48(122.6%)
1	Aninri	Oct. 2004	50,032,361.87	20,242,031.96(40.5%)	29,790,329.91(59.5%)
2	Enugu North	Oct. 2004	56,561,345.01	32,607,600.62(54.6%)	23,953,744.39(42.4%)
3	Nsukka	Oct. 2004	69,078,339.97	26,361,596.66(38.2%)	23,920,059.18(61.5%)
			175,672,046.85	79,211,229.24(133.3%)	77,664,133.48(163.7%)

1	Aninri	Jan. 2005	59,293,081.01	26,361,596.66(44.5%)	32,931,484.55(55.5%)
2	Enugu North	Jan. 2005	67,085,540.66	40,774,125.12(60.8%)	26,311,415.54(39.2%)
3	Nsukka	Jan. 2005	82,036,667.0	55,048,175.73(67%)	26,988,492.17(32.9%)
			208,415,289.57	122,183,897.51(172.3%)	86,231,392.26(127.6%)
1	Aninri	April, 2006	65,542,358.59	30,399,503.15(46.4%)	35,142,855.74(53.6%)
2	Enugu North	April, 2006	74,732,214.04	57,283,437.29(76.77%)	17,448,776.75(23.3%)
3	Nsukka	April, 2006	91,030,521.80	58,720,759.03(64.5%)	32,309,762.77(35.5%)
			231,305,064.73	146,403,699.47(187.67%)	84,901,395.26(112.4%)
1	Aninri	Sept. 2006	126,209,181.64	94,153,278.66(74.6%)	32,055,902.94(25.4%)
2	Enugu North	Sept. 2006	142,827,289.56	118,610,011.4(83.%)	24,217,278.12(17%)
3	Nsukka	Sept. 2006	174,478,179.81	150,430,810.7(86.2%)	24,647,369.07(13.8%)
			443,514,651.01	363,194,100.76(243.8%)	80,320,550.13(56.2%)
1	Aninri	Jan. 2007	62,323,331.39	28,687,073.25(46%)	33,636,258.18(54%)
2	Enugu North	Jan. 2007	70,576,416.47	43,150,893.87(61.1%)	27,425,522.60(38.9%)
3	Nsukka	Jan. 2007	86,203,716.22	58,189,229.87(67.5%)	28,014,486.35(32.5%)
			219,103,464.08	130,027,196.99(174.6%)	89,076,267.13(125.4%)
1	Aninri	April, 2007	69,172,119.84	48,091,829.69(69.5%)	21,080,292.15(30.5%)
2	Enugu North	April, 2007	79,037,418.26	65,049,565.09(82.3%)	13,987,853.17(17.7%)
3	Nsukka	April, 2007	97,842,037.42	86,068,494.51(82.3%)	12,773,542.91(13.1%)
			246,051,575.52	199,209,889.29(86.9%)	47,841,688.23(61.3%)

Source: Extracted from Eyo, (2011)[16] and modified by the researchers.

Table 7.3. Deduction from local government funds by Borno state government, between months of March 2002 and March 2003 (dollar) millions

LGA	*Gross Allocation*	*Total Deduction*	*Net Allocation*
Abadam	437.1	165(37.7%)	272.1
Askira/uba	504	325 (64.5%)	179.1
Barna	627	300(47.8%)	327.2
Banjo	390	156(40.0%)	234
Biu	558.0	303.4 (54.4%)	252
Chibok	361	185.4(51.4%)	175.4
Damboh	631	293(46.3%)	339
Dikwa	444	207.2(46.7%)	236.4
Gilbio	410	143.1(35.0%)	266.3
Guzamala	420	161.2(35.0%)	259
Gwoza	540	314(58.1%)	226.3
Hawul	500	356(71.2%)	144.2
Jere	7532	339.4(49.5%)	414
Kaga	431.2	213.4(49.5%)	218
Kala culge	343.1	167.3(48.8%)	176
Konduga	646.1	293(45.3%)	353.1
Kukawa	501	207(41.4%)	294
Kwaya ku sav	364	198(54.4%)	166
Mafa	419	183(43.6%)	236.3
Magumeri	487.1	142.4(39.5%)	295
Mmc	993	599.3(%)65.0	323.4
Marte	457	209(45.7%)	248
Mobbar	450.3	171(37.9%)	280
Monguno	441	207(47.6%)	234
Ngala	473	212.2(44.9%)	261
Ngaazai	385	150(38.9%)	235.1
Shani	421	189.1(44.9%)	252
Total	**13388.1**	**6440.7(48.4%)**	**6876.8**

Source: Ebo and Igboke, 2011.

claims and deductions, the total amounts accruable to the local government as their net amount for the months were ₦80,320,550.13, ₦89,076,267.13 and ₦47,841,688.23 representing 56.2% for the month of September 2006 25.4% for the month of January 2007 and 61.3% for the month of April 2007, respectively.

The implication from the given tables indicates that the more local government tries to addressing its developmental challenges, the more problem for local governments. The local councils in Nigeria had in the first time became conscripted and thwarted through the instrumentation and operation of joint account. It is only when local governments are released from the apron string called joint account, development in the rural areas by the local council becomes policy statements, illusion and myths (see table 7.3).

THEORETICAL FRAMEWORK OF ANALYSIS

The theoretical framework appropriated for the study is anchored on the decentralization theorem, an offshoot of fiscal federalism propounded by Samuelson,[17] in his book entitled, *The Theory of Public Good*. The ideas and writings of Samuelson were further elaborated and validated by the works of Musgrave,[18] Oates[19] and Tanzi.[20] The logic behind the postulation of decentralization theorem is that different levels of government provide different levels of public goods within their specific geographic scope. This is because one level of government cannot be efficient in providing public good on a large scope.

However, in order to achieve the aim of decentralization of functions, different levels of government need revenues and allocations to provide their respective public goods, and the need to grant access to the revenue stands at the centre of fiscal federalism. The fact that different tiers must deliver the needful based on the constitutional provision is problematic, owing to the position which local government occupies in the fiscal arrangement.

Sequel to the aforementioned context, the constitutional provision(s) have made the institution of local government in Nigeria impracticable. It is obtained that state government has been accorded constitutional rights, and locus standi to establish local government, and to define its structure and functions. This demonstrates that local government is a mere appendage or an agency created by the state government. It is important citing a clause of the Constitution, Section 7(7b) which states that the House of Assembly of state shall make provisions for statutory allocation of public revenue to local government councils within the state. This provision by the 1999 Constitution has a matter of fact necessitated the institutionalization and operation of the State-Local Government Joint Account (SLGJA). The account has become collective treasury of local governments within the state, under the sole control of state government through the state accountant-general.

Moreover, the aforementioned provision is a negation to the theorem of decentralization, since local government at the grassroots level has been conscripted and its autonomy lies in jeopardy. The implication remains that there is no way local government will strive to greater strengths towards development of its locales when the needed funds are not readily available.

FINDINGS

Arising from investigation to the developmental challenges and operation of state-local government account, nature and position of local government in delivering quality services to the people are the associated problems local government encounters in discharging its numerous functions to the locales.

The problems are holistically tie down to the nature of local government composition, the established fiscal relations and, inadequacy of the constitution in granting local government the needed autonomy like other levels of government in federal arrangement.

The implication is that there is no way that local government could rise and deliver beyond its expectations following the existence of fiscal arrangement which has conscripted it from exercising the needful to the local populace. The associated politicking of autonomization of local government may later give way for scrapping the institution of local government if adequate care is not taken.

CONCLUSION AND RECOMMENDATION

The study is an investigation to the position of local government in Nigeria in delivering needful services to the people at the grassroots level. Also, it appropriates the fiscal relationship between local government and the other tiers of government. The study significantly identified the associated problems and hurdles surrounding local government in discharging its numerous functions to the locales, which are holistically tie down to the nature of local government composition, the established fiscal relations and inadequacy of the constitution in granting local government the needed autonomy like other levels of government in federal arrangement. The study further discovered the inability of local governments to deliver as a result of the operation of joint account with the state government. The implication becomes the fact that local governments will find it difficult in meeting up with the expectations and aspirations of the locales in delivering quality services.

Therefore, the chapter recommends the following:

- It is high time the institution of local government in Nigeria become autonomous. This implies that the 'autonomization' of local authority in the use of available financial resources will help in delivering the needed safety frames and nets for the locales.
- The local government like every other tiers or levels of government should have its own separate accounts upon which statutory allocations and other payments shall be made.
- The various tiers of government should adequately engage in the spirit of equality in partnership. This will help in the consolidation of the dividend of democracy to every units and levels of government in the country.
- Also, the instrumentation of restructuring should be extended to the local government to accommodate yearnings and aspiration of the locales for better polity.

NOTES

1. Benedict Nwabueze, *Federalism in Nigeria under the Presidential Constitution* (London: Hurst, 1999), 2.
2. *Constitution of Federal Republic of Nigeria 1999* (Abuja: Government Printer, 1999), 5.
3. *Guideline for Local Government Reforms Acts 1976* (Abuja: Government Printer, 1976).
4. Ganiyu Orewa and Jibowu Adewunmi, *Local Government in Nigeria: A Changing Scene* (Benin: Ethiope Publishing, 1993), 68–72.
5. Elvis Meyer, 'Local Self Government', *India Journal of Local Government and Public Administration* no. 4 (1996): 47.
6. Emmanuel Ezeani, *Local Government Administration in Nigeria* (Enugu: Zik-Chuks Press, 2004), 28.
7. Peters Morgan, *Local Government and Local Administration* (London: Peterson Press, 2001), 19.
8. Ladipo Ademolekun, *Public Administration in Africa: Main Issues and Selected Country Studies* (Ibadan: Spectrum Books, 2002), 32.
9. Damilola Olowu, 'Local Government and Intergovernmental Relations in Nigeria', *Journal of Cross River State Public Service* 1 (1983): 42–3.
10. Regimus Ola, 'Thoughts on the Role of Local Government in Developing Countries', in *Local Government in West Africa since Independence*, ed. L. Adamolekun, D. Olowu and M. Laleye (Lagos: University of Lagos Press, 1988); 73.
11. Ugochukwu Ojukwu, Veronica Okeke and Anslem Obiora, *Comparative Local Government: Theory and Practice* (Nimo: Rex Charles & Patrick, 2014), 56.
12. Miriam Ikejiani-Clark and Fidelis Okoli, *Local Government Administration in Nigeria: Current Problems and Future Challenges* (Lagos: Mangrove Public, 1995), 67–9.
13. Damian Uzoma and Thomas Njemanze, 'The Operation of State Joint Local Government Account (SJLGA) in Nigeria: A Critical Evaluation', *International Journal of Research in Arts & Social Sciences* 8 (2015): 76–87.
14. Ogban Ogban-Iyam and Alfred Chukwu, 'The State Joint Local Government Account and the Federal Autonomy of Local in Nigeria', in *Key Issues in Local Government and Development: A Nigeria Perspective*, ed. Tony Onyishi (Enugu: Praise House Publisher, 2011), 27.
15. Eric Ebo and Emmanuel Igbokwe, *Economic Competitive across Nigeria States: The Challenges of Infrastructure and Utilities* (Enugu: Snapp Press, 2011), 33.
16. Oyovbaire Eyo, *Federalism in Nigeria: A Study in the Development of the Nigerian State* (Ibadan: Macmillan Publishers, 2011), 14.
17. Samuelson, *The Theory of Public Good* (New Delhi: Tata McGraw-Hill, 1955), 21–9.
18. Vans Musgrave, *The Theory of Public Finance* (NewYork: McGraw-Hill, 1959), 6–22.
19. Wright Oates, *Fiscal Federalism* (New York: Harcourt Brace Javanovich, 1999), 18–23.
20. Frank Tanzi, *Fiscal Federalism: A Review of Some Efficiency and Macroeconomic Aspects* (New York: Willey, 1996), 1–8.

BIBLIOGRAPHY

Ademolekun, Ladipo. *Public Administration in Africa: Main Issues and Selected Country Studies*. Ibadan: Spectrum Books, 2002.

Constitution of Federal Republic of Nigeria 1999. Abuja: Government Printer, 1999.

Ebo, Eric and Emmanuel Igbokwe. *Economic Competitive across Nigeria States: The Challenges of Infrastructure and Utilities*. Enugu: Snapp Press, 2011.

Eyo, Oyovbaire. *Federalism in Nigeria: A Study in the Development of the Nigerian State*. Ibadan: Macmillan Publishers, 2011.

Ezeani, Emmanuel. *Local Government Administration in Nigeria*. Enugu: Zik-Chuks Press, 2004.

Guideline for Local Government Reforms Acts 1976. Abuja: Government Printer, 1976.

Ikejiani-Clark, Miriam and Fidelis Okoli. *Local Government Administration in Nigeria: Current Problems and Future Challenges*. Lagos: Mangrove Public, 1995.

Meyer, Elvis. 'Local Self Government'. *India Journal of Local Government and Public Administration* 4 (1996): 47–53.

Morgan, Peters. *Local Government and Local Administration*. London: Peterson Press, 2001.

Musgrave, Vans. *The Theory of Public Finance*. New York: McGraw-Hill, 1959.

Nwabueze, Benedict. *Federalism in Nigeria under the Presidential Constitution*. London: Hurst, 1999.

Oates, Wright. *Fisçal Federalism*. New York: Harcourt Brace Javanovich, 1999.

Ogbaniyam, Ogban and Alfred Chukwu. 'The State Joint Local Government Account and the Federal Autonomy of Local in Nigeria'. In *Key Issues in Local Government and Development: A Nigeria Perspective*, edited by Tony Onyishi. Enugu: Praise House Publisher, 2011.

Ojukwu, Ugochukwu, Veronica Okeke and Anslem Obiora. *Comparative Local Government: Theory and Practice*. Nimo: Rex Charles & Patrick, 2014.

Ola, Regimus. 'Thoughts on the Role of Local Government in Developing Countries'. in *Local Government in West Africa since Independence*, edited by L. Adamolekun, D. Olowu and M. Laleye. Lagos: University of Lagos Press, 1988.

Olowu, Damilola. 'Local Government and Intergovernmental Relations in Nigeria'. *Journal of Cross River State Public Service* 1 (1983): 42–3.

Orewa, Ganiyu and Jibowu Adewunmi. *Local Government in Nigeria: A Changing Scene*. Benin: Ethiope Publishing, 1993.

Samuelson, *The Theory of Public Good*. New Delhi: Tata McGraw-Hill, 1955.

Tanzi, Frank. *Fiscal Federalism: A Review of Some Efficiency and Macroeconomic Aspects*. New York: Willey, 1996.

Uzoma, Damian and Thomas Njemanze. 'The Operation of State Joint Local Government Account (SJLGA) in Nigeria: A Critical Evaluation'. *International Journal of Research in Arts & Social Sciences* 8 (2015): 76–87.

Chapter 8

Nigeria and the Neo-colonial Dilemma: Rethinking the Challenge of an Unfinished Business

Obinna Innocent Ihunna

INTRODUCTION

'Seek ye first the political kingdom and all else shall be added unto you',[1] was the definitively stimulating *Freedom Proposal* offered by the late Kwame Nkrumah. A prompting from his pan-Africanist inertia, it soon became a testament in respect of the pursuit of African nationalism in diverse spaces. For Ghana, this proposal stimulated the gathering of storms of political struggles that eventually materialized in political independence in 1957. Plainly, it ushered a voice of hope, as well as, the needful anticipation of happiness in the possibility of realizing an esteemed goal that, at the time, seemed very elusive. Freedom, in eloquent term, was the focus of this proposal, and offering very powerful communication that not only found vast admiration among manybut also bore fruits beyond the confines of Ghana. Freedom, then, became the quintessence matter in that cliché informing early democratization drives within Africa of the immediate post–Second World War epoch.

Africa's most populous country, Nigeria,[2] got attracted and did not shy away from this compelling communication in enlisting painstaking efforts of its nationalists to respond to the subjections of British colonialism. First of October 1960 marked the point at which it assumed sovereignty, implying its attainment of freedom from colonial shackling. However, the way and manner of transfer of power therein must have set in motion emergent new tensions that appeared to render its freedom, from on set, as replete with dysfunctions. Thus, the hallmarks of its acquired unfertile freedom did not take long to manifest in plain inheritances of an intensely virulent and divisive immediate post-independence politicking (1960–1966), a protracted civil war (1967–1970), subsequent perturbations of military rule (January 1966–31 September 1978), a pitiable brief, if inauspicious, run of democratic rule

(1 October 1979–31 December 1983), another re-entry into military rule from December 1983 to 29 May 1999; and since 29 May 1999, a hurriedly packaged political process that assumes the nomenclature of democracy but best captured as subterfuge for disguising the continuation of military rule through retiree generals and their acolytes. Clearly, then, its democratization was set on a faltering path with untidy prospects in expectations.[3]

Listing the Nigerian state as defined by intensely divisive constituents, or, as a galore for coups and coupists, or a space of squandered hopes, seems appropriate, but more germane to our text is the fact that alongside these were combination of factors and forces revealing concrete interplays of Nigerian politics which had one particular victim it persistently attacked – the citizenry. Its implications for what is held as freedom, which ought to be beyond the caricatures it currently receives, suggest their pronounced state of helplessness, low level of articulation of their problems, a deluge of impoverished outcomes, and a befuddling inertia of parochialisms that is unwittingly deployed to ensure and assure that citizens never gets to think and act collectively aright. Indeed, any appreciation of the quality of its array of sufferable conditions must relate clearly to the deprecations in the value of freedom that is aimed specifically to achieve citizens perpetual disadvantage. Since this has been the prime preoccupation of its leading political elites at the helm of manipulations on the basis of ethnicity, or, the well-known shareholding rights of acolytes in corruption, it renders a lopsided image of freedom and makes necessary the emergent calls for 'second liberation struggles'[4] not only in Nigeria but also other African spaces.

The underlying fact, then, is that the conditions in the post colonies reveal vastly troubling situations compelling a revisit to the extant behaviours of hegemons in control of internal orders responsible for the vitiation and devaluation of freedoms. In that wise, it makes sense to understand the interests, nature and character of political relationships that tends to dominate such internal orders in which consent is considered relegate political capital. Given that power therein privileges violence rather than authority, it is this concern that Agbaje sought to succinctly underscore in observing that, with respect to the Nigerian State, she reveals 'the fact that the distinction between power and violence has not been widely acknowledged in theory or practice. . . . Nigeria's political history has shown that the polity has, by and large, been founded, propped up and prodded on not by a system of power (*read as due authority*) but by one of violence and threats of its use'.[5] Markedly, the dominance of such interest, which finds amplification in succeeding regimes, locates the state as one engulfed in the crippling grips of colonial inertia in which use of coercion and deception constituted the most veritable tools for it success.[6]

Therefore, it invites no surprise that the yearnings and yelling for freedom appears to have continued to inundate the Nigerian nation space from the aftermath of political independence till date. Note that the application of the neologism of *nation-space*[7] in this text derives from a careful invention from one of its most discerning minds, and meant to underscore the difficulty of a polity suffering from the surge of incapacitations that cumulate into collective citizen disillusionment. It is also one with the saddening effect that not only are the citizens struggling with believing and embracing the Nigerian project, but they are also doing wonderfully well to commit themselves to exiting from a supposed corporate whole.[8] The difficult conditions of social existence in the polity is not only reflected in the intensely divisive and disagreeable nature of its constituents, but, more pronouncedly, from the sufferable stance into which successive leaderships have sunk the citizenry into the Hobbesian order of *the poor, nasty and brutish*. It has left millions with no more choice than to wonder if exiting from the state is not the best option perceived in the rising profile of self-determination groups.

More importantly, the excruciating conditions of existence quite aptly informs renewed drives for redefining and reasserting freedom against the backdrop of perceived re-shackling of people authored by their internal political overlords. Perhaps this does not necessarily emerge because they cannot collectively find a common ground to cohere, but more particularly so for the fact that its leading political elites, through successive generations, have operated with a warped sense of order, progress and plainly oblivious of what it implies to contend that a state exist, first and foremost, for the good life of its citizenry. The dominance of self-serving purpose, the pursuit of personalization of power and cult adulation, takes precedence over objective interest in effective nation-building.

In what follows, we offer clarifications for some of the concepts we deploy in the text and consider an overview of the African neo-colonial order. Next, we place in perspective the case of neo-colonial conjecture in Nigeria, situating the nature, form and challenges it presents through the interrogation of regimes, agency roles and outcomes of governance on the people. Furthermore, we offer a critical insight on the trending fate of the fettered citizen in a postcolonial Nigeria to explain how governance engagements have led to material and mental incapacitations of citizens and constituting clear perversions of hope. Lastly, a conclusion.

ON CONCEPTUAL ISSUES

Conceptual clarifications have often been raised against the problem of imprecision in meanings of terms we deploy in diversity of texts meant for both communication and consumption. Within the domain of the social sciences, this concern proves somehow problematic in respect of attempts to attain apt or precise terms. Although such interest in precise use of concepts are always welcome, the field has since been left a profitable cautionary note about most of its terms bearing 'multi-fold meanings',[9] a case that renders them as fluid or 'contested concepts'.[10] Howbeit, fluidity in meaning to concepts may well not deter scholars from efforts to explain how or what they intend their concepts to mean in any given text. The key terms in the present intervention – neo-colonialism, colonialism, freedom, and citizenry – constitute familiar terms but not completely shorn of ambiguities in meaning even from the standpoint of contributions of a deluge of authors.

On *Citizenry*, the focus is on a collective social category that is deployed to capture the entire population of a state. More importantly, it needs be noted that it hardly implies that once there exists a state, then, there must exist citizens. It would, therefore, imply a qualified category of description that directs itself to the status of such population as free people. The notion of citizen invites a relational category to the fore that highlights a state and its people duly linked to the cause of 'common defense of personal (*and collective*) freedom'.[11] The best example has been the status of populations within a properly constituted democracy wherein the *consent of the people* is largely perceived as the actual foundation upon which the operations of the state is predicated. Thus, the category citizen is often raised in contra to 'subject'.[12] In the latter context, only the imaginations of freedom is possible; for, the people thrive at the behest of the hegemon in control of that space, and their opinion counts less to compel the attention of the hegemon. Thus, the stylized fact about the nomenclature of citizen derives its force from the democratic ordering of society, allowing us to figure and think of that category of persons as both rights bearing and definitive harbingers of consent upon which any exercising authority must take into cognizance in the business of rule.

Freedom has attracted a lot of attention from philosophers and social scientists alike wherein it assumes considerable adornment or embellishments. Yet shorn of the complexities of professional finesse, it points up to a valued abstract property that helps in defining man in the contest of meaningful association and existence. In this wise, freedom, which is derived from the word, free, or, being free, holds for a common vision of an unencumbered existence. Such concern is, however, imbued with a paradox. In this wise, it anticipates resistance to possible constraints to social existence which it foresees as weakening individual and collective social capacities. Yet to the extent that unrestrained expressions of individual freedom can result into collective dysfunctions, law gains relevance and meaning as a mechanism for legitimate regulation of social conduct of people within respective domains.

Therefore, the freedom basically emphasized, thrives on a utility potential which, under a democratically ordered society, cumulate into the fundamental law of the land that guides both managers of state power and the governed in what may pass as agreed norm of association. In that wise, freedom, as envisaged in this text, pertains to the relief of unencumbered modes of existences sanctioned by law within democratic societies. This is basically on the clear understanding that what emerges as law derives from public legislations that emanate from the representatives of the people, and guaranteed as consensual rather than arbitrary. In other words, freedom, as we intend it here, implicates the amplitude of guarantees aimed at ensuring and assuring for the good life of the people within the context of a democratic ordering of society, and must be seen as binding on all.

Colonialism is another among the significant terms of this text. Plainly, it is also one that is not spared the problem of ambiguity in meaning arising from diversity of author preferences. Howbeit, it directs attention mainly to a peculiar kind of political relationship that is, at best or worst, totalizing. By implication, the idea embedded in it speaks eloquently to a universal phenomenon that finds a place in all continents, and which has also gained universal condemnation even among its most ardent practitioners. The substantive defining factor of it can be gleaned from the engagement in unequal political relationship that emphasizes domination of one by another. The relationship so emphasized, therefore, implicates the colonizer and the colonized. Both trending interests tend to be laced with 'motives from the actions of the ruler and the ruled'.[13] In the context of its African experience, colonialism underscores the unequal relationship of political domination between Europe and Africa – one in which such lopsided arrangement of power accommodates the outsider to dominate the insider. Clearly, all instances of colonialism equals conditions of un-freedom for the colonized who becomes the dominated and an inferior partner in such socio-political process of rule relationship.

Neo-colonialism, then, can more appreciably be understood from the standpoint of colonialism from which it inheres. To this extent, it holds that it is a condition that emerges past colonialism. By implication, the understanding holds that colonialism was predicated on unequal political relationship of domination of the outsider over the insider, and that such exertion of rule was considered utterly pejorative to warrant its dismissal. The context gave cause for anti-colonial struggles to extirpate the process of external domination of the insider that was predicated on force and deception. If, then, neo-colonialism bears meaning, it is to the extent that it depicts the rejuvenation and re-invigoration of all particularities of the colonial order in a renewed context in which the dominant and the dominated own and share the same political space. Indeed, it is primarily about the tenacity of the pejoratives sustained within the context of a given space that implicates both members of that common space in unequal relationship of power and domination. Gonzalez aptly captured this trend in his averment that 'with the disappearance of the direct domination of foreigners over natives, the notion of domination and exploitation of natives by natives emerged'.[14]

What, then, constitute the logical nexus between these concepts? It is certainly not difficult to discern that the appropriate yearning of global peoples in political terms percolates around what happens to freedom. The latter can be found to define the quintessential social property necessary for the sustenance of meaningful political relationship between the governing and the governed. The challenge therein implicates the concern that only on grounds of legitimate legislation, that is, one perceived as having emanated from the people as consensual guarantees, can it be considered proper the constraining of individual or collective capacities. As envisaged, then, it is broached here that within the context of authoritarianism, by any pretext, neither citizenship nor freedom is an open possibility.[15]

The emerging difficult circumstance of un-freedom, therefore, has tended to requalify the citizen (*a prerogative social category applicable in a democracy*) into a subject class. The subject status is achieved in the event of brazen resort to arbitrary deployment of power to suit the whims and caprices of the leading hegemon and his acolytes rather than the people. To the extent that the behaviours of leading hegemons in diverse spaces impede the growth in social capacities of populations, the context of its exertions of power would aptly depict it as unduly domineering and constraining to permit the flight of freedom in the face of internal domination. This, as it were, underscores the trend in neo-colonialism, which is a shorthand expression for the continuation of inhibitive colonial practices in undue domination by indigenous inheritors of power over their fellow natives.[16]

OVERVIEW OF AFRICAN NEO-COLONIAL ORDER: AN UNUSUAL BACKDROP

Portugal, France, Belgium and Germany were the key colonial actors in the African political firmament overseeing to the near wholesale shackling of communities therein. These European states represented not just the signposts of a unique category of intimidators but also veritable examples of governments that, within their own domains, enjoyed the worth of self-rule laced in the consciousness of the value of freedom. Indeed, from the standpoint of their value for freedom, they were able to seriously exercise the duty of care to craft an admirable state – citizen relationship. In that wise, they clearly held the state as actually existing for the good life of their people since they had to work assiduously to ensure and assure that, through thoroughness in effective and efficient exploitation of foreign lands, and appropriation of their resources, they must bring home the booties to improve the social conditions of their people. Yet this freedom, ironically, was not thought a useful and adequate property for Africans that must be coerced, intimidated, and subordinated. Its implication was clearly felt in the imposition of that drudgery that was the colonial order.

The narrative of this peculiar engagement between Europeans and Africans earns the label, colonialism. It reveals a systematic political relationship that prides in stifling the 'other' of rights and privileges, holding in esteem the alien as master, and the native, a palpable servant. Such inverted order of political association yielded reservations, but more importantly, forced out the challenges of the short-changed to attempt resituating its social condition in seeking for its freedom from the shackles imposed by alien hegemons in a process called 'nationalism'.[17] Basically, the substantive ingredient of Nkrumah's communication can be located in the amplification of that common desire for genuine freedom for African peoples held down by that crippling force of colonialism. And by dint of the later, then, a justification was felt and found for a counter conjecture in African nationalisms which thrust aimed at reversing and retrieving lost freedoms of the people. It was believed to be politically correct the need for home rule, even if it were to be on the basis of an alien model. In other words, freedom was thought to be better served where a people managed their own public affairs unencumbered by any externalities. What was foreseen in this context was a condition in which collective social capacities would become enabled, and justice and equity find fertile ground within.

Indigenous Africans, however, were not oblivious of the snares of freedom as to note that this virtuous social good, in the light of possible perversions, could yield individual and collective disparagement. Such consciousness also became a part of the amplified realities in the course of political struggles for African independence that heightened apprehensions in all spaces. Such apprehensions were focused on possible constraints that may lead to freedoms falling far short of its anticipations. With zest and vigour, however, Africans were more tuned to ensure and assure for the effective extirpation of colonial rule in the clear hope that independence will usher true freedom for the effective and efficient development of human capacities in all spaces. More than anything else, their plain sensitivity to the fact that constraints to freedom can happen in instances wherein people's expectations remain largely un-met was taken into due consideration in the enlisting of support for African nationalism.

Hence, the struggles of African nationalism, for the promises it spelt and held, bore features of covenantal convictions providing the impetus for justifying the native's risks in terms of open support to early nationalist leaderships. To this end, then, the real price of their commitments was foreseen in the hope that the anticipated freedom would certainly blossom to their collective benefit rather than peril. It was not intended to mean the contumelious retention of the condemnable practices of the colonialists, nor was it ever focused on how the inheriting political classes will sustain and strengthen perceived constraints for which the people enlisted their support towards its extirpation. Unfortunately, the narratives of the post-colonial appears to reveal vast litters in the overwhelming presence of the disagreeable than the hopes and happiness the people so much desired.

The implication, from the foregoing, has been that the inheriting political elites, overtime, became the crucial sources informing and galvanizing the pathological conditions of social existence in Africa. Since the outcomes of their exploits in governance largely detracted from what was initially anticipated, it has become clearer today that, although the African Man was equally *born free*, it has actually been more betoken by persistent struggles to retake its freedom from assortment of colonialist's *chains*. For, the latter has become refashioned and re-brandished in the emergent contest of a postcolonial situation even in more pernicious terms, and revealing odd attributions in the exercise of power by internal hegemons in respective African locales. In consequence, then, it is not thought unusual the association of the African political landscape with negative freedoms anchored in the ease of deployment of coercion of both citizens and political opponents and the heightening of their disillusionments. The latter can be felt as outcomes from a rising profiles on poverty, disease, squalor and the status of debt peonage, a situation that permits the deployment of the phrase 'poverty in the midst of plenty'[18] for such exceptionally endowed country like Nigeria.

It is in the current blossoming of these many unwanted and unwarranted politically pathological interests affecting and limiting the lives of Africans that the notion of the neo-colonial is broached. Thus, it underscores not the stoppage, but the continuities that now ignore earlier *covenantal convictions*, or engagements enlisting perversions to the promises of independence, and the ensuing investments in all that were certified condemnable in the struggles for independence. The emergent neo-colonial situation appears to suggest carefully contrived shutdowns on earlier promises of freedom. Thus, contemporary circumstances of postcolonial betrayals reveal the continent as one that has received massive injections of disillusionment, despair, poverty, insecurity, squalor, diseases and desperation, to mention these few pejorative rewards of raging repressive governance engagements in diverse African locales.

As it were, it would imply that the *all else* that needs be *added unto them* only offered a disturbing and dissuasive profile in reverses that limits their anticipations of genuine freedom. Its plain outcomes became manifest in low-level human capacities, diseases, poverty, conflicts, insurrections and civil wars, among others, to suggest the neo-colonial order as intensely suffused with turmoil. Certainly, current situations also reveal perplexing dimensions underscored in the anomaly of 'political bankruptcy of these (African) regimes laced with repression of opponents and *the* inhibit(*ing*) *of* the emergence of alternatives'.[19] Its domination of the lives of Africans clearly evince the claim that what was not sought for, then, appears to have taken centre-stage in the public affairs of its respective nations and rendering the continent a galore of states embedded in confusion and disillusionment. The raging disquietude, therefore, can more appreciably be understood as a critical signpost in justification of massive devaluations of freedom in diverse African spaces that have left populations in profound pains.

Since the constraints of home-grown repressive orders (*outlined in authoritarian democracies and plain militarism*) dominated and constituted crucial helpmates in the process of deprecation of freedom, it does mean that the emergent order, in its institutionalization and amplification, proves an incontestable substitute for the colonial order – a fitting homologue per excellence in the actuations of the pejorative. The primacy of its strategy suggested itself in the ascendency of indigenous political elites to power positions in the post colonies, not with a view to avoiding the ills of yesteryears, but in its massive amplifications. They did so through unrelenting gravitations towards the short-changing of the African natives in the interplay of pursuit of self-serving interests of leadership, open neglect of the people, and in the ease with which it unleashes repression upon the populations who may wish to voice alternative opinions or condemn their wrongdoings.

It is within the foregoing context that plethora of hegemons in African states find criticisms as vile and unacceptable (*not virile and welcome*), and an affront that must be replied with disenabling coercion and intimidation of political opponents. In more general terms, it is for the same reason that the African citizenry is always looked upon as mere trivial *subjects* fit for scorn and handouts. Thus, the neo-colonial order underscores the presence and hyping of a perverse social process that yields immense benefits to emergent hegemonic elites and their cronies at the expense of the ordinary citizens that are persistently denied meaningful social existence. Indeed, the logic and foundation of a neo-colonial order ought to be appropriately understood from the standpoint of an inveterate political transition from the colonial to the post-colonial – one in which, to a very large extent, what appears to have changed suggests mere substitution of actors in power rather than the philosophy and modalities of operations or use of public power.

Of course, many postcolonial regimes (*immediate post-independence and thereafter*) were grandly bereft of any useful philosophical thrust to determine what constitutes their social purpose. And in being so remote from the realities of citizen expectations regarding creative conditions for enhancing their social capacities, inclusive of undeterred expressions of opinions about their public affairs, the social purpose of the good life for the African citizenry has remained an elusive good in current circumstances. Ironically, this implicates the leading elites relishing in affluence and ostentation, whereas the masses groan in poverty and squalor, and the society writ large defines itself in widening gaps between the rich and the poor. This is quite akin of the Nigerian state and makes it possible to speak of it in terms of a space defined by *poverty in the midst of plenty* to underscore the neo-colonial quagmire of the most endowed African nation. To a large extent, the narratives of African neo-colonialism bears considerably on continuities of debilitating attitudes and behaviours emergent from colonial political elites for which they earn massive condemnation, but which have been reinvented by inheriting indigenous political elites for dealing perniciously with co-natives.

THE NIGERIAN STATE: PERSPECTIVES IN THE NEO-COLONIAL CONJECTURE

How may we place the matter of neo-colonialism in Nigeria? The preceding question invites the matter of proof of existence and exertions of neo-colonialism which can be resolved by underscoring its minor and major manifestations. Since we hold the conviction that a neo-colonial situation prevails in instances that reveal stark continuities of the condemnable habits of erstwhile colonialist by inheriting new indigenous ruling elites, it is to the inordinate activities and operations of indigenous political elites of the African post-colonies that we must focus attention. This is to the extent that their habits and exertions constitute telling constraints on the social capacities of mass majority of African natives in diverse locales struggling to eke out meaningful existence.

To situate such concern is to immediately acknowledge that Africa's most populous country, Nigeria, represents a crucial signpost among African states in which wide-ranging citizen disillusionment has left its palpable marks in intense frustrations and irritations to place it as a valid candidate reeling in the neo-colonial quagmire. Thus, inundated with very high intensity of frills, it proves a crucial candidate for validating the measure and presence of unfreedom for a people profoundly ensconced in pathological effusions in both insidious and overt terms. Except freedom has now been redefined, and its new definition elevated to a pedestal where it underscores the freeness to do ill, then the current situation which captures Nigeria's political elites, who justify their heinous acts as what power gives and implies, would ultimately not speak to any disagreeable understanding of freedom. Unfortunately, this is certainly not the case, and that, as it were, accounts for continuing conversations reflecting intense worries in veracity of constituencies about why the focus on vast political prevarications by indigenous political elites must mean the short-changing and constraining of ordinary citizen.

By and large, there is no meaningful freedom for a people hemmed in on all sides by a deluge of incapacitations that prevent them from achieving the irreducible minimum that is collective happiness. That what presently exists has been at the expense of any endurable peace, robust growth, or serious improvements in standards of living, and even discernible improvements in infrastructural terms, it makes sense, then, Nigeria's rendition as a galore of both the imponderables and deplorable. It is in this wise that we broach the claim that since post-independence, the Nigerian mass majority has been *living a life not worth living* in the face of its persistent abuse and misuse, a key scheme that is extended to its enormous endowments which are unduly misappropriated by its leadership elites so adept in official and unofficial thievery.

Such chosen ill piety of its leadership elites was succinctly captured by Ayittey in his averment that 'corrupt African leaders have stolen at least $140 billion dollars . . . from their people in the decades since independence . . . *and that* over the postcolonial period, the African state has evolved into a predatory monster or a gangster state'.[20] There is no doubt that the Nigerian state is aptly implicated in this postcolonial African oddity. The implication of this uncanny indulgence can be figured in the comparable expropriation of capital from the indigenous to the metropolitan centres in the colonial order. Yet the more stunning reality is that this is coming from a people trusted to deliver the goods of politics to their own. The raging disappointments, therefore, have led to the intensification of social turmoil, as well as, the perpetuation of the impoverishment of indigenous natives by the leadership elite who steal the fiscal resources meant for collective development of the polity.

Basically, the matter of stealing of public resources and investing it in the state may seem an attenuated sinful cause unlike the prevailing habit in which resources, so much desired for internal development, are stashed away unused in foreign banks where many may never remember except at the sudden stroke of death. The case of late Gen. Sani Abacha, the former Head of State, who championed the notable policy of National Orientation for War against Indiscipline and Corruption (WAIC),[21] comes very handy to reveal the innermost bearings of many a post-colonial leaders in Nigeria. Of course, he eventually made history with his most pronounced loot in the annals of the Nigerian state, too striking to be ignored in the shortest possible time. While his monumental looting orgy is still being discussed in several global quarters in the hope of channelling repatriation to Nigeria, the lack of satisfactory account of what has happened to what has so far been recovered goes on to underscore the high presence of his likes in the system that the masses cannot trust anymore.

Besides, in noting that Gen. Abacha's disciplinary values were sharpened and helped earlier in the cause of his prominent participations in the Babangida era, the search light is yet to focus on an un-investigated Gen. Ibrahim Babangida, who, for eight or so years, managed the country's economy into a comatose state. It is an important part of prudent reasoning that it still remains an unfinished business to have only probed a dead Abacha while allowing wide leverage to a living profligate Gen. Babangida enjoying his unevaluated loot derived from his supposed unblemished services in power. The more ignoble dimension is the fact that nothing of this perturbs Gen. Babangida's memory as to explain his fresh relish in the dream of re-engaging in civic politics en route to Nigeria's presidency. Certainly, the former Head of State, like all the living others, must have thoughts about some unfinished business that needs be completed with a clear focus on the final decimation of the masses. This is in spite of his earlier admittance that the Nigerian economy under his lengthy regime *had defied all known solutions; albeit, not a conviction that can force him to resign from power*. Perhaps in the sobriety enforced on him in the period past his ignominious *Stepped Aside*, his unusual alchemy may have returned back to him to enlist the unleashing of his cronies to work towards the next strategy for re-engaging their icons political relevance and prepare the way for his next national liquidation project.

That the trending neo-colonial quagmire of the Nigerian state allows for the open flogging of a dead horse has been widely acknowledged in ignoring the value of his untendered accountability which received blessings through the succeeding Gen. Abdulsalami Abubakar, Gen. Olusegun Obasanjo, late Musa Yar'Adua, Goodluck Jonathan, and the incumbent Gen. Buhari. It is instructive to note that current interplays of democracy in the Nigerian state revolves around these aforementioned public figures and points the way towards a comity strongly attached to the goal of continuing the project of national liquidation of the ordinary citizen in Nigeria. Their services in power have seen to the growth of national disquisitions among many in clearly failing to elevate ordinary citizens and offering them a deplorable economy. Indeed, the raging odds of official thievery cannot be divorced from even the former Head of State and later President, Chief/Gen. Olusegun Obasanjo who, in the wake of Buhari's election victory in 2015, happened to have *carelessly and comically* voiced his intention to return some monies he *kept* in his custody belonging to Nigerians. That such unauthorized 'savings' was ever made, and would take over six years after he left office in 2007 to offer a national disclosure, implies clear breach of decent conduct justifying unofficial thievery and how open minded and true the leaders deal with citizens they govern.

In the light of several sordid experiences emerging from Nigeria's leadership elites, the matter of neo-colonialism here privileges the prevalence of conditions of unwarranted social mortgage – one in which the life of citizens has continued to be informed by diminishing values and dwindling fortunes. Since that is what makes news, it explains why *good news* is difficult to come by. It impresses also about its immersion into the ill fate of congeries of woes which, beyond pretension, speak aptly to its troubled and dissuasive status as a debt peon to international finance. Of course, rational anticipations ought to hope for something different from what presently confronts it except for its wide acceptance of an unfair bargain with baneful neo-colonialism. Indeed, there is no freedom for a debtor; what is available to it is acquiescence, meant to appease and please the master. That, in itself, is the grand fate into which Nigerians have been lodged by its post-colonial leaderships ensconced in perpetual borrowings till date, and with no serious efforts towards extricating from such neo-colonial string. In the light of further indebtedness incurred through wanton borrowings, it needs be understood, then, that the prime aims informing earlier colonial struggles and its attendant promises have become defeated too early in the day to compel calls for a second liberation.

Could such calls work in the region of financial independence for the people? There is considerable doubt that this will be so. In fact, Nigerians have been confronted with the plain understanding that it fits as homologue to the Greek fiscal quagmire in spite of ever flowing oil receipts. It is in this wise, then, that state governors, under the Buhari led presidency, found sufficient courage to declare themselves as incapacitated at meeting capital and expenditure needs to run their states and pay salaries of ordinary workers. Who needs be paid is the citizen who has offered his consent to the *lying governors* whose prime proclivities are outlined in stashing away development funds in faraway lands, quick declaration of empty treasuries, new interests in land acquisition to become formidable land moguls and the grand lure for ostentation.

The foregoing may well help to explain for why the state is far from arriving at the critical shore of meaningful democratic existence that prides in true freedom. Instead, current conditions reveal its place within the impoverishing shores of social disquisitions which internal colonialism renders. Clearly, it was for true democracy that the ordinary people had sued for independence, but un-freedom appear to take a heavy toll on them. Any such calls for a second liberation would surely be highlighting on their penchant to resume fresh struggles for true freedom, the focus is squarely on a reengagement or encounters with leaderships laced with admiration for ill personal valour rather than collective social purpose that yield betrayal of hopes. The latter can verily be perceived as provoking public angst from down trodden citizens. This ill disposition of neo-colonialism fits what its political elites readily embrace and work for by aligning with sustaining 'the legacy . . . *of* the colonial era, when political discourse excluded not only democracy but even the idea of good government and politics *which has been* reduced to the clash of one exclusive claim to power against another'.[22] In real terms, then, neither democracy nor true freedom fits as credible properties of its citizenry. In this wise, the democracy that now obtains thrives plainly as rhetorical or pseudo as it prides in the grand negation of citizens.

In respective spaces, it renders practices that are mostly illogical and confounding. It could not have been better in the light of outcomes of many equally pseudo institutional and behavioural implantations posed by leaderships in diverse African domains as these provide the fillip for the unhallowed presence of fictive democratic regimes established to appease the donor community (*to attract scarce funds*), or, were offered pretentiously as deceptive arrangements to suggest new and hurried converts into the comity of globalized democracies. In the light of rendering militarism an inutile force in the future management of state affairs in Africa and beyond since the early 1990s, the *chameleon* has appropriately adjusted its colours to suit its new environment. Nigeria's military political chameleons have wasted no time in taking their chances against the backdrop of growing unpopularity of military rule to creatively contrive an agreeable platform for the continuation of their 'veritable . . . strategic deception'.[23]

In the hurriedly packaged military authored transitions from 1985 to 1999, civilian politicians were only too happy to be invited to share ranks with, and as inferior partners in the process of transformations of the Nigerian society. The outcome, then, can clearly be figured in a contrived pseudo democratic arrangement in which the prime benefactors were the retired military. It calls for a close scrutiny to understand that current arrangements thrive basically on that violently toned social category to explain the intensification of the high presence of a militarized democracy in Nigeria since 29 May 1999. One after another, these retirees now take turns at the highest stakes, recruit their cronies when forces can no longer permit their continuation, and decide who gets what position.

It would seem, then, that current arrangements must be dictated by their whims and caprices rather than emanations from popular forces entrenched in the vastly short-changed and shut-out citizenry. The lily-livered stance of long emasculated civic elites appears to take its toll on how they can chart the course of their political participation. In this wise, since they failed to wrest power from the military in any clear struggles that can validly show them as victorious, it meant that in the new arrangement, they must serve as surrogates or inferior partners to 'transformed' militaries whose transformations speak only trivially to dropping the *Khaki* for *Agbada* than in attitudes of dialogue and compromise. At their behest, then, the emergent democracy is perceived to have been contrived to make for, and sustain, their less challenged corporate interest which must be protected to their utter benefits.

That is the implication of what is termed *negotiated transition* aimed at its protection. Part of the benefits of that protection is their settlement with vast allocations and control of Oil blocs, investments in Blue Chip companies, and important political appointment.

More crucially, they must control the parties, especially the major political parties, which seem likely to determine who controls power. Whether the one is leftist, right wing or centrist, retired militaries have all found places in the thriving political parties where they either overtly or insidiously call the shots. A check through the Board of Trustees (BOT) of Nigeria's political parties may produce useful evidence on *Who Is Who* on the comity of '*great financiers*' who must be credited with handsome rewards for their investment at the very expense of the people. In other words, the state appears to have been sold and bought by this irritant social category. Clearly this sale of the state became more pronounced under Gen. Ibrahim Babangida at whose behest Nigeria sunk into the depths of privatization and commercialization and, ironically too, through the strategy of Open Market Operations (OMO), which hardly allowed a space for the very poor to effectively participate in buying out interests from institutions hitherto built with monies of taxpayers. Such manifestations amount to the denigration and trivialization of citizenship and the idea of meaningful freedom that can help the cause of democratic relationships in respective African spaces.

Given that what the neo-colonial African state offered *ab initio* was not really focused on the good of the people per se, it can only help re-enact sowing 'the seeds of *new* postcolonial wars'[24] for real freedom of citizens. In consequence, not many of these regimes proved enduring enough as to escape military coups. Nigeria's fate offers a script in litany of coups to suggest its early reversal in barely six years of adversarial democratic politics from January 1966. Thereafter, it became a blossoming social canvass for coup competitions in diverse guises up to 29 May 1999; for, the Abubakar Abdulsalami hurriedly packaged entrepreneur project, was yet another grand ploy in the institutionalization of the disquisitions of dirty politics of the military in the Nigerian state that is always adept at negating values of probity and accountability. To think that his can be viewed as genuinely aligning with the democratic cause may be an ill prompted perception, but it can more plausibly be considered as the new *ameliorative* checkpoint for redesigning realignment of forces that must place emerging new democratic arrangements in the hands of the retired military. This, in the light of the growing unpopularity of military rule since the convulsions of late 1980s' Europe, produced an attenuation that sought to unduly glorify Nigeria as an emergent new convert to democracy wherein freedom now reigns supreme. Certainly, this would pass for a big mistake since its roots are unmistakably placed in the formulations of its irritant merchants of violence and coercion often having the people as its target.

THE NIGERIAN STATE: SOME EMPIRICAL ISSUES IN THE PROGRESSION OF NEO-COLONIAL EXPERIENCES

On the eve of Nigeria's independence on October 1, 1960, the *Round Table* had several remarkably kind words for the state which it described as the 'New star Turn'[25] in the continent. Even the caption of that article, 'Nigeria: The African Giant', must have spoken to the undiluted expectations of gigantic strides which the state was anticipated to champion. But that was fifty-seven years ago when it actually seemed like the inheriting political elites at the time had clearly understood the logic and demands for democratic ordering of society and were very ready to *add all else*. Unfortunately, what they understood better was how to intensify their divisiveness, enhancing their siege mentalities, and the pursuit of personality adulation and ostentation. If there was any outstanding credit in the initial winning of freedom in Nigeria, it was to the effect that the constituents, by dint of the peculiar drives of their respective leaders, were taught how not to respect or love each other, and never to hold the vision of unity as both valid and constant.

Perhaps for the foregoing reasons, it has been the most difficult matter discussing the viability of the state as an *indivisible corporate whole*. Whereas the intended corporateness of that whole called for concerted efforts in nation building, it is the case, however, that leadership in the state did so much to rather achieve Connor's idea of 'Nation-Destroying'[26]. For the avoidance of doubt, a number of objectively informed Nigerians have lent hands and voices in crafting the concrete picture of reality that agreeably mirrors the current situation. Among the many, three are of considerable attraction and germane to this text; it figures a pitiable outcry pointing in the direction of the state as befuddled by the ravages of internal political scavengers who show no pity even at foolishly lavishing its resources in the orgy of wanton appropriation that seizes every hegemon and its adjoining acolytes.

Since these ravages are actually thought to answer to the immediate interests of its perpetrators, they neither see anything wrong with depleting the state of resources, nor do they think it is about time to mount any rescue in a bid to salvage something from a persistently haemorrhaging social order that may soon collapse. Indeed, when this picture was raised, the state had bled terribly for twenty-five years, and with no clear assurances as to when this will end. In the views of this perceptive observer, the 'Nigerian . . . society . . . has seen the enthronement of corruption and the recycling of discredited politicians and rulers'[27] working to its utter disadvantage. It is basically because of the brazen malfeasance of its regimes that the state has been brought to its current status in which experiencing life in the Hobbesian order of the *poor, nasty and brutish* has become an incontestable reality. Indeed, sensitivity to the flurry of dissuasive appetites and dispositions of Nigeria's leadership became the very inaugural thesis of Professor John Ayoade with the title, 'Nigeria and the Squandering of Hope' in 1997.[28]

How far can the state thrive in the light of unending rancid political and economic effusions? It is a very difficult question to answer if judged against the backdrop of continuities of pathological effusions which has remained tenacious with successive leaderships. The palpable result can more clearly be felt in the state's location as a failed and ever failing state in which citizens continue to lose grips on political trust on a palpable set of lying leaders. It may well be convictions like this that brought Eghosa Osaghae to label the state, *The Crippled Giant*.[29] Thus, from the optimistic conjectures raised of it at the eve of independence, it now presents a cauldron of collective desuetude in which the citizens are beginning to give more attention to its dissolution that sustenance. The glaring implication of such choice is the fact that post-colonial situation has ushered an era that accords fillip to neo-colonialism, and compelling many to demand for a second liberation struggle. The latter is plainly to aim at internal political hegemons in that space that hardly sees any good in the good life of its citizens.

Basically, the situation has blossomed in the trivialization of the citizen to underscore his presence as marginal to the calculations of day-to-day governance. That, perhaps explains why if a citizen is cut for truth-telling, and perceived as doing excellently well at that, the one may be hounded for unfair co-optation or elimination by the hegemonic powers of the day. Co-optation will help in massaging the regimes ego, as did the enlisting of the services of Reuben Abati, the former editor of *The Nigerian Guardian*, under President Goodluck Jonathan; otherwise, the restiveness of a free press can always be brought to bear on public and private media outfits that fails to support and eulogize governments. Indeed, this has been the very irritable source of the confusion of reporting 'fictional wonderful things' that governments have done even where such do not really exist, or, the rage of disguised muzzling of press power by owing its workers (*those who work within government owned media outfits*), to constrain them to always say what 'good' governments are doing. As it were, these have become popular trending experiences that trivialize the democratic freedom that finds an uplift in a truly free press. It also explains why indigenous native populations want to prefer news from outside sources than what their local outfits often offer except for a few.

Indeed, the matter of negation of the importance of freedom to neo-colonial Nigeria has more than amply been demonstrated by vast histories of media shutdowns by regimes in the state often achieved in guises as stated earlier, it has, however, left the population with painful experiences to share that reminds them of how unfree they may be. Among the critical instances, the hounding of Radio Kudirat and the death of Dele Giwa proves the core attitude of neocolonial disquisitions of freedom. Indeed, when serious cases happen, it tends to matter far less to government how far one can go to investigating it. The case of a deceased, so long as it keeps the hegemon secured, may never be revealed. That, as it were, explains the inexplicability of the gory death of amiable a citizen like Dele Giwa.[30] It extends to the tragic fates of M.K.O. Abiola, and Kudirat Abiola, Ken Saro Wiwa, and a host of others who were forced into the stillness of the necropolis by their own post independent states. We dare hazard the thought that similarly disturbing fates may well await many in the current climate of un-freedom and adversarial politics that hems in a neo-colonial Nigeria.

It is difficult to speak of the difficulties of a neo-colonial Nigeria without a mention of institutional bottlenecks presented by state institutions of coercive hue. The army, navy, air force, police, immigration, customs and lately, civil defense corps, have all become crucial new irritants of intense proportions in the process of vitiating the freedoms of citizens. Of all these, the matter of the Police, which is charged with internal security of lives and properties of citizens, proves the most deplorable and utterly disturbing. To put the matter simply, it is not difficult to observe that the police sells security to any bidder, but often provides the lead for any bidding game to happen. This is what is implied when it persistently mounts illegal check points to extort monies from motorists. That this practice is done openly marks the trend as an incorporated culture of security in the discourse of neo-colonial Nigeria. Indeed, as at the time of writing this chapter, which involved movements through crucial sites for inquiry, and which also coincided with the federal governments deployment of forces to contain Indigenous Peoples of Biafra (IPOB) self-determinists in the Eastern part of the country, this toll practice appears to have become an attractive feature of interest for joint patrol teams of these forces placed at strategic sites. To now openly demand monies from citizen motorists, invariably, has been factored into the impoverishing subjectivization of national security interests. Clearly, for advancing a friendly ₦20 or ₦50 note, one may have fulfilled the rite of passage to pass unsearched even if one was carrying a human head.

In the light of such deplorable experiences, the citizens are often subjected to double taxation from the state whose agents have become un-dignifying conduit pipes for depleting scarce funds of highly impoverished citizens. This has been the fate of the underclass, but that of the cream of society in big business equally makes for close attention in respect of the ports through which contra-banned goods find their way into the state en masse. It is the case, then, that the paradox of security of the citizen in post-colonial Nigeria relates clearly the fact that he pays double taxes, and gets insults and intimidation from officers clothed and paid with tax payer's monies. To this end, the un-uniformed citizen in Nigeria is now included as part of the commodity for purchase since when harassed, such tempers can be ameliorated by the advancement of some few bills to buy back his freedom.

CONCLUSION

This chapter considered neo-colonialism in Nigeria and some of the ways it makes its presence felt in the lives of the people. The implication of its very presence, however, points up to thriving extant limitations in the incomplete claims of political independence which ought to assure for full freedoms for African peoples. It is the case, then, that such freedoms remain farfetched in current circumstances that have seen the blossoming and intensification of de-capacitating features authored and activated by hegemonic leaderships of Africa's neo-colonial regimes.

The Nigerian case offers a studied and instructive context in which the de-valorization of the citizen assumes precedence in defining the focal point of exertions of hegemonic exploitation and manipulation of natives. It represents not the end, but clear continuation of the logic of defiant colonialism in the persistent denials and constraining conditions in which the citizen is meant to operate within that space. It may well be that hegemonic leadership continues to take pride in the deployment of violence, exploitation and manipulations for which it equates the departing colonialists. If only they did it the same way the colonialists had done it – *carting away resources to their home countries for purposes of collective development of their citizens and communities*, it would be another matter. Howbeit, the neo-colonial stranglehold, as presently constituted, not only shares in wanton exploitation and manipulation of natives by natives but also would further insist on silencing them to the nearest necropolis in the event of any discernible resistance to hegemonic interests and proclivities. Hence, the value and validity of fresh claims for a second liberation in Africa is occasioned by the urgent need to 'resume from where colonialism left us'[31] in respect to acquiring true freedom in all African spaces.

NOTES

1. Kwame Nkrumah, *as cited* in Larry Diamond, 'Class, Ethnicity, and the Democratic State: Nigeria, 1950–1966', *Comparative Studies in Society and History* 25, no. 3 (1993): 457.
2. M.V. Stevovic, 'Nigeria: In the Run up to the Election', *Review of International Affairs* XXX no. 701 (1979): 27.
3. Eghosa Osaghae, 'Democratization in sub-Saharan Africa: Faltering Prospects, New Hopes', *Journal of Contemporary African Studies* 17, no. 1 (1999): 5–28.
4. Peter Ekeh, 'The Concept of Second Liberation and the Prospect of Democracy in Africa: A Nigerian Context' (Paper prepared for presentation at a conference on *Dilemmas of Democracy in Nigeria*, at the University of Wisconsin–Madison, United States, 10–12 November, 1995), 1–35.

5. Adigun Agbaje, 'A Century of "Power Sharing" Nigeria in Theoretical and Comparative Perspective' (working paper WP99/8, Development Policy Center, 13 August 1998), 4–5.

6. B. Ibhawoh, 'Stronger than the Maxim Gun: Law, Human Rights and British Colonial Hegemony', *Africa* 72, no. 1 (2002): 55–73.

7. Wole Soyinka, 'Between Nation Space and Nationhood', Text of a public Lecture delivered at as part of Centennial birthday celebration of Chief Obafemi Awolowo, Muson Center, Lagos. 3 March 2009. https://wwwnas-int.org/currentaffairs/public-lectures/299-between-nation-space-and-nationhood.

8. Eghosa Osaghae, 'Exiting from the State in Nigeria', *African Journal of Political Science* 4, no. 1 (1999): 83–98.

9. C.H. Titus, 'A Nomenclature in Political Science', *The American Political Science Review*, XXV, no. 1 (1931): 45.

10. W.B. Gallie, 'Essentially Contested Concepts', *Proceedings of the Aristotelian Society*, (1956): 167–98.

11. J.A. Scorza, 'Liberal Citizenship and Civic Friendship', *Political Theory* 32, no. 2 (2004): 86.

12. M. Mamdani, *Contemporary Africa and the Legacy of Late Colonialism* (New Jersey: Princeton University Press, 2002).

13. Peter Ekeh, *Colonialism and Social Structure* (Ibadan: University of Ibadan Press, 1983).

14. P. Gonzalez-Casanova, 'Internal Colonialism and National Development', in *Latin American Radicalism*, eds. Irving Horowitz, Jose de Castro and John Gerassi (New York: Vintage Books, 1969) as cited in Norma Chaloult and Yves Chaloult, 'The Internal Colonialism Concept: Methodological Considerations', *Social and Economic Studies* 28, no. 4 (1979): 85.

15. R.I. Rotberg, 'African Nationalism: Concept or Confusion', *The Journal of Modern African Studies* 4, no. 1 (1966): 33–46.

16. B. Turok, *Africa: What Can Be Done*? (London: Zed Books, 1987).

17. I.G. Shivji, 'The Rise, the Fall, and the Insurrection of Nationalism in Africa', (Paper from Keynote Address to the CODESRIA East African Conference held in Addis Ababa, Ethiopia, 29–31 October 2003), 114.

18. International Crisis Group, 'Nigeria: Want in the Midst of Plenty', Africa Report, no. 113, 19 July 2006, http://www.crisisgroup/org

19. Turok, *Africa*.

20. G.B.N. Ayittey, 'Nigeria's Struggle with Corruption', Testimony before the committee on International Relations subcommittee on Africa, Global Human Rights and International Operations, House Committee on Africa, U.S. House of Representatives, Washington, D,C, Thursday, May 18, 2006, 1–18.

21. O.P. Anwuluorah and S.C. Okafor-Udoh, 'The Perspective of Christian Moral Education for Good Governance in Nigeria', *Journal of Religion and Human Relations*, 7, no. 1 (2015): 63.

22. Claude Ake, 'Rethinking African Democracy', *Journal of Democracy* 2, no. 1 (1991): 32.

23. J.A.A. Ayoade, 'Nigeria and the Squandering of Hope', An inaugural lecture delivered at the University of Ibadan, Ibadan, Nigeria, 16 October 1997, 18.

24. Ali Mazrui, 'Pan-Africanism and the Intellectuals: Rise, Decline and Revival.' In Thandika Mkandawire (ed.) *African Intellectuals: Rethinking Politics, Language, Gender and Development*, 56–77. London: Zed Books, 2005.

25. Editorial Comments. 'Nigeria: The African Giant', Round Table, December 1959–September 1960, 2–3.

26. W. Connor, 'Nation-Building or Nation-Destroying', *World Politics* no. 3 (1972): 319–55.

27. O. Otite, 'Nigeria: Towards Salvaging a Ravaged Society', Postgraduate School Interdisciplinary Research Discourse, University of Ibadan, Ibadan, Nigeria. 18 July 1995, 1.

28. Ayoade, 'Nigeria and the Squandering of Hope'.

29. Eghosa Osaghae, *Crippled Giant: Nigeria since Independence* (Indiana: Indiana University Press, 1998).

30. B. Akinlaja, '30 Years after Dele Giwa's Murder, Nigeria yet to Unravel His Killer', Historical Flasback, October 5–November 1, 2016, 3–6.

31. Ogban Ogban-Iyam, 'Commencing from Where We Were Interrupted by Colonialism and the Need for Continuity with Our Pre-colonial Traditions with Adaptations and Modifications' (Presidential Address presented to the Twenty-First Annual Conference of the Nigerian Political Science Association, NPSA, 12–13 July, 1998), 1–15.

BIBLIOGRAPHY

Agbaje, Adigun. 'A Century of "Power Sharing" Nigeria in Theoretical and Comparative Perspective'. Working Paper WP99/8, Development Policy Center, 13 August 1998, 4–5.

Ake, Claude. 'Rethinking African Democracy'. *Journal of Democracy* 2, no. 1 (1991): 32–42.

Anwuluorah, O.P. and S.C. Okafor-Udoh. 'The Perspective of Christian Moral Education for Good Governance in Nigeria'. *Journal of Religion and Human Relations* 7, no. 1 (2015): 63–87.

Chaloult, Norma and Yves Chaloult. 'The Internal Colonialism Concept: Methodological Considerations'. *Social and Economic Studies* 28, no. 4 (1979): 85–98.

Connor, W. 'Nation-Building or Nation-Destroying'. *World Politics* no. 3 (1972): 319–55.

Diamond, Larry. 'Class, Ethnicity, and the Democratic State: Nigeria, 1950–1966'. *Comparative Studies in Society and History* 25, no. 3 (1993): 457–68.

Ekeh, Peter. *Colonialism and Social Structure*. Ibadan: University of Ibadan Press, 1983.

Gonzalez-Casanova, P. 'Internal Colonialism and National Development'. In *Latin American Radicalism*, edited by Irving Horowitz, Jose de Castro and John Gerassi. New York: Vintage Books, 1969.

Ibhawoh, B. 'Stronger than the Maxim Gun: Law, Human Rights and British Colonial Hegemony'. *Africa* 72, no. 1 (2002): 55–73.

Mamdani, M. *Contemporary Africa and the Legacy of Late Colonialism*. New Jersey: Princeton University Press, 2002.

Osaghae, Eghosa. *Crippled Giant: Nigeria since Independence*. Indiana: Indiana University Press, 1998.

Osaghae, Eghosa. 'Democratization in sub-Saharan Africa: Faltering Prospects, New Hopes'. *Journal of Contemporary African Studies* 17, no. 1 (1999): 5–28.

Osaghae, Eghosa. 'Exiting from the State in Nigeria'. *African Journal of Political Science* 4, no. 1 (1999): 83–98.

Rotberg, R.I. 'African Nationalism: Concept or Confusion'. *The Journal of Modern African Studies* 4, no. 1 (1966): 33–46.

Scorza, J.A. 'Liberal Citizenship and Civic Friendship'. *Political Theory* 32, no. 2 (2004): 86–93.

Stevovic, M.V. 'Nigeria: In the Run up to the Election'. *Review of International Affairs* XXX, no. 701 (1979): 27–31.

Titus, C.H. 'A Nomenclature in Political Science'. *The American Political Science Review*, XXV, no. 1 (1931): 45–66.

Turok, B. *Africa: What Can be Done*? London: Zed Books, 1987.

Chapter 9

Urban Redevelopment as a Metaphor for Gentrification in the Making of a Mega-City: The Forced Displacement of Otodo Gbame/Ebute Ikate Community, Lagos State

Bamidele Omotunde Alabi

INTRODUCTION

For most developing countries, including Nigeria, the surge in the development of slums, squatter settlements, shanties and blighted areas in the major cities is the key recipe for urban decay, which has continued to constitute daunting challenge for the appropriate authorities. In Lagos, for example, these informal settlements are often sited in such highly susceptible places like waterfronts, creeks, lagoon banks, water-logged areas, river edges and road fringes, where the living conditions are often squalid and the residents are vulnerable to all forms of physical, environmental and health perils. The existence of such settlements is often inimical to the society at large as they portend several social and environmental maladies. As such, in its bid to tackle the menace of urban decay, urban redevelopment/regeneration schemes have been one of the frequently used policy response by different regimes in Lagos. In fact, many seminal works have shown that successive governments in Lagos have employed various urban regeneration schemes over the years.[1] Indeed, urban regeneration is one of the standard panaceas deployed in Nigeria to address the malaise of urban decay, and this much has been affirmed by Nwana as follows:

> Most often, the Nigerian government's response is demolition or slum clearance after the eviction of residents. Such efforts are largely undertaken to improve the city's international public image, or justified for health reasons or as maintaining standards.[2]

Along this line, it has been established that the major hallmark of urban regeneration policy execution schemes in Nigeria is the forcible eviction of the people living in the areas marked for renewal, and such exercises often lead to population displacements, with attendant negative aftermaths.[3]

To the extent that urban redevelopment (also known as urban renewal, urban regeneration, urban revitalization, or urban rehabilitation) and gentrification both refer to the process of reversing and transforming the decay within a typical urban space, the line of distinction between the two has in practical terms been rendered rather amorphous by the manner in which they are manifested in many parts Africa. It is perhaps for this reason that it has been convenient to consistently cloak gentrification with the garb of urban redevelopment in most places in the region where there have been a plethora of urban decay, which chiefly stems from the development of slums, shanties and blighted areas in the major cities. For proper appreciation and better understanding of the dialectics between the two, it becomes vital at this juncture to attempt an explication of the meaning of these concepts.

While urban regeneration has been variously defined across disciplines, Lee in 2008 encapsulated it as follows:

> Urban renewal is a process that includes clearance of slum or blight areas, urban development, urban revitalization, building rehabilitation, preservation and conservation to improve urban fabric and meet some economic and social objectives.[4]
>
> Akin to this is Agbola's viewpoint which considers urban regeneration as:
>
> A relatively comprehensive community redevelopment program through which a particular city seeks to re-fashion and rebuild the physical structures of a particular segment of the city in order to enable it to cope more successfully with the problems confronting it.[5]

The aforementioned perspectives present the sense that urban regeneration is a populist process, often executed for the overall good of a vast majority of the affected society. Evidences have, however, shown that despite the intended beneficial aftermaths of urban regeneration schemes, it can also have adverse effects on social and physical environments, particularly displacements (usually by forcible evictions).

However, it is from the point after people are forcibly displaced from their usual places of abode for purposes of upgrade and regeneration that the thin line of distinction between urban regeneration and gentrification start to become discernible, for while both processes aim at reversing and transforming decay within a typical urban space, the major motivation for gentrification is often profit. This viewpoint has been aptly underscored by Nwana thus:

> However, it could be argued that this (*gentrification*) is about profit maximization when a settlement is located on prime development land, which a number

of slums are. After evictions and demolitions, such areas are often redeveloped into condominiums such that the former residents cannot afford the new properties. This transformation, I would argue, is a form of gentrification in Lagos.[6]

Gentrification is a term which was developed in the 1960s by Ruth Glass to basically explain how rich people from the countryside literally invaded the city in search of central locations, and being unable to settle down in the already-wealthy areas, took working-class neighbourhoods and, slowly in the beginning but accelerated once the process is started, refurbished the existing buildings and changed the dynamics of the area.[7] Succinctly therefore, gentrification literally means an orchestrated shift in the population dynamics of a specific urban space such that its new dwellers are of higher socio-economic status than the displaced dwellers. Along this line, Kilmartin aptly captures the concept as that process by which higher-income inhabitants displace lower-income dwellers of a community, thereby completely changing the fabric of the environment. Therefore, implicit in Kilmartin's encapsulation is the distinctive features of gentrification including the displacement of original residents often through forcible evictions, the physical transformation of the area, which ultimately lead to change in the general outlook of the area.[8] While the realities of gentrification have been gleaned from different perspectives, it shall in this chapter be gleaned from the context explicated by the glass, that is, of government policy associated with major urban redevelopment schemes that trigger the low- to middle- or upper-class transformation of residents.[9]

It is to this end therefore that this chapter argues that relics of colonization are replete in the policy frameworks of nations across Africa, particularly as regards the preponderance of urban regeneration schemes, wherein gentrification is often cloaked with the garb of urban redevelopment, the execution of which is often achieved through forcible evictions, typified by intimidation, coercion and violence. In arguing that urban redevelopment is a mere metaphor for gentrification in this part of the world, this chapter examines the dynamics, mechanisms and outcomes of the latest in the series of such exercises by the Lagos state government, which involved the forcible eviction of residents of Otodo-Gbame and Ebute Ikate communities in Eti-Osa local government area between November 2016 and April 2017.

TRAJECTORY OF URBAN DECAY AND REGENERATION IN LAGOS

While debates about the actual population figures of Lagos State Nigeria lingers, it is still one of the fastest-growing cities in the world, and it has been classified by the Population Divisions of the United Nations (Department of Economic and Social Affairs-UN DESA) in its highlights of the 2014 revision of the World Urbanization Prospects as one of the only three megacities in Africa, alongside Cairo and Kinshasa.[10] With an estimated population of over twelve million and ranking nineteenth in the 2014 global urban agglomeration, the city is expected to become the ninth-largest city in the world by 2030, as its population will be over twenty-four million, growing at an annual rate of 3.9%.[11] Although with a much higher figure of 23.3 million and an annual growth projection rate of 3.2% as at 2014, the Lagos State Bureau of Statistics (LBS) has further accentuated the fact that Lagos is indeed densely populated.[12]

The import of these statistics is that not only is population growth in Lagos very rapid, but that it is urbanizing at rather fast rate.[13] As such, with the growth rate projected for the city of Lagos, it goes without saying therefore that the challenges of urban population explosion, including among other things, the upsurge in the number of urban poor, culminating to the increase in informal developments, often typified by slums, shanties and blighted areas, which are already manifest in some areas, will likely continue to escalate.

Indeed, these challenges have been encapsulated by the LBS as it estimated that 66.9% of residents in Lagos lived below the poverty line of US$1 a day.[14] Along this line, the Lagos State Urban and Renewal Agency (LASURA), has affirmed that the state has hundreds of informal settlements, consisting of a number of densely populated slums and shanties along its various waterfronts.[15] The slums and shanties in Lagos are believed to have a density of between 790 and 1240 people per hectare, as against the average residential density for Lagos as a whole, which are 260 people per hectare.[16] The consequence of the swarming population of Lagos, relative to its small land mass is thus recipe for a significant housing challenge.[17] This much has been corroborated by the Lagos State Ministry of Economic Planning and Budget as follows:

> There is a massive housing deficit in Lagos due to considerable slum housing, overcrowding and unmet demand from middle and high income households . . . there is a massive backlog of unmet [housing] need, probably in excess of 2 million housing units. . . . The housing areas of the poor are thought to accommodate over 70% of the Lagos population, i.e. about 15 million people'.[18]

The foregoing presents a prevalent myriad of challenges to which there have been successive proposals or actual executions of different urban regeneration policies and programmes to address them by the relevant authorities.

In fact, attempts at regenerating the Lagos urban space is not nascent, as it can be traced to the colonial times when Lagos was still a colony under the British Protectorate. Years after serving as the main slave harbour and a major commercial hub for foreign and local merchants where it was increasingly involved in the circulation of people, goods, ideas and technologies along the coastal West African sub-region, Lagos was annexed as a British colony in 1861 and it became the administrative and military settlement for the Colonialists.[19] Lagos was annexed officially to stop the slave trade, but more pragmatically to be used mainly for the conquest of the hinterland regions in what was later to be known as Nigeria.[20]

The phenomenal growth in the population of Lagos began as agricultural and commercial activities thrived upon the abolition of slave trade, and the port in Lagos became the main interface between Britain and the African colony, eventually becoming headquarters of the Federation of Nigeria, after the merging of three former colonial administrative entities: the colony of Lagos, the protectorate of Northern Nigeria and the protectorate of Southern Nigeria.[21] It was believed that the gradual replacement of the slave trade with the palm oil, cocoa and cotton industries and the consolidation of the position of Lagos on the West African coast attracted European merchants, freed slaves from Brazil and Cuba, slaves freed by the British on the coast and refugees from the interior, thereby contributing to its progressive population growth.[22]

Specifically, the regeneration of Lagos first occurred in 1929 after a severe bubonic plague that lasted six months broke out in 1924. In 1929, Lagos Executive Development Board (LEDB) was established in an effort to combat the spread of the plague. The board was especially established to undertake a Town Planning Scheme of the worst affected area, upon which the first slum clearance of 400 unhealthy shacks that relocated thousands from the indigenous community to the mainland was undertaken. In the said exercise, over fifty acres of derelict properties were demolished in within the Lagos Island precinct, to pave the way for good roads and other amenities.[23] Another epochal regeneration exercise was the pre-independence demolition of Isale-Eko, the main objective of which was to afford the visiting Queen of England a pleasing view of the area.[24] According to Agbola and Jinadu, series of other post-independence clearances were to follow in the 1970s, including the Idioro evictions of over 500 people in 1973 and the 1975 evictions of over 5000 people from their various homes and work places in Adeniji Adele, and the eviction of another 5000 in Iponri from their homes and workplaces. Another major clearance was carried out by the state government in Oba Akran in 1976 and Central Lagos where 10,000 people were evicted in 1976, and in the same year, the eviction of over 10,000 people in Ketu as well as Apongbon took place. In 1977, over 20,000 were cleared from Alaba Market, while another 10,000 were evicted in Oworonshoki in 1980. Yet other, a large number of settlers were evicted from Somolu/Bariga 1982, and in 1990, there was the celebrated eviction of over 300,000 people from the sprawling Maroko community, which was the totally demolished by the government.[25] In a similar vein, over 9000 people were forcibly evicted from an estimated

2237 households, made of about 266 structures that served as homes and business outlets by the urban renewal exercise carried in Badia East in 2013.[26] Lately, between 19 March 2016 and 22 April 2017, there occurred a series of seven forced evictions of more than 30,000 residents of Ilubirin/Otodo-Gbame, Ebut Ikate communities by the Lagos state government.

URBAN REGENERATION AND GENTRIFICATION

Extant literatures particularly from the 1990s have become increasingly fascinated with the relationship between urban redevelopment and gentrification, so much that pertinent questions have agitated the imagination of scholars in the area. Not only have there been questions about where the boundary lies between gentrification and urban, it has also been queried if every situation of renewal connotes gentrification and whether there is a possibility of urban renewal introducing new population and maintaining the existing residents. It has also been asked if this process reshaping the conception of urban growth and re-directing the transformation of cities.[27] Indeed, it has been argued that processes of urban renewal and gentrification are part and parcel of the continuous reshaping of the built environment to create a more efficient arena for profit making.[28]

In 2017, a review produced evidence for various pathways linking urban renewal to gentrification[29] and the findings indicate that urban renewal can indeed drive gentrification due to increasing land values and lifestyle costs, resulting in the displacement of long-term residents unable to cope with these changes.[30] Following from the foregoing is the idea that gentrification is a direct fall out of urban regeneration. As such Jorge López de Obeso submits that the phenomenon called gentrification has usually been considered as the result of the speculation, which after a successful renewal makes attractive the zone for richer population, creating a dynamic in which the prices of land and built context rise and therefore becomes unaffordable to the current residents, who have the risk to be expelled by the new condition.[31] Perhaps, the most apposite question at this juncture could be to ask how and why urban regeneration schemes lead to gentrification. It is instructive to note that many seminal works have indeed lent credence to the suggestion that changing urban policies from social welfare to market-led outcomes in larger cities led to an increase return on profitable land.[32] The aftermath of these is thus reflected in changes in rent and lifestyle increases resulting in certain populations, largely low-income, racial and ethnic minorities or seniors, being displaced more disproportionately compared to other populations.[33]

While urban regeneration exercises have been to known to beget its unique dire social and economic consequences, particularly for the displaced persons, gentrification has been reported to create its peculiar challenges, including loss of social diversity, loss of cheap shelter for low-income earners, owing particularly to the inevitable commercialization of housing in the gentrified communities and other areas within its precincts. As such, it has been argued that displacement, often the aftermath of urban regeneration and gentrification exercise, is not the major challenge, but that the real challenge is the social cost of gentrification to the affected communities.[34] With the passage of time, the scope of gentrification has widened to become not only global and diverse in outlook, but also from interest in residential to commercial buildings, and from individual stakeholders to corporate real-estate concerns, including governments.[35] For the Nigerian environment, the involvement of government and key corporate players is of particular significance.

Theoretically, this chapter will consider three perspectives with respect to gentrification as follow: demand-side explanation or consumption-side theory (offshoot of the urban ecological theory); supply side explanation or production-side theory, and economic globalization perspective. Succinctly, gentrification has its roots in the urban-ecological perspective, made popular by Ruth Glass,[36] wherein it submitted that gentrification is a process of displacing the original lower-income dwellers of a place by rising costs and other composite mechanisms attributable to new wealthier residents.[37] This perspective is further underscored by Ley in the demand-side explanation, in which the focus was on preferences, motives and sociocultural factors that make high-income earners to seek inner city, centrally located housing.[38] The supply side perspective is the same as the neo-Marxists, with the argument proffered by Smith about gentrification being the fall-out of the uneven development of many major Western industrial cities, which causes the overvaluing of the suburbs relative the downtown.[39] Smith formulated the rent-gap theory, which asserts that capital flows in the direction where the return on investment is the highest, thus explaining that with the incessant diminution in the values of the downtown, capital begins to move to the suburbs, thereby creating the rent gap. In other words, the theory simply explains how gentrification is indeed the outcome of the decline in the values of properties in the downtown caused largely by suburbanization and de-industrialization. As such, rent gap ultimately creates the economic opportunity for the relevant real estate investors (including developers, landlords, private investors and others) who take advantage of the surplus value left by the disparity between the exchange value and the use value of the property for profit. Finally, the economic globalization side believes that the city has become a field where social, cultural and economic factors are played out, thus creating inherent inequalities in urban areas and providing a basis for gentrification. The centrality of the modern global city makes it rather inevitable that government and corporate organizations would be the key players.[40]

STUDY LOCATION

At this point, a brief overview of the profile of the study location becomes inevitable, as this will afford a deeper appreciation of what the community was prior to the displacement of its residents. Otodo Gbame and Ebute Ikate can be said to be one community, as they were both within each other's precinct. Indeed, the entire community within the proximity was referred to generally as Otodo Gbame. The community was an informal settlement inhabited by at least 60,000 people at the edge of the lagoon in Lekki area of Lagos state. Otodo Gbame was believed to have been in its location for over a hundred years. The community comprised various ethnic groups, including Yoruba, Igbo, Ilajes, Egun, Ijaw and other people of mainly fishing communities, who prefer to settle near rivers because of their love of fishing which serves as a source of livelihood for them. In addition, immigrants from neighbouring countries in the West coast of Africa, including Benin Republic, Togo, Ghana and Cote d'Ivoire, were also resident in Otodo Gbame and were known to own their own houses in the community.

The community was indeed rustic as it was made up of was of spontaneously made lean structures, majority of which were constructed with woods/planks and zinc. There were very few houses made with bricks in the location, many of which were more on the lagoon than on land. Despite its close proximity to the highbrow Lekki Phase 1, Lagos, Otodo Gbame community presented a very sharp contrast to the opulence around it, as all over are modern, state of the art buildings complemented by first-class facilities. As such, the community did not enjoy the provision of basic infrastructures or amenities and services. The community had no source of potable water and it was not electrified. Prior to the forcible evictions of the inhabitants, they were known to make provision of water and electricity by and for themselves individually. The residents relied on water from wells dug all about the community for their water needs. However, because of the proximity to the lagoon, water from the well was not consumable as it had been contaminated, and as such, is used for non-consumption purposes. It was said that in the time past, the community enjoyed episodic public electricity supply through a formal connection and they paid a collective communal bill. This arrangement was later discontinued. As such, for potable water, they were known to have patronized water vendors in tankers for potable water and they got electricity through the use of small generators.

The community turned its closeness to the lagoon to an asset which they used for sanitation and sewage purposes. As they had no connection to public sewerage or any official waste disposal arrangements, they made use of bucket toilets which were periodically emptied into the lagoon once it filled

Figure 9.1. Satellite image of Otodo-Gbame taken on 11 May 2016. *Source*: Amnesty International, March 2017.

up. There were no proper drainage systems and such, some of their wastewater drained back into the lagoon. Wastes were burned, buried or turned into the lagoon to dispose them. All of these indeed added to the squalid environmental conditions of the community. There were no roads leading into the community but only through footpath. Also there were no public health facilities at all, the only infirmary available to the community was owned by one of the residents.

A vast number of residents were young adults and middle aged mostly in age group twenty to fifty-nine, with an admixture of monogamous and polygynous family setting. The highest educational attainment of the majority of the people is primary school leaving certificate. The community had five private primary schools, all privately owned by the residents. Many of the residents were engaged mostly in fishing, artisanship and trading and so forth.

RESEARCH DESIGN

This is a qualitative study and it employed a combination of in-depth and key informant interview, two key ethnographic methods, to generate primary data from the samples. The samples were purposively drawn from among the forcibly evicted victims of Otodo Gbame/Ebute Ikate communities and officials of the relevant agencies like Lagos State Urban Renewal Agency (LASURA), the Lagos State Environmental Sanitation Enforcement Agency (Taskforce) and the Lagos State Building Control Agency. Since for a study of this nature, smaller but focused samples rather than large samples are often most appropriate, the sample size for the study was thirteen persons, consisting of ten victims and three officials. Six of the evictees were male, while four were females. All the government agency officials interviewed as key informants were males. In selecting the samples from the evicted victims' population, the study employed different apposite purposive characteristics as age, residency status, length of stay in the community and, most importantly, availability. The issue of availability becomes important at this point as all of the respondents were interviewed in places other than Otodo Gbame/Ebute Ikate. They were all interviewed in the different locations they had escaped to seek shelter after their displacement from the community like, Makoko, Oko Baba, Ikorodu, Snake Island, Apapa, Badagry and so on. As for the officials the bases used to select the samples include relevance, and hierarchy in the agencies. Four research assistants, who themselves were residents of Otodo Gbame were deployed in this process of gathering data from the samples and the interviews were conducted over a five-week timeframe (5th May–1st June 2017). The major instrument employed in eliciting information from the interviewees is the unstructured interview guide. The guide contained the different relevant questions as were administered to the respondents to elicit information relevant to the study. The data gathered for this chapter were largely qualitative. Verbal responses by some of the interviewees were rendered in both the local language and pidgin English. These have been appropriately transliterated for ease of interpretation and analysis. The data gathered in this study were analysed employing appropriate qualitative data analysis tool. This study followed a careful presentation and meaningful interpretation of data, in such a way that it proffers deep understanding of the subject matter of this chapter.

FINDINGS

This study argues that urban redevelopment is a mere metaphor for gentrification in Nigeria, and in testing the argument, it examines the dynamics, mechanisms and outcomes of the recent regeneration exercise in Otodo Gbame/Ebute Ikate Communities of Eti Osa LGA. The study thus focuses on the methods and the instrumentalities deployed by the government to effect the exercise, as well as the real reasons behind the exercise.

EMPLOYING THE INSTRUMENTALITY OF THE STATE TO DISPLACE OTODO GBAME

This study finds that the displacement and consequent appropriation of Otodo Gbame had been systematically and sequentially orchestrated in a manner that is symptomatic of state-led gentrification. Indeed, the instrumentality of the state was methodically deployed to achieve this objective.

Findings of this study established that a covert move to appropriate the community began almost three years prior to the actual eviction of the residents. This much was echoed in the responses of some of the evictees thus

> the plan to grab our land began about three year ago when the Elegunshi family and some other powerful people in government started dredging the lagoon and filling up the place in such a manner that would have eventually encroached our land. (Evictee, sixty-one years old, male)
>
> They had it all figured out amongst themselves since the courts gave Elegunshi family the order to take over the land which our forebears started living upon over 100 years ago, and the house of assembly in Lagos also supported the move. (Evictee, forty-nine years old, male)

The aforementioned assertions were indeed corroborated by the report of Amnesty International that a reclamation project was embarked upon by a prominent royal family (Elegushi) and others.[41] The said reclamation project was found to not only have the approval of the Lagos state government through its relevant agency, but the process was also reported to be backed by a court order in October 2016 granting the royal family and other interested parties the right to take possession of Otodo Gbame community.[42] In furtherance of the use of organs of government in this instance, the legislative arm of the Lagos state government structure passed the following resolution:

> The said land called Otodo- Gbame is historically called Ebute-Ikate which is part of Ikate land that belongs to Elegushi family and not the petitioners. More so, the petitioners who inhabited Otodo-Gbame are (mostly from Egun tribe of Cotonou and Togo) squatting in the area without the consent or permission from the Elegushi.[43]

Consequent to the stated subtle moves, there was a massive fire incident which destroyed over a third of Otodo Gbame on 9 November 2016. The scale of the destruction was such that it prompted the Lagos state government to announce the take-over of the community, upon which the Ministry of Physical Planning and Urban Development moved in to clear the rubbles caused by the fire and demolish the remaining structures.[44]

Figure 9.2. A section of Otodo Gbame on fire in the background. *Source*: Amnesty International, March 2017.

While the fire in the morning of 9 November 2016 was believed to be caused by a clash between youths in Otodo-Gbame/Ebute Ikate community, some of the interviewed evictees, however, believed otherwise. Two of them stated thus:

> We all know that what happens when the Lagos State government wants to take over a place is that they set fire in such places, and there are many such instances like Balogun market, Tejuosho market, Mushin market and many more. . . . It is the same strategy they decided to adopt with our community. (Evictee, thirty-two years old, male)
>
> Look, it is the government and Elegushi family that burned down our houses and I know what I am saying because I saw it all with my own eyes how their agents carried out the nefarious activities, and even the police helped with setting our houses on fire that morning while we watched helplessly (Evictee, forty-one years old, female)

Findings revealed that immediately following the fire incident, demolition exercises began on houses and different structures in the community. Bulldozers and pay-loaders were deployed to the area with active supervision of police officers, military personnel (the Military Police) and the Nigerian Security and Civil Defense Corps (NSCDC), as well as other people in plain clothes, with officials of such agencies as Lagos State Urban Renewal Agency (LASURA), the Lagos State Environmental Sanitation Enforcement Agency (Taskforce) and the Lagos State Building Control Agency. The exercise lasted for over forty-eight hours and structures that could not be demolished by bulldozers were set ablaze by the demolition team which worked till Friday, 11 November 2016.

As is typical of forced eviction exercises, the Otodo Gbame episode was believed to have violated the rights of residents to adequate housing, life, dignity of person, family life, education and freedom from cruel, inhuman and degrading treatment or punishment. Concomitantly, there were casualties recorded in the process. This as is affirmed by some of the evictees:

> There is no better way to describe what the government has done to us other than an infringement on our fundamental human rights as prescribed by not only the constitution of Nigeria, but also as pronounced by the law courts and as recommended by the United Nations basic principles on evictions (Evictee, forty-eight years old, male).
>
> . . . this place was like war zone during the exercise as there were armed men everywhere, with police were shooting live ammunition and teargas at the people and some of those hit by the bullets died, while some who tried to escape through the water drowned in the lagoon, such that a number of people are still missing till now (Evictee, fifty-one years old, female).

It was found that after the exercise, over 90% of the residents had been forcibly evicted, while some of them, particularly those with structures on the lagoon stayed back and had some others squat with them.

However, since the earlier eviction exercise in Otodo Gbame did not totally displace the entire resident, some of those who remained gradually regrouped and erected makeshift shelters on the location and continued to live theirs live, while as a community, thirteen other waterfront communities approached the law court for protection. The court, in a landmark judgment delivered by Hon. Justice S.A. Onigbanjo of the High Courts in

Figure 9.3. Images of the instrumentality of government fully deployed in the eviction process. *Source*: Amnesty International, March 2017.

Lagos, on Thursday, 26 January 2017, did grant a temporary protection by the way of an interim injunction restraining the government and its agents from demolishing the homes of the claimants, pending the hearing of the case, while ordering the parties to explore an out of court settlement through mediation.

Prodded as to the communities view on the judgement, an evicted victim reacted thus:

> This is Nigeria where the rule of law is hardly respected by the government. . . . I am not surprised that Lagos state did not obey the ruling of this court restraining them from further actions and advising the parties to settle out of court . . . they withdrew from the settlement process and returned to finish the annihilation process they began four months earlier. (Evictee, sixty-one years old, male)

In defiance of the court order and without prior consultation or notice, the government and its agencies were said to have returned to Otodo Gbame to conclude the exercise of evicting the people and appropriating the land. Typically, between March 17, 2017 and April 9, 2017, in a sequenced exercise, all the paraphernalia of government needed to enforce forcible evictions were deployed. Some of the evicted victims related the experience as follows:

> They came back after the court judgment and the whole of this place was filled with police, army, KAI brigade, TASKFORCE, CIVIL DEFENSE people and other men armed with machetes, axes and guns, bringing bulldozers to demolish

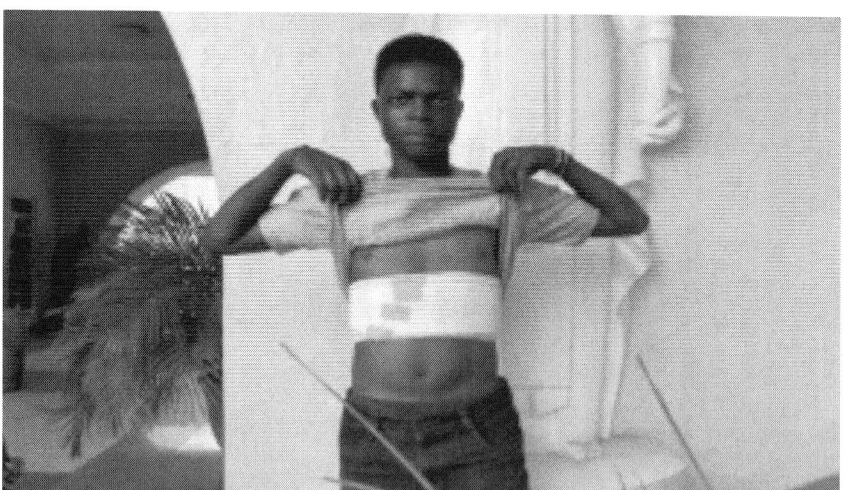

Figure 9.4. The rubbles that became of Otodo Gbame and the mortality/morbidity in wake of the forcible eviction. ***Source*****: Amnesty International, March 2017.**

everywhere . . . the sad part is one of my neighbors was shot dead in the process while another sustained gunshot injuries. (Evictee, fifty-seven years old, male)

The police shot live ammunition, teargas to drive away those who tried to resist by protest as they showed the restraining order from the court, just as some thugs, hoodlums and miscreants working for the Elegushi family beat and stabbed people . . . not only were our home turned to mere rubbles, many people were injured and over a dozen were detained by the forces. (Evictee, thirty-two years old, female)

OFFICIAL POSITION OF THE STATE ON THE FORCED EVICTION IN OTODO GBAME

The study sought the position of the government of Lagos state on the forced eviction in Otodo Gbame/Ebute Ikate community from respondents drawn from the three agencies involved in the exercise. Findings of the study revealed that government did justify the forced evictions. In preferring their justification, an official of the LASURA stated as follows:

> The government has the responsibility of identifying areas requiring urban redevelopment, draw up schemes for redevelopment programme, monitor, coordinate and implement redevelopment activities and interventions. . . . Lagos state government being a responsible government is attempting to do just that with Otodo Gbame/Ebute Ikate community. (KII, male, official, Lagos)

Another official of one of the agencies offered this:

> A responsible government will be interested in the security of its citizens, and there are reliable information that many communities along the waterfronts and creeks in the state including Otodo Gbame/Ebute Ikate, are becoming the hideout of criminals, robbers and militants . . . let us not forget the dastardly robbery attack in Lekki in 2015 and how the criminals used the lagoon and the creeks as their cover and escape route . . . once bitten, twice shy they say. (KII, male, official, Lagos)

The security justification for the eviction of Otodo Gbame/Ebute Ikate community was supported by another official who also noted that

> maintaining law and order in the state is one of the key social contracts the government owes its citizens and in a situation where there is breakdown of law and order caused from the ethnic clash between the Egun and Yoruba residents within the community that is capable of threatening the peace, what should the government do? . . . A good government will readily move in to arrest the situation and that is what the government did in this instance. (KII, male, official, Lagos)

In justifying the actions of the government on the community, one of the officials interviewed stated as thus:

> Many of the inhabitants were indeed living in a harmful environment and the government needed to save them from utter degradation . . . you will agree therefore that government's action in this regard was in the overriding public interest not only of the people of the community but also of the proximal communities. (KII, male, official, Lagos).

Figure 9.5. The Periwinkle estate. *Source*: The Imperial International Business City.

THE GENTRIFIED OTODO GBAME/EBUTE IKATE COMMUNITY: PERIWINKLE ESTATE/IMPERIAL INTERNATIONAL BUSINESS CITY

Months after the displacement of the residents of Otodo Gbame/Ebute Ikate unfolding happenings have revealed that the justifications offered by the government are indeed suspect. Indeed, it has been found that the forceful eviction of residents of Otodo-Gbame/Ebute Ikate and other waterfront communities is a part of the pursuit of the state government's policy to ape the modernity of Dubai in the city. It has been revealed that the Elugushi royal family with the help of the Lagos state government has divided the land into two highbrow luxury estates, namely the 'Periwinkle estate' (so-called because of the lagoon sand burrow is full of periwinkle shells) and the 'Imperial International Business City'.

Periwinkle, it was reported, is to comprise 100 plots of size between 500 square metres and 2000 square metres with a commanding price of between ₦45 million and ₦200 million (approximately $150,000 and $620,000) each for a piece of land. The imperial International Business City is said to be a 150 hectares new super-luxury only similar in grandeur with the Eko Atlantic City off Victoria Island.

Indeed, the timeline of these projects appeared to be the major reason the Lagos state and the Elegushi royal family was desperate to evict the inhabitants of Otodo-Gbame, as findings showed that the approval for the development of the property had been obtained from the government prior, which informed the reclamation projects that the inhabitants protested even to the court of law.

CONCLUSION

It becomes evident from the findings that irrespective of whether the process is urban renewal or gentrification, the issues of physical displacement as well as social and economic alienation from the city is an aspect that is of particular significance in a place like Nigeria. This often leads to capital-induced gentrification, which makes the urban areas exclusive for cultural production and class differentiation[45] with the potential of eroding cultural diversity especially in inner city areas, thus engendering over commercialization of housing both in the central cities and the suburbs. Upon critical analysis of the events leading to the study, as well as the series of urban regeneration exercises that have taken place in Lagos, it is convenient to state that gentrification fits well as a term and explanation for them, as indeed they all bore the semblance of capital-led gentrification. As part of government infrastructural development, it can be argued that gentrification holds a lot of prospects for urban regeneration especially in urban slums, shanties and blighted areas in a place like Lagos, particularly since the government is mostly involved in urban regeneration vide state-led processes. However, there is evidence that the processes have over the years been usurped by people with positional and financial advantages who with their vast resources take over the locations purposed for revitalization, build private properties on them with the sole purpose of maximizing profit from the real estate investments.

While events are still unfolding on this particular ongoing gentrification exercise, it becomes instructive to note that while the redevelopment of the area can indeed have positive impacts in terms of infrastructural upgrade and massive capital injection in the real estate sector, it's negative consequences cannot be discountenanced, and these includes displacement which causes homelessness, isolation and social dislocation. In most instances, particularly in the Otodo Gbame/Ebute Ikate's case, victims are never given resettlement considerations and as such are often left destitute, while the performances in school of their children who would have to change schools will be negatively impacted upon. Another major challenge is relocation expenses, which many of the victims of eviction may not be able to afford. There are also emotion difficulties likely from the disintegration of the family, as it is likely that many of them may not have the opportunity of continuing to stay together as one family.

This study therefore argues that while gentrification may have its positive contributions to a society, its negative aftermath often outweighs these positive ones particularly in an environment like Nigeria where it is done without any consideration for the affected victim. As such, the study concludes therefore that the Lagos state government had not made adequate plans to compensate the evicted people particularly since the real estate venture they have embarked on will generate revenue. The study also notes that conscious had not been made to rehabilitate the victims. In conclusion therefore, the study anticipates that future exercises of urban redevelopment by the state would be made to have a human face.

NOTES

1. Tunde Agbola and A.M. Jinadu, 'Forced Eviction and Forced Relocation in Nigeria: The Experience of those Evicted from Maroko in 1990', *Environment and Urbanization* 9, no. 2 (1997): 271–88; Raphael Olawepo, 'Perspectives on Urban Renewal and Transportation Development in Lagos: Implications for Urban Development in Nigeria', *African Research Review* 4, no. 1 (2010): 273–87; Olu Sule, 'Recent

Slum Clearance Exercise in Lagos (Nigeria): Victims or Beneficiaries?' *GeoJournal* 22, no. 1 (1990): 81–91.

2. Chinwe Nwanna, 'Gentrification in Nigeria: The Case of Two Housing Estates in Lagos', in *Global Gentrification: Uneven Development and Displacement,* edited by L. Lees, H. B. Shin and E. Lpoez-Morales, 311–26 (Bristol: Policy Press, 2015).

3. Bamidele Omotunde Alabi, 'Urban Renewal Schemes and the Plight of Internally Displaced Persons in Nigeria: A Study of Oke Ilu-Eri, Badia East, Lagos State', in *The African Metropolis: Struggles over Urban Space, Citizenship, and Rights to the City,* edited by T. Falola and B. Falola, 126–75 (New York: Routledge, 2018).

4. Grace Ka Lee, 'Factors Affecting Urban Renewal in High Density City: A Case Study of Hong Kong', *Journal of Urban Planning and Development* 134, no. 3 (2008): 140–8.

5. Tunde Agbola, 'Institutional Constraints on Housing Development: The Urban Areas of Ngeria: The Land Use Decree and the Building Plan Approval Processes', *Habitat International* 11, no. 2 (1987): 113–20.

6. Nwanna, *Gentrification in Nigeria*, 318.

7. Ruth Glass, *Cliches of Urban Doom* (London: Basil Blackwell, 1989).

8. Christine Kilmartin, *Port Phillip: Change and Gentrification* (Victoria: Urban and Regional Research Department of Sustainability and Environment, 2003).

9. Ruth Glass, 'Introduction: Aspects of Change', in *Center for Urban Studies* (London: MacGibbon and Kee, 1964).

10. United Nations, Department of Economic and Social Affairs (UN DESA), *World Urbanization Prospects: The 2014 Revision* (New York: Population Division, 2015).

11. UN DESA, *World Urbanization,* 91.

12. Lagos Bureau of Statistics (LBS), *Poverty profile of Lagos State* (Lagos: Ministry of Economic, Planning and Budget, 2014).

13. Josephine Abiodun, 'The Challenge of Growth and Development in Metropolitan Lagos', in *The Urban Challenge in Africa: Growth and Management of Its Large Cities*, eds. C. Rakodi, 192–222 (New York: United Nations University Press. 1997); Abass Owoade, 'Rapid Urbanization and Coping Strategies: The Case of Lagos', *Nigeria,* thesis submitted to the Department of Urban Planning and Environment Division of Urban and Regional Studies (Stockholm: Kungliga Tekniska Högskolan, 2007), 1–42; Olugbenga Akinmoladun and Jacob Oluwoye, 'An Assessment of why the Problems of Housing Shortages Persist in Developing Countries: A Case Study of Lagos Metropolis, Nigeria', *Pakistan Journal of Social Sciences* 4, no. 4 (2007): 589–98; Olusegun Akiyode, 'Urbanization and Human Security in Developing Economy Mega-City: A Case Study of Lagos. Nigeria', *Journal of Sustainable Development and Environmental Protection* 2, no. 3 (2012): 76.

14. Ministry of Physical Planning, Lagos State Urban Renewal Agency, 'Introduction' (Lagos: Ministry of Physical Planning and Urban Development, 2016).

15. World Bank, Project Appraisal Document on a Proposed Credit in the Amount of SDR 13 8.10 Million (US$200.00 Million Equivalent) to the Federal Republic of Nigeria for the Lagos Metropolitan Development and Governance Project (7 June 2006), 2.

16. Ibid., 2.

17. Lagos State Government, 'Lagos State Development Plan, 2012–2015' (September 2013), 48–9.

18. Laurent Fourchard, 'Lagos', in *Capital Cities in Africa: Power and Powerlessness*, edited by Simon Bekker and Göran Therborn (Pretoria: Human Sciences Research Council, 2012).

19. Fourchard, *Lagos* in *Capital Cities,* 67.

20. Robin Law, 'Trade and Politics behind the Slave Coast: The Lagoon Traffic and the Rise of Lagos, 1500–1800', *Journal of African History* 24 (1983): 321–48.

21. Fourchard, *Lagos* in *Capital Cities,* 67.

22. Ibid., 67.

23. Ayodeji Olukoju, 'Population Pressure, Housing and Sanitation in West Africa's Premier Port-City: Lagos, 1900–39', *Journal of the Australian Association for Maritime History* 2 (1993): 91–106.

24. Agbola and·Jinadu, 'Forced Eviction', 272.

25. Ibid., 272.

26. Lekan Oyefara and Bamidele Omotunde Alabi, 'Socio-economic Consequences of Development-induced Internal Displacement and the Coping Strategies of Female Victims in Lagos Nigeria: An Ethno-Demographic Study', *African Population Studies* 30, no. 2 (2016): 2520–32.

27. Jorge López de Obeso, *Urban Renewal and Controlled Gentrification: Housing and Urbanism* (London: Architectural Association London, 2003).

28. David Harvey, *Social Justice and the City* (Baltimore: Johns Hopkins University Press, 1973).

29. Roshanak Mehdipanah, Giulia Marra, Giulia Melis and Elena Gelormino, 'Urban Renewal, Gentrification and Health Equity: A Realist Perspective', *European Journal of Public Health* 1, no. 5 (2017): 1–5.

30. Mathias Bernt, Dieter Rink and Andrej Holm, 'Gentrification Research in East Germany: Conceptional Problems and Research Gaps', *Berichte Zur Dtsch Landeskd* 84 (2010): 185–203; Hamish Kallin and Tom Slater, 'Activating Territorial Stigma: Gentrifying Marginality on Edinburgh's Periphery', *Environmental and Plannning* A 46, no. 6: 1351–68; Rachael Granger, 'What Now for Urban Regeneration?' *Proceedings of the Institution of Civil Engineers in Urban Design and Planning*, 163 DP1 (2010).

31. Obeso, *Urban Renewal and Controlled Gentrification*, 48.

32. Bernt et al., 'Gentrification Research in East Germany'; and Hamish and Slater, 'Activating Territorial Stigma'.

33. United Nations, Department of Economic and Social Affairs (UN DESA). *World Urbanization Prospects*; Lagos Bureau of Statistics (LBS), *Poverty Profile*; Smith. 'Toward a Theory of Gentrification'.

34. Granger, 'What Now for Urban Regeneration', 9–16.

35. Heeji Lim, Jeeyeop Kim, Cuz Potter and Woongkyoo Bae, 'Urban Regeneration and Gentrification: Land Use Impacts of the Cheonggye Stream Restoration Project on the Seoul's Central Business District'. *Habitat International* 39 (2013): 192–200.

36. Glass, 'Introduction: Aspects of Change'.

37. Chinwe Nwanna, 'Gentrification in Lagos State: Challenges and Prospects', *British Journal of Arts and Social Sciences* 5, no. 2 (2012): 163–76.

38. David Ley, 'Gentrification and the Politics of the New Middle Class, Environment and Planning', *Society and Space* 12, no. 1 (1994): 53–74.

39. Neil Smith, 'Toward a Theory of Gentrification: A Back to the City Movement by Capital Not People', *American Planning Association Journal* 45, no. 4 (1979): 538–48.

40. Saskia Sassen, 'The Global City: Introducing a Concept', *Brown Journal of World Affairs* XI, no. 2 (2005): 27–43.

41. Amnesty International, *The Human Cost of a Megacity: Forced Evictions of the Urban Poor in Lagos, Nigeria* (London: 2017), 20.

42. Amnesty International, *The Human Cost of a Megacity*, 21.

43. Ibid., 21.

44. Ibid., 21.

45. Chandrasiri Niriella, 'Social Mobility and Class Formation: An Analysis of the Housing Market in Colombo, Sri Lanka', (Paper presented at the International Conference on Sustainable Built Environment, Kandy, Sri Lanka, 14–16 December 2012).

BIBLIOGRAPHY

Abiodun, Josephine. 'The Challenge of Growth and Development in Metropolitan Lagos'. In *The Urban Challenge in Africa: Growth and Management of Its Large Cities*, edited by C. Rakodi. New York: United Nations University Press, 1997.

Agbola, Tunde and Adele Jinadu. 'Forced Eviction and Forced Relocation in Nigeria: The Experience of those Evicted from Maroko in 1990'. *Environment and Urbanization* 9, no. 2 (1997): 271–288.

Agbola, Tunde. 'Institutional Constraints on Housing Development: The Urban Areas of Nigeria: The Land Use Decree and the Building Plan Approval Processes'. *Habitat International* 11, no. 2 (1987): 113–120.

Akinmoladun, Olugbenga and Jacob Oluwoye. 'An Assessment of why the Problems of Housing Shortages Persist in Developing Countries: A Case Study of Lagos Metropolis, Nigeria'. *Pakistan Journal of Social Sciences* 4, no. 4 (2008), 589–598.

Akiyode, Olusegun O. 'Urban and Human Security in Developing Economy Mega-City: A Case Study Of Lagos. Nigeria'. *Journal of Sustainable Development and Environmental Protection* 12, no. 5 (2010): ISSN: 1520-5509.

Alabi, Bamidele Omotunde. 'Urban Renewal Schemes and the Plight of Internally Displaced Persons in Nigeria: A Study of Oke Ilu-Eri, Badia East, Lagos State'. In *The African Metropolis: Struggles over Urban Space, Citizenship, and Rights to the City*, edited by T. Falola and B. Falola. New York: Routledge, 2016.

Amnesty International. *The Human Cost of a Megacity: Forced Evictions of the Urban Poor in Lagos, Nigeria*. London: Amnesty International, 2017.

Bernt Mathias, Dieter Rink and Andrej Holm. 'Gentrification Research in East Germany: Conceptional Problems and Research Gaps'. *Berichte Zur Dtsch Landeskd* 84 (2010): 185–203.

Fourchard, Laurent. 'Lagos'. In *Capital Cities in Africa: Power and Powerlessness*, edited by Simon Bekker and Göran Therborn. Pretoria: Human Sciences Research Council, 2012.

Glass, Ruth. *Cliches of Urban Doom*. London, Basil Blackwell, 1989.

Glass, Ruth. 'Introduction: Aspects of Change.' In Center for Urban Studies (ed.) *London: Aspects of Change*, i–xix. London: MacGibbon and Kee, 1964.

Granger, Rachael. 'What now for Urban Regeneration?' *Proceedings of Institution of Civil Engineers in Urban Design and Planning*, 163(DP1), 2010.

Harvey, David. *Social Justice and the City*. Baltimore: Johns Hopkins University Press. 1973.

Heeji Lim, Jeeyeop Kim, Cuz Potter and Woongkyoo Bae. 'Urban Regeneration and Gentrification: Land Use Impacts of the Cheonggye Stream Restoration Project on the Seoul's Central Business District'. *Habitat International* 39 (2013): 192–200.

Ka Lee, Grace. 'Factors Affecting Urban Renewal in High Density City: A Case Study of Hong Kong'. *Journal of Urban Planning and Development* 134, no. 3. https://doi.org/10.1061/(ASCE)0733-9488(2008)134:3(140)

Kallin, Hamish and Tom Slater. 'Activating Territorial Stigma: Gentrifying Marginality on Edinburgh's Periphery'. *Environmental and Planning* 46, no. 6 (2014). https://doi.org/10.1068/a45634

Kilmartin, Christine. *Port Phillip: Change and Gentrification*. Victoria: Urban and Regional Research Department of Sustainability and Environment, 2003.

Lagos Bureau of Statistics (LBS). *Poverty Profile of Lagos State*. Lagos: Ministry of Economic, Planning and Budget, 2014.

Lagos State Government (LSG), *Lagos State Development Plan, 2012–2015*. Lagos: LSG, 2013.

Law, Robin. 'Trade and Politics behind the Slave Coast: The Lagoon Traffic and the Rise of Lagos, 1500–1800'. *Journal of African History* 24, no. 3 (2009): 321–348.

Ley, David. 'Gentrification and the Politics of the New Middle Class, Environment and Planning'. *Society and Space* 12, no. 1 (1994): 53–74.

López de Obeso, Jorge. *Urban Renewal and Controlled Gentrification. Housing and Urbanism*. London: Architectural Association, 2003.

Mehdipanah, Roshanak, Giulia Marra, Giulia Melis and Elena Gelormino. 'Urban Renewal, Gentrification and Health Equity: A Realist Perspective'. *European Journal of Public Health* 1, no. 5 (2018): 243–248.

Ministry of Physical Planning, Lagos State Urban Renewal Agency. *Introduction*. Lagos: Ministry of Physical Planning and Urban Development, 2016.

Niriella, Chandrasiri. 'Social Mobility and Class Formation: An Analysis of the Housing Market in Colombo, Sri Lanka'. Paper presented at the International Conference on Sustainable Built Environment, Kandy, Sri Lanka, 14–16 December, 2012.

Nwanna, Chinwe. 'Gentrification in Lagos State: Challenges and Prospects'. *British Journal of Arts and Social Sciences* 5, no. 2 (2010): 163–176.

Nwanna, Chinwe. 'Gentrification in Nigeria: The Case of Two Housing Estates in Lagos'. In *Global Gentrification: Uneven Development and Displacement,* edited by L. Lees, H. Shin and E. Lpoez-Morales. Bristol: Policy Press, 2015.

Olawepo, Raphael. 'Perspectives on Urban Renewal and Transportation Development in Lagos: Implications for Urban Development in Nigeria'. *African Research Review* 4, no. 1 (2010). DOI:10.4314/afrrev.v4i1.58226

Olukoju, Ayodeji. 'Population Pressure, Housing and Sanitation in West Africa's Premier Port-city: Lagos, 1900–39'. *Journal of the Australian Association for Maritime History* 15, no. 2 (1993): 91–106.

Owoade, Abass. *Rapid Urbanization and Coping Strategies: The Case of Lagos, Nigeria.* Thesis submitted to the Department of Urban Planning and Environment Division of Urban and Regional Studies. Stockholm: Kungliga Tekniska Högskolan, 2007.

Oyefara, Lekan and Bamidele Omotunde Alabi. 'Socio-economic Consequences of Development-Induced Internal Displacement and the Coping Strategies of Female Victims in Lagos Nigeria: An Ethno-Demographic Study'. *African Population Studies* 30, no. 2 (2016). https://aps.journals.ac.za/pub/article/view/863

Sassen, Saskia. 'The Global City: Introducing a Concept'. *Brown Journal of World Affairs* XI, no. 2 (2005): 27–43.

Smith, Neil. 'Toward a Theory of Gentrification: A Back to the City Movement by Capital Not People'. *American Planning Association Journal*, 45, no. 4 (2007): 538–548.

Sule, Olu. 'Recent Slum Clearance Exercise in Lagos (Nigeria): Victims or Beneficiaries?' *GeoJournal* 22, no. 1 (1990): 81–91.

United Nations, Department of Economic and Social Affairs (UN DESA). *World Urbanization prospects: The 2014 Revision*. New York: Population Division, 2015.

World Bank, *Project Appraisal Document on a Proposed Credit in the Amount of SDR 13 8.10 Million (US$200.00 Million Equivalent) to the Federal Republic of Nigeria for the Lagos Metropolitan Development and Governance Project.* (New York: World Bank, 2006).

Chapter 10

Railway and the Transformation and Modernization of Kafanchan, 1927–1993

Gaius Jatau

INTRODUCTION

Transport is basic and essential for all societies and economies, at all times. For any economy to operate effectively and profitably, the regular movement of people and goods must be taken into consideration. More so, the importance of the transport sector must be seen in its capacity to promote an increasing proportion of the economy by absorbing a significant proportion of labour, capital and entrepreneurship among other resources. Generally, modern transportation systems in Nigeria started with British colonial rule, mainly for British imperialists' purpose. At independence in 1960, the Nigerian government inherited a transport system set up for the global interest of the British imperialists. The most popular was the railway system. However, not all towns or cities were linked with the railways. Kafanchan was one of the towns the railway system traversed, though it was later overtaken by road transport.

The railway transport system pre-dates its road counterpart in Nigeria. The simple reason for this is the fact that the development of the transport sector in Nigeria by the colonial administrators was primarily directed at evacuating the produce of the Nigerian economy. Railway a transport system capable of conveying bulky goods over long distances became naturally attractive. As a means of achieving the imperialists' objectives, the need to establish the railways was inevitable. The survey for the establishment of the eastern railway from Port Harcourt to Kafanchan ended in 1921, immediately after the survey, the construction started and ended in 1926, and by 1927, the railway began to operate until its decline in the early 1990s.[1] Kafanchan served as one of the biggest railway stations; because of its strategic location, it was linked by the eastern railway and the Baro-Kano rail lines. The railways enhanced socio-economic development of Kafanchan and environs in the colonial and post-colonial era.

To understand the role of the railway in the transformation of Kafanchan, this chapter is divided into following sub-sections: 'Theoretical framework', 'The construction of railway in Kafanchan', 'The railway and the socio-economic transformation of Kafanchan', 'The railway and social transformation of Kafanchan' and 'The railway and economic transformation of Kafanchan'.

THEORETICAL FRAMEWORK

This historical analysis on the railway and the transformation of Kafanchan needs theoretical explanation as a guide. There has been and still a debate on colonialism and its colonial infrastructures in Africa. Some argued it was for the development and civilization of African societies, while others argued, it was for their exploitation and underdevelopment.

This chapter uses the modernization theory for its analytical framework. The modernization school of thought view African societies before colonialism as being static, underdeveloped, uncivilized and barbaric. Therefore, the idea of modernization initially comes from a view of societies as having a standard evolutionary pattern by evolving inexorably from barbarism to ever greater levels of development and civilization.[2] By this view, it means to be modern or civilized, is the ability to replace African traditional ways of development with the Western type, so the supporters of modernization, typically view only Western societies as being really modern and civilized compare to non-western societies.

Though this perspective of modernization is western, it was what its proponents claimed that countries in Africa looked up to in achieving or attaining socio-economic development. By doing so, suggests African over dependence on the west in terms of economic development. In support of this, David Lerner argues that modernization refers to

> the process by which the less developed societies acquire certain characteristics common to the more developed societies which is activated by international or interstate relations whose component is to effect economic development.[3]

In social science, modernization refers to a model of an evolutionary transition from a 'pre-modern' or 'traditional' to a 'modern' society. Modernization theory explains the process to modernity within societies. The theory looks at the internal factors of a country while assuming that, with assistance, 'traditional' or 'pre-modern' societies can be brought to development in the same manner more developed societies have.[4] Modernization theory attempts to identify the social and economic variables such as schools, health centres, railways and others, which contribute to social and economic development of societies. This was the case of Kafanchan, for example, as a result of the railways; Kafanchan was transformed from a village to a sub-urban and full town in the 'Middle Belt Region' of Nigeria.[5]

CONSTRUCTION OF RAILWAY IN KAFANCHAN

Kafanchan is strategically located. It is the present headquarters of Jema'a Local Government Area in Kaduna state of Nigeria. It is located between Latitude 90 North and 90 7′N, and Longitude 80 2′E and 80 6′E, and occupies approximately 3072 square miles. It lies on the escarpment of the Jos Plateau 900 metres above sea level. It experiences climatic conditions similar to that of the savannah forests. Rain falls from March to October with an average fall between 136 and 162 mm annually, although sometimes it reached a maximum of 172 mm. Kafanchan town is bounded to the east, by Kagoro, to the north, by Zonkwa, to the west, by Gwong and Jaba (Kwoi), to the south, and south-east, by Sanga.

Kafanchan like Zonkwa, Jagindi-Station, Tsaunin-Kura and Kakuri-Kaduna became very important railway stations, centre of commerce and administration in the colonial period. The railway lines were constructed to link not only the major towns named earlier but also the neighbouring villages either by virtue of their location or relocation to rail areas. These areas were opened up for social and economic activities.

Baro-Kano Railway and the Nigerian Eastern Railway were significant to Kafanchan. However, the eastern railway line which took its roots from Port-Harcourt traversed Kafanchan and most areas in the southern part of Kaduna. The line reached Enugu in 1916, Markurdi in 1924 and Kafanchan in 1927.[6] In Kafanchan, and its environs, the railway construction began with a survey by two Railway Survey Parties namely, Mr Fleming party and Brown's. Fleming, the engineer in charge of the first party, entered the Province from the North and established himself at Fadan Kagoro, some miles north of Kafanchan (Jema'a); here he was joined by Mr Collingwood with a number of assistants. The second party led by Mr M.E. Brown, the District Engineer, entered the Province at a point about four miles south of Kaderko in Lafia Division, and thirty-six miles from Benue. The route followed by this party passed close to Lafia town and thence via Keffi, Wamba, to near the left bank of the Mada River which flows across the Jema'a (Kafanchan) and to Jagindi and Fadan Kagoro. The survey of the route through the province of the Nigerian Eastern Railway was practically completed at the end of December 1921.[7]

After the survey, construction commenced immediately at Kafanchan and was completed by 1927. Rail head reached Lafia at the end of 1923 and went over to Keffi-Akwanga road the same year 1923, at the end of 1924 reached Kogum River, Wasa to Jagindi in 1925, to Kafanchan-Kagoro-Manchok in 1926 and completed in 1927.[8] The rail line was extended in 1927 from Kafanchan to Jos, Kaduna and from Zaria to Kaura Namoda in 1929, and eastwards from Kano to Nguru in 1930.[9]

The railway was constructed and maintained regularly by the colonial administration using the community labour on the order of the district heads or the village chiefs and headmen. The colonial administration was very keen on the maintenance of the railway and other infrastructure because of their significance to the colonial economy that had to be achieved by all means at the expense of the indigenous people. The establishment and extension of the Eastern Railway line from Kafanchan to some major railway stations like Zonkwa, Iri, Tsauni-Kura and Kakuri-Kaduna fostered development in the socio-economic of Kafanchan, which transformed it in diverse ways. Such developments are discussed explicitly in the next section.

THE RAILWAY AND THE SOCIO-ECONOMIC TRANSFORMATION OF KAFANCHAN

The transformation of Kafanchan by the railway deserves special attention here. The extension of the Eastern Railway from Enugu to Kafanchan in 1927 was not without consequences for the socio-economic transformation of Kafanchan town. It resulted in the gradual phasing out of the pre-colonial economy that was based on the caravan trade and long-distance trek on foot. The railway which was supplemented by road transport replaced the donkey as means of transportation for long distance journeys. Far from being an end in itself, railway transport was a means to an end, the end being the evacuation of agricultural and mineral produce from the interior to the country of the coast by the colonialists and improved socio-economic activities of the indigenous people. This objective, however, was realized in the development of railway for the evacuation of ginger from Kafanchan region, groundnuts from far north, palm produce from the south and many others. To underscore the section on the transformation of Kafanchan by the construction of the railway, we here examine the social and economic factors.

THE RAILWAY AND SOCIAL TRANSFORMATION OF KAFANCHAN

The railway played a dominant role not only in bringing about structural changes in the economy but also in the social changes. This was witnessed in the movement of the population away from traditional urban centres and villages to new emerging centres along the railway lines and stations. Many sub-urban centres emerged around Kafanchan as a result of the railways, for example, the extension of the Eastern Railway line to Kafanchan in 1927 led to the development of the following major railway stations: Kogum-River, Jagindi-Station, Kafanchan, Kagoro, Manchok, Fadan-Atakaad, Madakiya, Zonkwa, Kamuru-Station, Kurmin-Biri, Iri-Station, Tsauni-Kura and Kaduna.[10] Some of these stations transformed to urban centres and modern cities.

Kafanchan is best example of the relationship between population movements and the emergence of sub-urban centres. The establishment of Kafanchan as a railway station attracted people from within the area and around the country. From 1927 onwards, Kafanchan experienced a rapid population growth leading to structural expansion. Colin R. Walter, Esq., district officer in charge of Jema'a Division reported that 'originally Kafanchan Railway Junction is a busy and important junction, it inevitably grew and attracted settlers, traders, contractors and other people to the area'.[11] The migrants to Kafanchan as railway junction town were from various ethnic nationalities such as Igbo, Yoruba, Ibibio, Ijaw, Edo, Nupe, Idoma, Tiv, Jukun, Ekoi, Igala, Gbagy, Chamba, Kanuri, Hausa, Fulani, Kadara, Kurama, Koro, Biram, Eggon and Mada.[12] Most of them were railway workers and traders and thus increased the population of Kafanchan, turning it into one of the largest settlements of not only railway workers and traders, but of other migrants in search of better economic opportunities.[13] Indeed, during the early stages of the development of Kafanchan, its population had a significant number of migrants from other parts of the country and a few whites that came as a result of the railway construction work and colonial rule. Of all the ethnic groups or nationalities mentioned, there were considerable numbers of Igbo, Yoruba and Hausa. Many of these immigrants provided various services at the railway station, as railway workers or traders and a good number of them acquired plots of land to build their personal houses.[14] For example, a ninety-six-year-old Alhaji Umar Mohammed, a trader in local goods like slippers, wallets, trousers, and shirts from Kano, popularly known in Kafanchan town as Baba Umaru, remembered the glorious days of Kafanchan as a railway town, which attracted him. He claims:

> I sold all the goods without stress and that was how I started coming to trade from Kano. I was not the only one coming. Traders were bringing their goods from the west and east for trading. Our business was booming, and I decided to relocate with my family from Kano to Kafanchan, to consolidate on my growing business.[15]

Since 1940, the number of Igbo immigrants kept increasing dramatically in Kafanchan. Some are permanently settled in Kafanchan who came there as railway staff, traders or businessmen. Between 1940 and 1991, the number of Igbo in Kafanchan and environs rose to over 8000 though the number reduced during the civil war in 1967–1970 as some of the Igbo retired back to their indigenous home and returned after the civil war.[16] After the civil war (1967–1970), their numbers increased until the recent perennial crises that reduced their numbers in Kafanchan to slightly above 2000.[17] Today, some of them are permanent 'settlers' in Kafanchan. Chima Okoli a businessman is over eighty years of age, is permanently based in Kafanchan and is the Igwe (chief) of Igbo in Kafanchan. Deacon Awoniyi, a seventy-year-old man says:

> We came to Kafanchan in the 1950s principally because of the railway constructed in 1927. I was a Head teacher and retired into business and remain in the business till date. Some of my kinsmen came as railway workers, traders and businessmen in terms of trading and contract work. Today, we are close to 500 in Kafanchan town.[18]

Having a community of different people from various areas of the country promoted socio-economic development and enhanced the integration of Kafanchan people with other Nigerians. The immediate impact of immigration into Kafanchan was its emergence and transformation as a sub-urban centre. In providing the background into the construction of the Kafanchan railway station, Abdulrauf Akinwoye, the public relations officer of the Nigerian Railway Corporation in Kafanchan, stated that available records showed that it was the railway that founded Kafanchan as a town. He argues that before the advent of the Railway Corporation in Kafanchan, hence, the popular slogan of the Nigerian Railway Corporation in Kafanchan: 'No railway, no Kafanchan'. He further states, 'Railway discovered the town Kafanchan like many other towns in the country'.[19] According to him, the Nigerian Railway Corporation by virtue of its influence acquired vast land in Kafanchan for building projects and other facilities. For example, the Kafanchan township stadium was built for the railway football club before it was relinquished to the government.

These accounts do not mean that Kafanchan did not exist as a settlement; they only show the importance of the railway in transforming Kafanchan from a village to a sub-urban status. For example, Ibrahim James maintains that what the immigration facilitated by the railway did to Kafanchan was to transform it from a village to become one of the largest settlements of railway workers and traders in the Middle Belt Region of Nigeria.[20] In support of Ibrahim James, Baba Umaru, a migrant trader, says that Kafanchan as a railway junction became transformed into a town with the coming of more people. Before its transformation to a town, Kafanchan lacked tarred roads and electricity; they came with the railway. As more people came to Kafanchan, so did business expand, this informed him to relocate from

Kano to Kafanchan with his wife and two children because of business along the railway.[21]

The movement into Kafanchan because of the railway promoted marriages which enhanced intergroup relations between the nationalities and the indigenous Kafanchan people. Musa Gaiya, a retired railway worker in support of these relations maintains that the railway increased the population of Kafanchan and other areas like Zonkwa and Kaduna since its construction up to the early 1980s. Many of the nationalities moved to settle in Kafanchan, some worked with the railway; some were traders and have since become well established traders up to date in Kafanchan.[22] For example, Patrick Ozemoya from Edo whose father was a railway worker settled in Kafanchan got married to a Kagoro woman, an indigene of Kafanchan area, and today they are resident in Kafanchan and Kagoro. Patrick maintains:

> Railway is the heart of Kafanchan. . . . Fifty to sixty percent of non-indigenous people . . . the Igbo, Yoruba, Delta, and Edo are based today in Kafanchan, their parents were railway staff that stayed and gave birth to them in Kafanchan. A great number of them got married to natives of Kafanchan, I as an example, married to a Kagoro woman.[23]

Marriages and the formation of associations and cultural groups in Kafanchan since the 1960s to the early 1980s promoted integration, intergroup relations and cultural heritage where people learn to appreciate and respect not only their group but other groups for unity and peaceful co-existence. This is a clear indication that in the early years of the railway system, and after independence, people from different areas in Nigeria found themselves in Kafanchan either as traders, businessmen and women or as railway workers. Having different people from various areas of the country promoted socio-economic activities and enhanced cultural integration of Kafanchan people.

The population of Kafanchan kept increasing, this is exemplified by the 1991 Population Census of Nigeria's Population Distribution in Local Government Areas, where the number of households in Jema'a (Kafanchan) numbered 25,884 while the distribution by sexes goes for 72,239 (Males), and 66,481 (Females) giving the total of both males and females 138,720.[24] The continuous migration and increase in the population of Kafanchan town was not without the demand for social facilities. There was the need for more social and communication services such as health, schools, post-office and electricity to take care of the increased population. Thus, the small general hospital which was already in use since 1929 to cater for the health of the railway workers, traders, the entire district, and the surrounding villages was expanded first in the late colonial period and also in the post-colonial period to cater for thousands of people in Kafanchan and environs. For example, in

1957 Kafanchan hospital had two thirty-bed wards, two sixteen-bed wards, a few doctors and nurses.[25] Between 1960 and 1993, the same hospital had become transformed with well-equipped modern facilities and standard bed wards that accommodated the over 120 in patients with many doctors and nurses.[26]

Educationally, the railway opened up Kafanchan to more schools established by the missionaries who were waiting for opportunity to preach the gospel through schools. The incessant influx of the immigrants as a result of the railway provided the dare need for more schools and other infrastructural facilities in Kafanchan and environs. The Christian missions that came with the railways were pioneers in establishing schools in the area. The missionaries in different denominations, which included the Roman Catholic Mission (RCM), the Sudan Interior Mission (SIM), the Christian Missionary Society (CMS), the Sudan United Mission (SUM) and many others, augmented the colonial government's effort by establishing schools between 1934 and 1940, while some missions established both schools and churches in Kafanchan; some established churches and health centres.[27] One of the philosophies of the RCM was that they waited until the area is opened in terms of increase in settlement and population then they will develop schools. The railway that opened up Kafanchan made them together with the Evangelical Missions (EM) under the SIM and the Anglican Mission opened schools in Kafanchan. For instance, they established College of Mary Immaculate Kafanchan in 1939.[28] Many people in the surrounding areas of Kafanchan moved to Kafanchan for school and settled their either temporary or permanently. This development enhanced rapid growth in population, increased social activities and expansion in settlements.

Another social infrastructure that was introduced as a result of the railway in Kafanchan was the post-office. The post office had a departmental sub-office in 1928 which rendered postal services to customers apart from money savings. The postal system as a means of communication was used to receive and dispatch messages, articles and other transactions including money, prior to the banking system. For example, in 1949, a bigger post-office was built in Kafanchan and centrally located adjacent to the railway station for easy handling of mails.[29] This helped to improve communication and greatly contributed to the development of Kafanchan and environs. Similarly, in Zonkwa and Kaduna, post offices were built for the same purposes during the period.

The accounts on the social infrastructure and communication networks established at the beginning to cater for a small population received a boost in the post-colonial era especially in the 1970s through the 1990s, because of the increasing population. The railway in Kafanchan promoted and transformed not only the social but as well the economic activities of the people in different ways. Some of the migrants and indigenous Kafanchan people were employed to work with the railway and post office as clerks, messengers, attendants and cleaners.

THE RAILWAY AND ECONOMIC TRANSFORMATION OF KAFANCHAN

The introduction of the railway system in Kafanchan encouraged the production of ginger in large quantities. Ginger, one of the widely cultivated crops in Kafanchan area like cotton in Zaria region, was cultivated in large quantity for export by railing from Kafanchan railway station to the ports for shipping. Ginger was one of the major cash crops produced and railed, this transformed the economy and benefitted the people of Kafanchan area, they were able to pay their taxes and send their children to school, from ginger produce. According to colonial report, between 1940 and 1952, there was rapid increase in the volume of railway cargos of green, fresh ginger from Kafanchan to the ports. The increase is illustrated in table 10.1.

The illustration in the table shows the volume of green and fresh ginger railed from Kafanchan and other areas within the region. The volume as noted kept increasing after every three years since the inception of the railway in 1927. Kafanchan over the years was second to Kurmin Biri in terms of the volume of green and fresh ginger railed to the ports. This helped to foster trade and the development of trading centres not only in Kafanchan but in areas like Zonkwa, Kamuru, Kurmin-Biri and Kachia, which served as both producing and collective centres for ginger. The chief producing centres in Kafanchan area alone were mainly: Jaba, Kagoro, Moroa, Tum, Kagarko, Koro, Kafanchan, Kurmin-Biri, Gidan-Waya, Godogodo, Jagindi and Kagoma.[30] These areas produced the kind of ginger in quality and volume required for export during the colonial period and even up to date, the same areas still produce and market ginger as the main cash crop.

Table 10.1. Green ginger railing in tons within the region, 1927–1953

Years	*Kafanchan Station*	*Zonkwa Station*	*Kamuru Station*	*Kurmin Biri*	*Total*
1927–1931	81	83	23	450	**637**
1932–1935	273	95	77	466	**911**
1936–1940	469	114	166	560	**1309**
1941–1944	545	183	117	617	**1462**
1945–1948	786	239	263	850	**3600**
1949–1952	878	348	271	1020	**2517**
1953	210	34	59	73	**376**
Total	**3242**	**1094**	**976**	**4036**	**10812**

Source: National Archive Kaduna (NAK) ZARPROF MKT/ 6 Ginger MKT.

Apart from ginger, other crops like cotton and groundnuts were cultivated in Kafanchan area, but in small quantities because of the nature of soil compared to Zaria and the far north whose soil allowed mass cultivation of these crops. This is confirmed in the statement of one colonial administrator, Mr J.E.C. Blackeney, who says:

> Although, due to the nature of soil in some areas, not all polities produce the desired cash crops in large quantities, frequently groundnuts, cotton, and tobacco were grown close to the hut of the village itself. In the neighborhood of Karshi in Jema'a, groundnuts are grown in an extensive scale, while cotton was but little grown.[31]

This is a clear indication that although cotton and groundnuts were grown in Kafanchan area, it was on a small scale compared to ginger that received wide cultivation because of the nature of the soil in the area. However, with the establishment of the Native Authority in Kafanchan, the headquarters of Jema'a division, the Authority under Zaria Province invested in the cultivation of cash crops like cotton, ginger and groundnuts. This was done through the provision of selected seeds on loan basis to be paid in similar quantities to the Native Authorities through district heads and village heads, and through propaganda by the trained staff of Agricultural Department in the extension service for improved production.[32]

The monetization of the economy and the introduction of a unified currency as a means of exchange imposed new basis of trade and socio-economic relationships in Kafanchan and environs. The producing and trading centres earlier mentioned, thus, led to the accumulation of wealth which became a mark of social status in Kafanchan.[33]

Apart from the role played by the Native Authority in the expansion of agricultural produce, the missionaries, following the establishment of the railway in 1927, improved in the development of Kafanchan lay-out and the extension programmes in agriculture. The Christian Missions initiated modernization and urbanization and influenced agricultural production in Kafanchan and environs. Individual missionaries planted fruit trees around their compounds and made vegetable gardens as well. These practices had demonstration effects on the indigenous communities and generated innovation diffusion. The SIM, SUM, Church Missionary Society (CMS), and the RCM, indeed sent out agricultural experts as missionaries. Kafanchan and communities around adopted the practice of planting economic trees around their compounds. Hence, the rapid growth and expansion of settlements in this region due to rising population brought about the replacement of gallery forest in the area with fruiting plants and economic trees.[34] Today, in Kafanchan and its surroundings, fruit plants and the planting of economic trees are common practices by the indigenous people.

The net effect of the railway was the rapid transformation in trade and commerce which was occasioned by the extension of both the local and long-distance trade routes. As the railway began to take shape, new trading and commercial centres were developed at strategic points on the lines most especially on the railway stations to link Kafanchan. For instance, Jagindi, Zonkwa, Kamuru, Dutsen-Bako, Kogum-River, Manchok, Kakuri-Kaduna (Railway Station), Tsaunin-Kura (Sabon-Tasha Kaduna) and nearly every railway station became large trading as well commercial centres; Kafanchan and these areas mentioned as a result of the expansion in trade and commerce became not only modern trading centres, but permanent settlements up to date.[35]

Increase in agricultural produce in these areas provided the need for exchange through trade and marketing and the means to enhance this was the railway. The railway also engendered inter-group trade between Kafanchan as a giant railway station with some areas like Zonkwa, Ugwar-Rimi, Kachia and Kurmi-Biri. They produced maize, corn and been-cake; the people of Gwong, Jagindi and Wasa-Station produced yams, cassava, maize and corn; and Kamuru, Dutsen-Bako, Iri and Kankumi produced livestock like goats, pigs and fowls, which were commonly needed by the people as means for livelihood.[36] The railway in its usual characteristics was the means for the transportation of these products, moving from one centre of exchange to another. For example, moving from Wasa to Kafanchan, to Zonkwa, Kamuru, Dutsen-Bako, Kachia, Kaduna and even to the far north.[37]

We could argue that with the aforementioned discourse on agriculture, trade and commerce as the main economic activities of Kafanchan, the railway played a vital role in this aspect of economy. It was through the railway that these products – ginger, cotton and groundnuts – were easily and cheaply evacuated not only within Kafanchan area but the North at large to the ports.

Importantly to note is that in as much as the railway played this vital role in the transformation of Kafanchan, it was not without the negative consequences on the socio-economic lives of the people. The railway had its negative impact on the socio-economic, and people of Kafanchan area. For instance, it is pertinent to note that the same railway system that boosted agriculture also affected its production. For example, the construction work on the railway affected farming work because the people had combine farming with construction, putting in some weeks for the construction and some weeks off for farming.[38] Indeed, labour recruitment for the construction of the railway in the area did not take into consideration the farming calendar of the people and made the farmers to lose some times they would have put on their farms to construction work. In fact, even after the construction work, some able men and women were still used for maintenance work at the railway side continuously.

Another development that affected agriculture during this period was the need to develop Kafanchan lay-out. The establishment of the railway in 1927 gave rise to the need for land to develop a lay-out in Kafanchan. The indigenous farmers who owed land most especially in the vicinity of Kafanchan junction was taken over for the construction of railway camps by the government without compensation. To confirm this, one of the Divisional Officers of Jema'a (Kafanchan) reports:

> A construction camp is merely a temporary camp of grass huts and usually destroyed by the construction authorities as soon as they have no further need of it, no compensation being paid to the rightful owners of the land for temporary use of their land. In this case, the camp was not destroyed and has gradually been grown owing to the influx of traders; contractors . . . these 'squatters' have in some cases started farming and have deprived the native community of Kafanchan pagan village of the use of their farm lands without right whatsoever.[39]

Of course, the non-indigenous people perhaps, after the construction work could not be engaged in doing one thing or the other, and cannot afford to rent a house, had no option than to live in old railway abandoned camps which also deprived the indigenous people of their farmlands for agricultural purposes; this invariably affected cash crops and food production in the area.

CONCLUSION

This chapter underscored the railway and its socio-economic transformation of Kafanchan in the colonial and post-colonial periods. The railway led to the growth in size and population of Kafanchan area, improved trade and commerce, agriculture, labour and socio-cultural integration over the years. The development of railway transportation system changed both the direction and structure of the economy and social status of Kafanchan and environs. While to the colonial authorities, the value of the railway was seen only in terms of the volume of import and export commodities it conveyed. To the indigenous Kafanchan people and migrants, its most telling effects was in the areas of fostering inter-group relations, integration and improved social and economic activities. This is to say that the provision of social and economic infrastructure, especially the railway by the colonial government, transformed Kafanchan. Though, the railway was meant to achieve the colonial interest, Kafanchan people found it beneficiary as they used it to develop themselves socially, economically and otherwise. Kafanchan like Zonkwa, Jagindi-Station, Tsaunin-Kura and Kakuri-Kaduna became very important railway stations, centres of commerce and administration in the colonial period.

The railway lines were constructed to link not only the major towns named earlier but also the neighbouring villages, either by virtue of their location or relocation to rail areas. These areas were opened up for social and economic activities.

Importantly, the colonial railway development in Nigeria is more than a single-way draining devise. It is an expandable framework for temporal and spatial interaction, for innovation spread and movement of people, goods and services in different directions. The positive impact of the railway on Kafanchan would be replicable, should the modern model of this rail transport network be introduced and its policies fully implemented not only in Kafanchan but in every part of Nigeria.

NOTES

1. T.F. Carlyle, 'National Archive Kaduna (NAK): Nasarawa Province Annual Report' no. 85 (1924): 34–35.
2. Abdullahi M. Ashafa. and Maryam, M. Jungudo, 'Understanding the Paradox of Modernization and Dependency in the Nigerian Defense System, 1970–90s', in *Studies in the Economic History of Nigeria since the Nineteenth Century*, eds. A. Olayemi O.O. Okpeh and W. Terhemba, 388–9 (Ibadan: HSN, 2017).
3. David Lerner, *Modernization and Change for the Third World,* (New York: 1972), 386–387.
4. Abdullahi and Maryam, 'Understanding the Paradox of Modernization and Dependency', 389.
5. Gaius Jatau, 'Railway Infrastructure and the Socio-economic Transformation of Southern Kaduna, 1927–1960', in *The Transformation of Central Nigeria, Essay in Honor of Toyin Falola*, ed. Sati U. Fwatshak (Austin: Pan-African University Press, 2017), 185. Also see Ibrahim James, *Studies in the History, Politics and Cultures of Southern Kaduna Peoples Groups* (Jos: Ladsomas Press, 1997), 119.
6. Ibrahim, *Studies in the History,* 119.
7. National Archive Kaduna (NAK): ZARPROF, 105P/1921 Zaria Province Annual Report for 1921.
8. T.F. Carlyle, 'National Archive Kaduna (NAK): Nassarawa Province Annual Report 1924' no. 85 (1924): 34–35. Also see Francis Jaekel, '*The History of the Nigerian Railway Vol. 2 Network and Infrastructures* (Ibadan: Spectrum Books Ltd., 1997), 189.
9. Ibrahim, *Studies in the History,* 119.
10. Gaius, 'Railway Infrastructure', 185.
11. National Archive Kaduna (NAK): JOSPROF 61/1928 Report No. 41 for year ending 31st.
12. December, 1927, para 18, 7.
13. Gaius, 'Railway Infrastructure, 185. Also James, *Studies in the History,* 121.

14. National Archive Kaduna (NAK): PLAPROF, 234 Resettlements Plan, Jema'a Division, 1931.

15. Maman Moses, 'Levels and Differentials in Fertility of Kafanchan: A Study in Population Geography' (M.A. Geography, Diss. ABU, Zaria, 1985), 51–54.

16. Ismail Mudashir, 'The Decline of Kafanchan Railway Town', 20th September 2009. https://dailytrust.com/the-decline-of-kafanchan-railway-town

17. Chima Okoli, interviewed in Kafanchan, September 2013.

18. Okoli, interviewed September 2013.

19. Deacon Awoniyi, interviewed in Kafanchan, September 2013.

20. Ibrahim James, *Studies in the History, Politics and Cultures of Southern Kaduna People Groups.* Jos: Ladsomas Press, 1997.

21. John Shiklam, *Kaduna Blazes Trail on Metro Rail Reference, http://www.allafrica.com/stories/2009o90793.html*, accessed on 20/09/2009.

22. John shiklam, *Kaduna Blazes Trail on Metro Rail Reference: allafrica.com/stories/2009o90793,html* 20th September 2009.

23. Musa Gaiya, interviewed at Kamuru-Ikulu, 24th April 2012.

24. Patrick Ozemoya, interviewed at Kafanchan, April 2013.

25. National Population Commission- 1991 Population Census of Nigeria Population Distribution in LGAs by Sex and Number of Households, 23.

26. National Archive Kaduna (NAK): ZARPROFMed/61 Kafanchan General Hospital, 1957.

27. Rahab Goroh, interviewed in Kafanchan General Hospital, 4th April 2013.

28. James Kantiyok, 'The Establishment and Development of Kafanchan Town, 1927–57', (B.A. History Project, ABU Zaria, 1975), 54.

29. Ibrahim, *Studies in the History*, 132–137.

30. NAK: ZARPROF 1734 Annual Reports, Zaria Province, 1952. Also 'Railway Infrastructure and the Socio-Economic Transformation of Southern Kaduna, 1927–1960', in *The Transformation of Central Nigeria, Essay in Honor of Toyin Falola*, 185.

31. Gaius, 'The Impact of the Colonial Economy', 2003, 58.

32. National Archive Kaduna (NAK): SNP10191P/1920 Nassarawa Province Jema'a Emirate, Jema'a District.

33. Christopher M. Turu, 'Imperial Policies and Ginger Industries in Colonial Nigeria: A Study of the Development and Marketing of Ginger Crop in Libi Ham of Southern Part of Kaduna State, Nigeria 1920–1960' (M.A. thesis, University of Jos, 1988), 171.

34. Paul M. Bonat, *Chiefdoms and Emirate in Southern Kaduna, A Historical Perspective,* (Kaduna: Image Printers, 2010), 30.

35. James, *Studies in the History*, 143.

36. James, *Studies in the History*, 119; Tobayas Idi, interviewed in Kafanchan, 14 April 2013.

37. Patrick Ozemoya, interviewed in Kafanchan, April 2013.

38. Ozemoya, interviewed, 2013.

39. 'National Archive Kaduna (NAK): ZARPROF, Zaria Province Report' no. 63 (September 1914), Memo No. 1133/14 from Ag. Resident Zaria Province, 28–9.

BIBLIOGRAPHY

Ashafa, Abdullahi M. and Maryam M Jungudo. 'Understanding the Paradox of Modernization and Dependency in the Nigerian Defence System, 1970–1990s'. In *Studies in the Economic History of Nigeria since the Nineteenth Century*, edited by A. Olayemi, Okpeh O. Okpeh and Terhemba Wuam, 386–405. Makurdi: Aboki, 2017.

Awoniyi, Deacon, interview by Gaius Jatau. 2013. *Railway in Kafanchan* (12 September).

Bonat, Paul. *Chiefdoms and Emirates in Southern Kaduna: A Historical Perpective*. Kaduna: Image Printers, 2010.

James, Ibrahim. *Studies in the History, Politics and Cultures of Southern Kaduna People Groups*. Jos: Ladsomas Press, 1997.

Jatau, Gaius. 'Railway Infrastructure and the Socio-Economic Transformation of Southern Kaduna, 1927–60'. In *The Transformation of Central Nigeria: Essays in Honor of Toyin Falola*, edited by Sati U. Fwatshak, 363–85. Austin, TX: Pan-African Press, 2017.

Kantiok, James. 'The Estblishment and Development of Kafanchan Town'. *Unpublished BA Project, Ahmadu Bello University, Zaria,* 1975.

Lerner, David. *Modernisation and Change for the Third World*. New York, 1972.

Moses, Mamman. 'Levels and Differentials in Fertility of Kafanchan: A Study in Population Geography'. *Unpublished BA Project, Ahmadu Bello University, Zaria,* 1985.

Turu, Christopher M. 'Imperial Policies and Ginger Industries in Colonial Nigeria: AStudy of the Development and Marketing of Ginger Crop in Libi Ham of Southern Part of Kaduna State, Nigeria 1920–1960'. *Unpublished MA Thesis, University of Jos,* 1988.

Chapter 11

Institutions, Inequality and Crisis of Developmental Regionalism in Africa

Ernest Toochi Aniche

INTRODUCTION

Inequality is natural, a fact of life, and in fact, as old as man, and yet contentious. It pervades all human societies. Inequality is hierarchy, diversity, relative, differential, dialectics and natural. Thus, inequality is not entirely or totally dysfunctional except when it becomes extreme or arises as a result of exploitation. Unfortunately, the modern world is defined by extreme inequality. Extreme inequality therefore is dysfunctional but moderate inequality is not. Moderate inequality is in fact developmental. There is need for the world to move from extreme inequality to moderate inequality.[1]

From economic, social and political points of view, the world is still defined by extreme inequality at individual, group or state levels. Economic, social and political inequalities remain extreme in all ramifications leading to economic disparity in terms of income, wages, assets, wealth and consumption; social exclusion, discrimination, classification and marginalization in the form of status, age, ethnic, race, gender, religion, education, intergenerational and social class; and political apathy, alienation and emasculation by way of political passivity, uneven political participation, unequal political opportunities, unfair political recruitment and unjust political power acquisition.

Globally, from the point of economic inequality, for example, the distribution of income remains uneven. In 2010, high-income countries with only 16% of the global population were estimated to generate 55% of global income. Whilst low-income countries with 72% of world's population (most of whom are in Africa) generated just above 1% of global income. An average gross domestic product (GDP) per capita of $2,014 in sub-Saharan Africa in 2010 compared unfavourably with regional GDP per capita of $27,640 in the European Union (EU) and $41,399 in North America. Indeed, the magnitude of income disparities across countries as well as across individuals and groups within a country is large. For example, inequality in disposable income rose in 65 out of 130 countries from 1990 to 2012. Income distribution has become increasingly unequal in most of countries in the past twenty years, particularly in African countries.[2]

From all indications, economically, socially and politically, there is widening international inequality between developed and underdeveloped countries of which Africa belongs to the latter. Whilst international politics is characterized by extreme inequalities, international inequality has been deeply politicized. Thus, the politicization of international inequality has fostered inequality of international politics. Extreme global inequality has serious implications for regional integration in Africa. To be sure, extreme international inequality here refers to the huge inequality gap between the developed countries of the west and underdeveloped countries of Africa.

Whilst, the literature on international inequality abounds but the point of departure of this study is to interrogate the nexus between extreme inequality of international politics as embedded in global political economy and worsening crisis of African integration. The research question investigated by this chapter is: Has extreme inequality of international politics deepened crisis of African integration? The chapter examines the option of post-neo-functionalism or post-neo-nationalism as a viable solution for resolving crisis of African integration.

UNDERSTANDING INTERNATIONAL RELATIONS AND INTERNATIONAL POLITICS

International relations or international politics takes place across national frontiers or state boundaries irrespective of how it is defined. However, it is noteworthy to state at this juncture that international relations or international politics has been defined variously. As such there is no one definition of international relations or international politics. Thus, there is need to classify and systematize these definitions for proper understanding. Thus, Aniche identified two main perspectives in the conceptualization of international relations and international politics which are state-centric and materialist perspectives or definitions.[3] Let us begin with state-centric definitions of international relations or international politics.

The two main common features of state-centric perspective of international relations or international politics irrespective of ideological persuasion are state-centric and power-centric. Thus, scholars who defined international relations and international politics from the perspective of state-centric definitions emphasize the primacy of state actors and argue that state is the most significant actor in the international relations and international politics, and defined international relations as simply inter-state relations or international politics as inter-state politics. Also, scholars who conceptualize international relations and international politics from the point of view, state-centric perspective see the essence of international relations and international politics as primarily struggle for political power, and thus, defined international politics as simply power relations.[4]

For example, Wright conceives international politics as 'relations between powerful groups, and these powerful groups are the states'.[5] Also, Morgenthau defines international politics as 'the struggle for power among nations'.[6] Thus, international politics can be seen from state-centric perspective as 'the struggle for state power which transcends state boundary'.[7] Similarly, Obasi Igwe refers to international relations as 'relations between international actors, especially but not exclusively state'.[8] In the same vein, Nnoli avers that 'international relations may be properly conceived as interactions among independent centers of force, and these independent centers of force are states'.[9]

For Nnoli, the state is the most significant actors in the international relations for the following reasons; one, the state monopolizes the legitimate use of force in any country, and thus, it is inconceivable to have another independent actor within the same territory, which acts against the wishes of the state. Two, it is the state that mobilizes the internal resources for participation in the international relations. Three, the participation of the state is crucial in making binding agreements or treaties, for determining custom duties or tariffs, and for fixing foreign exchange. Four, and last, the state carters for the welfare of the citizens at home and abroad, protects them from internal attack and extends the foreign enterprises wishing to invest in the country non-material assistance through the embassies of the state located in the foreign countries.[10]

However, Asobie enumerated certain defects of state-centric definitions of international relations and by extension in international politics. One, state-centric perspective is state-centred, and therefore, conceives international relations as essentially inter-state or inter-governmental relations. Two, state-centric definitions conceive international relations in abstract terms, and as such, see the object of international relations and international politics as struggle for power. Three, state-centric approach is superficial and results to a shallow conception of international relations and international politics by focusing on the states and activities of inter-governmental organizations. Four, state-centric perspective is essentially preoccupied with stability, and thus, hardly considers or unable to unmask the processes through which international relations and international politics are altered. Five, and last, state-centric approach does not focus on the primacy of material condition of existence such as objects of labour, instruments of labour, labour power and so forth. Therefore, it does not reveal the inter-connectedness of social phenomena. In other words, it does not expose the hidden forces behind international relations and international politics.[11]

On the other hand, Asobie materialist perspective of international relations and international politics is non-state-centric and not power-centric. It is rather human-centred and recognizes just like state-centric definitions that international society is formally divided into entities called state, but depart from state-centric view in that it does not regard the state as the critical or significant actor in international relations and international politics rather it sees social groups as the significant actors in international relations and international politics. Materialist or non-state-centric definitions also recognize that for activities of social groups to be described as international, they must cut across the boundaries of either state or similar independent political entities such as empires, colonies and so on belonging to different powers.[12]

Following from the aforementioned context, Asobie defines international relations from materialist perspective as 'the totality of political, economic and social interactions and processes among social groups that takes place across the territorial boundaries of state and other relatively autonomous political units or independent political communities'.[13] In the same vein, Ken Ifesinachi defines international politics from materialist conception as 'the struggle over means of sustenance which political actors pursue within the state and within the relationships of super-ordination and subordination transcending the boundaries of a nation-state'.[14] Similarly, Okolie defines international politics as 'a struggle over means of sustenance within the context of super-ordination and subordination relationships within the state and across state boundaries'.[15]

The import of the aforementioned definitions of international politics is that domestic politics and international politics are closely linked or intricately related that one cannot distinguish one from the other or demarcate the boundary between the two. It is indeed difficult if not impossible to determine or pinpoint where domestic politics ends and where international politics begins, vice versa. As demonstrated by linkage politics approach, the boundary between domestic politics and international politics is blurred because while domestic politics influences international politics, international politics shapes domestic politics.[16]

However, Asobie identifies explanatory merits of materialist definitions as follows; one, materialist perspective of international relations and international politics is human or people-centred in that it conceives international relations and international politics as inter-people relations or inter-group politics. Two, it studies international relations concretely since it regards the object of participating in international relations in terms of material condition of life such as objects of labour, instruments of labour and labour power. Three, it focuses on the primacy of the social condition of existence, and therefore, has a deeper insight into the nature and character of international relations and international politics. Four, as corollary to the aforementioned context, it exposes the hidden forces behind international relations and international politics and present in their nakedness as social classes or social movements. Five, it provides a comprehensive view of international relations and international politics in the sense that it encompasses the activities and interactions of state and non-state actors of transnational transactions and international non-governmental organizations. Six, and final, materialist perspective is preoccupied with change by dealing with social forces and their contradictions enabling it to identify and unveil the processes through which international relations or international politics is altered. Consequently, he insisted that materialist conception is superior to state-centric perspective.[17]

CONCEPTUALIZING AND MEASURING GLOBAL INEQUALITY

Inequality is the harbinger of class or put in another way, class is a product of inequality. Aniche defines class as 'a socio-economic and political stratification or division of societies on the basis of unequal or asymmetrical or differential access to social influence, economic resources and political power'.[18] Thus, class reflects all these divisions, stratifications, classifications or distinctions that are essentially based on unequal or differential access to social influence, economic resources and political power in every society. The aforementioned definition emphasizes the social, economic and political dimensions of class.

Just like class, inequality has social, economic and political dimensions. Economically, inequality is typically viewed as differential in income, wage, wealth and consumption.[19] Sen defines economic inequality as 'the fundamental disparity that permits one individual, certain material choices, while denying another individual those very same choices'.[20] Mckay noted that the aforementioned definition encompasses both inequality in opportunities and inequality in outcomes.[21]

Economic inequality therefore refers to how economic metrics are distributed among individuals in a group, among groups of the country, or among countries of the world. Generally, the three metrics of economic disparity or inequality include wealth, income and consumption. In other words, wealth inequality, income inequality and consumption inequality constitute as well as cause economic inequality. But wealth, income and consumption inequalities are closely interwoven and mutually inclusive.[22] Economic inequality is thus unequal or uneven distribution of economic resources like wealth, income and wage.

Litchfield defines inequality from economic point of view as 'the dispersion of a distribution, whether that be income, consumption or some other welfare indicator or attribute of a population'.[23] Economic inequality varies between societies, historical periods, economic structures and systems. Thus, it refers to cross-sectional distribution of income or wealth at any period of time.[24] Kuznets argued that levels of economic inequality are largely due to stages of development.[25]

Social inequality occurs when resources in a given society are distributed unequally or asymmetrically through norms of distribution that engender specific patterns along lines of socially defined categories such as gender, class, age, race, ethnic and religion. Social inequality is thus associated with racial inequality, gender inequality, age inequality, generational inequality and other status characteristics or categories and other forms of social exclusion and disparity.[26] Social inequality also connotes inequality of access to social services and social influences. Inequality, variation or disparity of access to education is an important factor in the creation of social inequality.[27]

Political inequality suggests differential or asymmetrical access to political power or inequality of opportunities to political recruitment. It is unequal access to binding decision-making apparatus of the political society. Political dimension of inequality is the inequality of political opportunities to political recruitment process of occupying authoritative decision-making machineries of the state. This connotes differing levels of political participation in democratic and electoral politics. It involves political marginalization and emasculation of certain group of people in the political decision-making process. For instance, women are under-represented in political and decision-making processes in most states.[28] Accordingly, Stiglitz noted that the reason for widening inequality is the use of political power created from wealth by certain groups to shape public policies that are materially beneficial to them.[29]

Apart from economic, social and political inequalities, there are individual inequality, group inequality, regional inequality, international inequality and global inequality. In other words, there are inequality of individuals, inequality of groups, inequality of households, inequality of regions or communities within a country, and global inequality between countries.[30] In this chapter, we are primarily concerned with international or global inequality which includes essentially though not exclusively inequality of individuals, groups, countries and regions in the world or globe.

Milanovic defines international inequality as 'inequality between countries'[31] or economic disparities between rich and poor countries. The economies of the world have developed historically unevenly such that entire geographically regions were left mired in poverty while others were able to minimize poverty rapidly or comprehensively. This aptly reflects the post–Second World War North-South divide between developed and Third World countries.[32]

For example, global economic inequality has been steadily rising since the early nineteenth century. Milanovic noted that global income inequality increased constantly from 1820 to 2002, with a significant rise from 1980 onwards.[33] Also, Cornia noted that inequality gap widened globally between the early 1980s and 1990s.[34] Ortiz and Cummins stated that given the huge global economic asymmetric; financing an equitable development agenda requires a degree of transfer from wealthy to the poor across three levels, namely, North-South transfers, South-South transfers and national transfers.[35] The justification for more equitable international distribution is stronger in this era of globalization. For globalization to be accepted, it will have to be globalization that benefits the majority, a globalization for all and not just for a privileged few. However, South-South transfers are already occurring in three main forms, and the most relevant to this chapter is regional integration.[36]

There are many indices demonstrating the extreme inequality within and between countries. There is growing body of evidence that economic inequality within and between countries has been increasing over the past two decades.[37] Indeed, income and wealth inequalities have been rising for some years.[38] A study of the World Institute of Developmental Economic Research at the United Nations University demonstrates this widening global inequality.[39]

From the foregoing, therefore, international or global inequality is not just inequality between countries but also inequality between individuals and groups within and outside countries. It is also inequality between regions of the world or globe vis-à-vis economic, social-cum-political inequalities. International inequality is cross-country, and cuts across countries of the world at individual, group, state and regional levels. Incidentally, it is geographically demarcated. Geographically, there is a widening gap between the North and South of the globe.

THEORETICAL PERSPECTIVE FOR EXPLAINING INTERNATIONAL INEQUALITY

One major theoretical perspective for understanding international inequality is neo-Marxism, which encapsulates four major variants or versions of dependency theories such as institutional, structural, centre-periphery and world-system theories. For instance, the institutionalists are concerned with inequality of states within the institutional framework of international organizations such as United Nations Security Council (UNSC), International Monetary Fund (IMF), World Bank and World Trade Organization (WTO). In the UNSC (by far the most powerful organ of the UN), any of the five powerful countries constituting the permanent membership can veto the decision of the UNSC on substantive matters. Also, both IMF and World Bank have weighted voting and absolute systems based on the economic strength of members as determined by their GDPs. In other words, the voting power or strength depends on the quota system and special drawing rights (SDR) which, in turn, are determined by the respective member states' economic strength as expressed in GDP. Each member qualifies for 250 basic votes and additional one vote for SDR from every 100,000 of its quota. Thus, the higher a member's quota, the larger its votes and stronger its influence on the policy and management of the institutions. Therefore, a member's influence on the policies and activities of the institutions depends on its voting power or the number of votes it controls.[40]

Consequently, the most influential members of the twin Bretton Wood Institutions (BWIs) are the 'Big Five'. The big five alone control over 40% of the votes and thirty-five countries can produce a majority vote of over 53% out of 181 members. Also, few highly industrialized countries control 47.58% votes while developing countries control just 37.68% votes in 1989. Africa countries in BWIs control only 8.60% in 1989. The implication is that the decisions and resolutions of the IMF and World Bank are determined by the richest and most influential members and not the conventional majority of the total number of member states. Thus, the United States in concert with few other developed countries (e.g. G.7) controls the decision making apparatus of the BWIs. There is in fact unequal participation or access to the decision-making machineries of members in the BWIs. The fact that the developed countries dominate the organizational structure of the UNSC, IMF and World Bank also put them in the position to dominate the decision-making process in these international institutions to their advantage and in their economic interest.[41]

The structural theory of Raul Prebish and Hans Singer is another version of dependency theory which argues that the world is composed of a few industrialized or developed countries of the North (mainly Western Europe and North America) and a larger less industrialized or developing countries of the south (mainly Africa) along international division of labour. Thus, while the industrialized countries of the North produce and export manufactured products to the less developed countries of the South, conversely, the less industrialized countries of the South produce and export primary goods to the industrialized countries of the North. This engenders unequal or asymmetrical exchange relations between these two sets of countries in favour of the industrialized countries of the North.[42]

For example, while the less industrialized countries export the primary products at very low prices to the industrialized countries; the industries in these industrialized countries transform these primary goods into manufactured products and export them at very high prices to less industrialized countries. The difference between these two sets of products constitutes a surplus which is appropriated and accumulated by the industrialized countries. The relationship is thus asymmetrical, skewed, unequal or dependent not just in exchange relations (terms of trade) but also in trade volumes. The implication of this international division of labour is that less industrialized countries of Africa (linked through colonial and neo-colonial ties) trade more with the industrialized countries of the North than with their African counterparts in spite of many years of regional integration in the continent. The import of the aforementioned is that African economies are historically (colonially) linked, vertically integrated, structurally dependent on and neo-colonially tied to the western economies, thereby fostering relationship of dependence or inequality.[43]

This produces a situation where the most multinational corporations (MNCs) or transnational corporations (TNCs) originated from the developed countries of the North (particularly the Triad) such as United States, EU and Japan. The technical and strategic operations of these MNCs/TNCs are located in their home countries while their activities in the developing countries of the South such as Asia, Africa and Latin America are restricted mainly to the production of primary goods which are externally determined including the prices of primary goods. Thus, the structuralists focus on these factors of global capitalism which tend to preserve or actually increase inequalities between developed countries and underdeveloped countries in terms of economic, political, social and technological gap.[44]

Thus, it has been sufficiently demonstrated that in tandem with international division of labour, international division of the world into two sets of countries fosters relationships of dependence and inequalities. As a result, the industrialized countries with 13% of the world's population of about 500 million people receive 45% of the world's Purchasing Power Parity (PPP) income of over $11,500 annually. The developing countries comprising India, Indonesia and rural China with 42% of the global population of about 2.1 billion people receive only 9% of the world PPP income amounting to under $1,000 annually.[45] Also, with respect to wealth inequality, a 2006 report based on data from 2000 indicated that India dominated the bottom third of the global wealth distribution while the middle third of the distribution belonged to China.[46] More recent data in 2019 by World Poverty Clock showed that Nigeria overtook India to become global capital of extreme poverty. From the foregoing, the structuralists focus on inequalities among countries of the world, and not on inequalities among individuals within a country or across countries.

The centre-periphery model is another version of the neo-Marxist dependency theory of Andre Gunder Frank and Samir Amin. Centre-periphery (C-P) model of dependency theory divides the world into two, namely, the centre-nations (C) and the periphery nations (P). The centre nations (C) are the developed or industrialized countries of Western Europe and North America. The periphery nations (P) are the underdeveloped and less developed or developing countries of the Asia, Latin America and Africa. Unlike structural theory, the model went further to divide or subdivide the C and P into two classes of people or groups of people.[47] So within the centre nations, there are two classes namely the bourgeois and the proletarian classes. The bourgeois class occupies the centre of the centre nations and thus is the centre of the centre (CC) while the proletarian class occupies the periphery of the centre nations and therefore is the periphery of the centre (PC).[48]

Similarly, in the periphery nations (P), there are two classes, namely the indigenous bourgeois class (consisting comprador or petty bourgeoisie) and the proletarian or working class (Frank 1981). The indigenous bourgeois class occupies the centre of the periphery nations, and therefore, is the centre of the periphery (CP) while the proletarian class occupies the periphery of the periphery nations, and as such, is the periphery of the periphery (PP). The implications of the aforementioned postulations are enormous and can be portrayed as follows: one, there is harmony of interest between the CC and the CP. Two, there is conflict of interest between the PP and the CP. There is also a clash of interest between the CC and the PC. Four, there is disharmony of interest between the PP and the CC. Lastly, there seems to be however disharmony of interest between the PC and the PP.[49]

This last assertion is, however, paradoxically because both PC and PP occupy the same position in the social relations of production but the contradiction is easily resolved if one reckons with the fact, that, one, the PP is subjected to double exploitation by both the CP and CC. Two, the surplus generated from the exploitation of the periphery nations (P) by the CC is sometimes used for the welfare or wellbeing of the PC.[50] In other words, PC indirectly benefits from the surplus generated from the indirect exploitation of PP by CC and direct exploitation of PP by CP. It is this very fact that makes it impossible or difficult for the PP and PC to heed to the clarion call of Karl Marx for them to unite and overthrow the existing socio-economic formations through proletarian international movement or international movement of the working class or socialist/Marxist internationalism.[51]

However, the bottom-line of the entire argument is that the working class of the Third World countries is subjected to abject poverty and lack of access to basic necessities of life.[52] So, it presents a scenario where the working class of the developed countries of the North is living above poverty line, while their counterpart in the Third World countries like Africa are living below poverty line. There is indeed unequal and exploitative relationship between centre nations (C) and periphery nations (P). Furthermore, there are extreme inequalities between CC and PP and between CP and PP but moderate inequalities between CC and PC, and between CC and CP.

The next version of neo-Marxist dependency theory is world-system theory of Immanuel Wallenstein which he enunciated in response to some critiques levelled against dependency theories.[53] Unlike centre-periphery model which divided the world into bimodal system comprising the centre and periphery, world-system theory divides the world into a tri-modal system consisting of the core, semi-periphery and periphery.[54]

In the world systems theory, the semi-periphery lies between the core and periphery and is exploited by the core while it exploits the periphery.[55] The periphery suffers double exploitation from the core and semi-periphery in the unjust and unequal exchange relations. In other words, the periphery nations are being exploited directly by semi-periphery nations and both directly and indirectly by core nations in an asymmetrical trade relations.[56]

Therefore, the world-system theory captures the tri-modal economic relations existing among developed economies of the West, developing economies like China (arguably), India, Brazil and so on, and underdeveloped economies of Africa with possible exception of South Africa.[57] This tri-modal division of the world for Immanuel Wallenstein explains and compares the level of industrialization among countries.[58] In the end, there is more extreme inequality between the centre and periphery than between the core and semi-periphery or between the semi-periphery and the periphery. There could even be more inequality gap between the semi-periphery and the periphery than between the core and semi-periphery. This is because the periphery suffers double exploitation from the core and the semi-periphery. The periphery is exploited both directly and indirectly from the core, and directly from the semi-periphery.

INTERNATIONAL INEQUALITY AND DEEPENING CRISIS OF AFRICAN INTEGRATION

Indeed, the world is characterized by rising inequalities such as widening inequality gap between individuals, groups, states or even regions of the world like North and South, developed and underdeveloped countries, industrialized and less industrialized countries; and the First World and Third World countries. Thus, globally, the distribution of income remains very unequal. As a result, high-income countries with minority of the global population generate greater percentage of global income while low-income countries create much lesser of global income with overwhelming majority world's population. Also, an average GDP per capita in sub-Saharan Africa pales into insignificance when compared to regional GDPs per capita in the EU and North America.[59]

Extreme inequality arising from unequal exchange relations between industrialized countries of Western Europe and North America and underdeveloped or less industrialized African countries has serious implications for African integration. Indeed, the crisis of African integration is not unconnected with the rising international inequality between the North and South divide of the global politics or global political economy. The resultant effect is decimation, fragmentation and disintegration in Africa. As an indication of the aforementioned context, Africa accounted for least of world trade out of which non-oil exports accounted for greater percentage. The level of intra-African trade is also low which was 10% (on the average) compared to about 40% of North America and about 60% in Western Europe. Africa has the highest export product concentration coupled with a high export market concentration compared with other continents. This reflects continued reliance on primary product exports mainly to the EU, the United States and China. The African markets thus remain fragmented or decimated preventing emergence of regionally integrated industries and supply chains. This is in spite of over five decades of regional economic integration in Africa.[60]

More so, in most African countries, the contribution of manufacturing value-added (MVA) to GDP continues to be negligible. Manufacturing in the region is also generally dominated by the production of low-technology products such as clothing, textiles, leather, footwear and food stuffs; and very few of them like from South Africa have been able to participate significantly in the medium and high technology (MHT) segments of global manufacturing. Thus, most African countries remain heavily reliant on the production and export of a narrow range of agricultural, fuel and mining products.[61] Only few countries like South Africa has a complex manufacturing base.

Following this, African countries have similar economic structures and thus produce, import and export similar products. Rather than complementarities, there are competitions among them. Therefore, the scope of complementarities in their trade relations is often very limited partially related to why they currently trade so little with one another. The implication is the deepening vertical linkage and external or structural dependencies of African economies. Also, due to rentierism of most African economies, there is intra-regional dependencies in which some African economies are dependent on few others like South Africa. The point being made is that most of the African states are export-oriented primary producers whose primary products are in very little demand within the region.[62]

Africa is still confronted with some major development challenges, including pervasive poverty and marginalization in global trade. Also, Africa is currently confronted by a number of trade-related challenges. The share of Africa's exports in total world exports is only about 4%. Other challenges include poor infrastructure and supply-side constraints. Essentially, African exports are directed outside the continent. At 10.2%, the share of trade that is intra-African is very low compared with the fact that about 40% of North American trade is with other North American countries and 63% of EU trade is with other EU countries. Still, agricultural products (along with few other industrial goods) are the products most likely to be traded within the region.[63] The point is that intra-African trade is weak partly because basic elements of trade logistics are deficient. Trade constraints such as inadequate infrastructure make trade physically difficult.[64]

Therefore, infrastructural challenges in Africa remain indisputably frightening. For example, Africa with about 14% of the global population produces only about 3% of the world's electricity. Power consumption in Africa is only about 10% of the developing world. Also, in most African countries, power shortages are the norm. This causes Africa's firms to lose a significant percentage of their sales, while the economic costs of power outages in Africa are huge.[65] Africa accounts for only about 3% of global trade. The level of Africa's intra-regional trade is the lowest among the regions of the world.[66]

In addition, the market concentration of African exports is strong. For example, the share of Africa's exports to other regions of the world shows a concentration in primary goods and a lack of export diversification. African products exported outside the continent are mainly to just a few partners.[67] Thus, Africa registers balance of trade deficits. Comparing Africa's exports to the rest of the world against its imports from the world also suggests a certain lack of self-sufficiency in basic foods.[68]

Already, the role of regional hegemons like South Africa and Nigeria in promoting regional integration is causing tension as other countries perceive them to be pushing their domestic or national interests at the expense of regional interest.[69] Asymmetrical product complementarities in the region means that the more advanced economies of South Africa, Egypt and perhaps Nigeria are in much better position to market their exports leading to economic polarization and disparity as investments are attracted towards these economies thereby undermining African integration.[70]

Most African countries are dependent on tariff and other trade taxes for fiscal revenues frustrating tariff liberalization ultimately regional economic integration.[71] This is coupled with the fact that regional trade agreements are often not backed up by implementation, enforcement and support at the national level or by member countries.[72]

The subnational centrifugal tendencies like conflicts, violence, ethnic nationalism, religious intolerance, terrorism, insurrections and insurgencies, occasioned by various forms of inequalities and marginalization, are impeding Africa integration and in fact contrary to it. The political instability in some African countries renders the region risky for investments.[73] This is exactly what Echezona was referring to when he averred that the intractable conflicts within the member states of African Economic Communities (AEC) and the refuge crisis which they cause are the constant reminders that the African states are too fragile to engage in the pursuit of regional integration.[74]

Despite the recent formation of African Continental Free Trade Area (AfCFTA), there has been lack of progress, and in fact setbacks in African integration. Consequently, AEC has not been able to achieve its set out targets. Some good examples are EAC and SACU which surpassed a free trade arrangement by achieving customs union but are now jettisoning it to join SADC and COMESA in forming a tripartite free trade area (T-FTA) or tripartite EAC-SADC-COMESA free trade area as well as the newly formed AfCFTA.[75]

Thus, under AEC watch, the regional economic organizations have proliferated and steadily fragmented into various subgroupings leading to multiple memberships of African countries in the regional economic communities (RECs). Consequently, regionalism in Africa has been significantly undermined by overlapping memberships, several sub-groupings and proliferation of regional economic bloc. The resultant effects of all these is crisis in African integration engendered by extreme global inequality at individual, group, country and regional levels.

THE OPTION OF POST-NEO-FUNCTIONALISM

It is perhaps germane to state here that post-neo-functionalism or post-neo-nationalism is not a theory of nihilism that is to say that it does not advocate total or complete dismantling of regional integration in Africa. It only says that given the scale of global inequality that Africa is not yet ready for integration particularly in the areas of economy and politics, or put in another way that African states are not prepared for economic and political integration. In addition, post-neo-functionalism is not in sync with Marxism or neo-Marxist dependency theories that advocate delinking. However, post-neo-functionalism may be closer (especially at the initial stage) to mercantilism or economic nationalism than Marxism and neo-Marxism, and still distinct. Essentially, post-neo-functionalism is a synthesis of neo-nationalism, post-nationalism and humanism. The theoretical approach is essentially though not necessarily a two-phase approach to regional integration. In other words, post-neo-functionalism is a mixture of neo-nationalism, post-nationalism and humanism. Put differently, the first phase or stage of post-neo-functional approach to African regionalism is neo-nationalism and post-nationalism. This means that political-cum-economic nationalism (neo-nationalism) and regional security cooperation (post-nationalism) must be applied concurrently. There must be simultaneity in the adoption and application of nationalism in political and economic spheres and regionalism in security matters. This requires further clarification.[76]

For example, neo-nationalism is a blend of a new form of nationalism and protectionism. This means that neo-nationalism is a hybrid of political nationalism and economic nationalism. More importantly, neo-nationalism is geared towards the struggle against neo-colonialism, rentierism and dependency. It can also help in tackling the global extreme inequality as well as resolving the perennial conflicts in Africa.[77]

Therefore, there are two major components of neo-nationalism, namely, modern political nationalism and economic nationalism. As stated earlier, both of them constitute one of the two legs of the first stage of the two-phased post-neo-functional approach to African integration. Political nationalism is predominantly the political aspect of neo-nationalism, while protectionism or economic nationalism, on the other hand, is the economic sphere. Modern political nationalism is aimed at fostering national unity and integration through state-building and good governance in order to eliminate or at least reduce civil conflicts in Africa. This involves resolving national question of ethno-religious violence that pose enormous security challenges in Africa.[78]

The clog in the wheel of African integration is that countries that cannot achieve unity and integration at the national level cannot logically pursue integration at the regional level because charity begins at home. It is in vain that African leaders begin their own charity abroad. Thus, neo-nationalism side of post-neo-functionalism is proposing that economic and political integration should start at the national level (national integration) then progressively and logically proceed to regional level (regional integration), and possibly finally moved to global level (global integration or globalization).[79]

Whilst modern political nationalism is aimed at achieving national unity and integration, economic nationalism is geared towards achieving national development and perhaps industrialization. Economic nationalism does not advocate for complete closure of the economy from external economies. Rather it advocates partial closure of the economy and opening it up when the African economies must have been industrialized enough or close the inequality gap to the level of competitive advantage with other economies. Strategic or partial closure here suggests imposing tariff barriers or total ban on certain commodities (especially those ones which importation will be detrimental to achieving industrialization and national development). This requires protecting local industries against unfavourable competition from abroad. Check the history of today's industrialized economies and you will observe that they have at one point or the other practised protectionism before preaching free trade and liberalism. These include Britain, Germany, and the United States, and the newly industrialized countries (NICs) like China, and Asian Tigers. Therefore, protectionism should be targeted more on regulating free trade (i.e. importation of commodities and movement of migrant workers) than on free movement of capital (i.e. foreign direct investment). It is yet to be seen a state or a region which climbed the ladder of industrialization through regional integration.[80]

Perhaps what can be distilled from the aforementioned context is that African countries are not yet ready for regional economic and political integration owing to the fact that they are confronted by rentierism, mono-product economy, primary producing economy, de-industrialization, and as well as being decimated by internal armed conflicts. Most of European states that embraced neo-functional approach to regionalism that led to EU have transcended challenges of national unity, de-industrialization and national insecurity. Almost all the African countries are operating at the same level of productive activities and therefore have nothing to protect because those who do not produce have nothing to protect. This is the reason why there has been marginal progress in regional economic integration in the continent. This state of affairs reinforces international division of labour or relationships of dependence or inequality, rather than relationships of interdependence or equality.[81]

The next aspect of post-neo-functionalism is post-nationalism. This is the other leg of the two-staged theoretical approach to regional integration in Africa which must be operated simultaneously with neo-nationalism. It therefore transcends nationalism. In this regard, post-neo-functionalism prescribes regional cooperation in security matters at the inception which is a short-term strategy for curbing the tremendous security challenges in many states in Africa at the regional level. The achievements of ECOWAS and AU in peacekeeping, and the recent multinational forces of the four neighbouring countries (Nigeria, Niger, Chad and Cameroun) in combatting terrorism are all good examples. In other words, it advocates that regional security cooperation should precede regional economic integration, and even regional integration in political sphere. Some of the existing sub-regional and regional security organization like ECOWAS Monitoring Group (ECOMOG) and African Peace and Security Architecture (APSA) can be repositioned, strengthened, fortified and synergized to ensure continental peace and security. This is in tandem with neo-nationalism insistent that Africa is not yet prepared for regional economic and political integration and should proceed with national integration until such a time the continent is ripe for integration at the regional level in economy and politics.[82]

Humanism is another element of post-neo-functionalism. This is the second and final stage of post-neo-functional approach to African integration. It advocates that once the continent is ready for integration in the economic and political matters, that such regional integration should not only be allowed to evolve gradually but should as well be humane, humanistic, man-centred, people-driven or private sector-led so as to ensure people-to-people integration and bottom-up integration rather than the present state-driven, state-centric, top-bottom, public sector-led or inter-governmental integration of neo-functionalism.

It posits that regional economic integration should be championed by civil society organizations (CSOs) or non-state actors like African business persons and investors as well as labour unions. In this case, regional economic integration should be aimed at encouraging free movement of Africans and their businesses, investments, finances, capital and labour. By so doing, African businesses and firms become multinational and transnational, enabling them to bypass and circumvent both TBs and NTBs. It should be targeted at promoting large-scale merging or integration of African businesses, finances and capital into big conglomerates and cartels to compete with non-African MNCs and TNCs within and outside the continent or intra-regionally and extra-regionally. This will naturally render TBs and NTBs within Africa useless and common external tariff (CET) impotent. Logically, direct tax dependency will gradually replace tariff dependency in Africa.

This means that regional economic integration in Africa should not be integration of African economies or integration of economies of Africa per se. But rather it means that regional economic integration in Africa should foster integration of African businesses, firms, finances, and capital into African MNCs and TNCs bringing them up to speed with their non-African counterparts. In this way, the regional MNCs and TNCs will garner the competitive leverage regionally and globally. This may create inequality at individual and group levels within the continent but it will bridge the huge inequality gap between Africa and developed regions of the world. However, the rapid economic growth and development can be distributed in such way as to tickle down so as to reduce extreme inequality and engender moderate inequality between individuals and groups in the region through efficient social welfare policy.

The role of the state or government should only be to facilitate. In other words, the function of the states in African integration at this stage should be regulative. One of the positives of post-neo-functionalism is that it does not support artificialization of regional integration rather it suggests that regionalization should be allowed to evolve naturally. Post-neo-functionalism does not advocate artificial and fast-tracking of regional integration. The import of this is that once African integration is allowed to evolve gradually as driven by the African people and facilitated by the governments of African states, the incidence of multiple, duplicative and overlapping memberships, and subgroupings would not arise.[83] Post-neo-functionalism if adopted is likely to enable Africa to bridge the huge inequality gap in all ramifications and dimensions. Indeed, post-neo-functionalism is a panacea to extreme inequality within Africa and between Africa and developed regions of the world.

CONCLUSION AND RECOMMENDATIONS

We have noted that the modern world is defined by extreme inequality. Extreme inequality therefore is dysfunctional or defective but moderate inequality is not. Moderate inequality is in fact developmental and progressive. There is need for the world to move from extreme inequality to moderate inequality.

International inequality is not just inequality between countries but as well inequality between individuals and groups within and outside countries. It is also inequality between regions of the world or globe vis-a-vis economic, social and political inequalities. International inequality is cross-country, and cuts across countries of the world at individual, group, state and continental levels. Incidentally, it is geographically delineated. Thus, by focusing on primarily though not exclusively international inequality, this chapter concludes that extreme inequality of international politics as embedded in international political economy deepens crisis of African integration. The chapter argues that the current Eurocentric neo-functional approach to regional integration in Africa is not just a recipe for worsening crisis of African regionalism but also for widening the massive inequality gap between Africa and developed regions of the world.

The chapter recommends that post-neo-functionalism or post-neo-nationalism is a viable option for resolving crisis of African integration. This is a desideratum for reducing extreme inequality and engendering moderate inequality between individuals and groups in the region through efficient social welfare policy. It is the *conditio* sine qua non for alleviating extreme inequality within Africa and between Africa and developed regions of the world.

NOTES

1. National Archive Kaduna (NAK): No. K3079/5 SNP/1927, by the Divisional Officer Jema'a 28th September, 1927; Ernest Aniche, *A Modern Introduction to Political Science* (Onitsha: Desvic Publishers, 2009).

2. James Galbraith, *Inequality and instability: A Study of the World Economy just before the Great Crisis* (New York: Oxford University Press, 2012); Branko

Milanovic, 'Global Inequality Recalculated and Updated: The Effect of New PPP Estimates on Global Inequality and 2005 Estimates', *Journal of Economic Inequality* 10, no. 1 (2012): 1–18; Joseph Stiglitz, *The Price of Inequality: How Today's Divided Society Endangers our Future* (New York: W.W. Norton & Company, 2012); Engelbert Stockhammer, *Rising Inequality as a Root Cause of the Present Crisis* (working paper no. 282, Political Economy Research Institute, Massachusetts, 2012); Wu Hongbo, *Inequality Matters* (New York: UN Department of Economic and Social Affairs World Social Situation, 2013).

3. Aniche, *A Modern Introduction to Political Science*. See also Assisi Asobie, *Re-inventing the Study of International Relations: From State and the State Power to Man and Social Forces* (Nsukka: University of Nigeria Press, 2007). Derived from Asobie's classification as orthodox and radical perspectives.

4. Ibid.

5. Quincy Wright, *The Study of International Relations* (New York: Appleton-Century-Crofts, 1955).

6. Hans Morgenthau, *Politics among Nations: The Struggle for Power and Peace* (New York: Alfred A. Knopf, 1978), 6.

7. Aniche, *A modern Introduction to Political Science*, 6.

8. Obasi Igwe, *Politics and Globe Dictionary* (Enugu: Jamoe, 2002), 210.

9. Okwudiba Nnoli, *Introduction to Politics* (Ibadan: Longman, 1986), 200.

10. Ibid.

11. Asobie, *Re-inventing the Study of International Relations* cited in Aniche, *A modern introduction to Political Science*. Note that Aniche refined Asobie's classification from orthodox and radical perspectives to state-centric and materialist perspectives, respectively.

12. Ibid.

13. Ibid., 417.

14. Ken Ifesinachi, 'Collection of Lecture Notes & Mimeos' (n.d.), Department of Political Science, University of Nigeria, Nsukka, cited in Aniche, *A modern Introduction to Political Science*, 7.

15. Aloysius-Michael Okolie, 'Collection of Lecture Notes & Mimeos' (n.d.), Department of Political Science, University of Nigeria, Nsukka, cited in Aniche, *A Modern Introduction to Political Science*, 8.

16. Vincent Okeke and Ernest Aniche, 'Internal Political Environment of Nigerian Foreign Policy and Implementation of Citizen Diplomacy under Yar'Adua/Jonathan Administration (2007–2011): A Linkage Political Approach', *American Journal of Social Issues and Humanities (AJSIH)* 4, no. 1 (2013): 72–83.

17. Asobie, *Re-inventing the study of International Relations* cited in Aniche, *A Modern Introduction to Political Science*, 418.

18. Aniche, *A Modern Introduction to Political Science*, 67; Joshua Goldstein and Jon Pevehouse. *International Relations*. New York: Pearson Longman, 2008.

19. Andrew McKay, 'Inequality Briefing: Defining and Measuring Inequality' (briefing paper 1, Overseas Development Institute, London, 2002).

20. Amartya Sen, *Inequality Re-examined* (Oxford: Oxford University Press, 1995), 5.

21. McKay, 'Inequality Briefing'.

22. Anthony Atkinson, *The Economics of Inequality* (Oxford: Clarendon Press, 1983); Amartya Sen and James Foster, *On Economic Inequality* (Oxford: Oxford University Press, 1997); Serge Svizzero and Clem Tisdell, 'Income inequality between skilled individuals', *International Journal of Social Economics* 30, no. 11 (2003): 1118–30; William Easterly, 'Inequality Does Cause Underdevelopment: Insights from a New Instrument', *Journal of Development Economics* 84, no. 2 (2007): 755–76; Jonathan Ostry, Andrew Berg and Charalambos Tsangarides, *Redistribution, Inequality, and Growth* (Washington, DC: IMF, 2014).

23. Julie Litchfield, 'Inequality: Methods and Tools'. In *Inequality, Poverty, and Socio-economic Performance* (Washington, DC: World Bank, 1999).

24. Thomas Piketty and Emmanuel Saez, 'Income Inequality in the United States, 1913–1998', *Quarterly Journal of Economics* 118, no. 1 (2003): 1–41; Bram Lancee and Herman van de Werfhorst, 'Income Inequality and Participation: A Comparison of 24 European Countries' (discussion paper no. 6, Amsterdam Center for Inequality Studies, GINI Amsterdam, 2011); Anthony Atkinson, *Inequality: What Can Be Done?* (Massachusetts: Harvard University Press, 2015).

25. Simon Kuznets, 'Economic Growth and Income Inequality', *American Economic Review* 45, no. 1 (1955): 1–28 cited in Atkinson, *Inequality*.

26. John Goldthorpe, 'Analyzing Social Inequality: A Critique of Two Recent Contributions from Economics and Epidemiology', *European Sociological Review* 26, no. 6 (2010): 731–44; Dennis Gilbert, *The American Class Structure in an Age of Growing Inequality* (Los Angeles: Pine Forge Press, 2011); Christopher Doob, *Social Inequality and Social Stratification in US society* (New Jersey: Pearson Education, 2013); Scott Sernau, *Social Inequality in a Global Age* (Thousand Oaks, CA: SAGE, 2013).

27. McKay, 'Inequality Briefing'. See also Isabel Sawhill, 'Do We Face a Permanently Divided Society?' In *The Economics of Inequality, Poverty, and Discrimination in the 21st Century*, ed. Robert Rycroft (Washington, DC: The University of Mary, 2012).

28. Samantha Brennan, 'Feminist Ethics and Everyday Inequalities', *Hypatia* 24, no. 1 (2009): 141–59; Hadas Mandel, 'Winners and Losers: The Consequences of Welfare State Policies for Gender Wage Inequality', *European Sociological Review* 28, no. 2 (2012): 241–62.

29. Stiglitz, *The Price of Inequality*.

30. McKay, 'Inequality Briefing'.

31. Branko Milanovic, 'True World Income Distribution, 1988 and 1993: First Calculation Based on Household Surveys Alone', *The Economic Journal* 112, no. 476 (2002): 51–9. See also en.wikipedia.org/inequality. Accessed on 01/04/2020.

32. Nancy Birdsall, *Why Inequality Matters in a Globalizing World* (Helsinki: UNU-WIDER Annual Lecture, 2005); Branko Milanovic, *Global Income Inequality: The Past Two Centuries and Implications for 21st Century* (Washington DC: World Bank, 2011); Isabel Ortiz and Matthew Cummins, 'Global Inequality: Beyond the Bottom Billion – a Rapid Review of Income Distribution in 141 Countries' (working paper, UNICEF Social and Economic Policy, New York, 2011); Kim Weeden and David Grusky, 'The Three Worlds of Inequality', *American Journal of Sociology* 117, no. 6 (2012): 1723–85.

33. Branko Milanovic, 'Global Inequality and the Global Inequality Extraction Ratio: The Story of the Past Two Centuries' (working paper 5044, World Bank Policy Research, Washington, DC, 2009).

34. Giovanni Cornia, 'The Impact of Liberalization and Globalization on Income Inequality in Developing and Transitional Economies' (working paper no. 14, International Labor Office, Geneva, 2003).

35. Ortiz and Cummins, *Global Inequality*.

36. Branko Milanovic, *Worlds Apart: Measuring International and Global Inequality* (Princeton: Princeton University Press, 2005).

37. McKay, 'Inequality Briefing'.

38. Branko Milanovic and Shlomo Yitzhaki, 'Decomposing World Income Distribution: Does the World Have a Middle Class?' *Review of Income and Wealth* 48, no. 2 (2002): 155–78.

39. Ibid. See also Scott Neuman, *Oxfam: World's Richest 1 Percent Control Half of Global Wealth* (Washington, DC: National Public Radio, 2014).

40. Julius Aghohowa, 'The Marginality of Developing Member Countries in IMF's Policy Implementation Process: An Explanation', *African Political Science Review* 1, no. 1 (2000): 51–81; Vincent Okeke and Ernest Aniche, 'World Bank and public Sector Reforms in Nigeria (1999–2007)', *International Journal of Development Studies* IV, no. II (2012): 1–10.

41. Aja Akpuru-Aja, *Selected Themes in International Economic Relations: Understanding Trends of Globalization and Regionalization* (Enugu: Rhycee-Kerex Publishers, 2001); Ernest Aniche, 'The "Calculus" of Integration or Differentiation in Africa: Post-neo-functionalism and the Future of African Regional Economic Communities (RECs)', *International Affairs and Global Strategy* 36 (2015): 41–52.

42. Raul Prebisch, 'Commercial Policy in the Underdeveloped Countries', *American Economic Review* 49 (1959): 251–73. See also John Toye and Richard Toye, 'The Origins and Interpretation of the Prebisch-Singer Thesis', *History of Political Economy* 35, no. 3 (2003): 437–67.

43. Ibid. See also Joseph Love, 'Raúl Prebisch and the Origins of the Doctrine of Unequal Exchange', *Latin American Research Review* 15, no. 3 (1980): 45–72; Nduba Echezona, *International politics in Post-Cold War Era* (Awka: Meks Publishers, 1998).

44. Echezona, *International Politics in Post-Cold War Era*; Okeke and Aniche, 'World Bank and Public Sector Reforms in Nigeria'.

45. Danny Quah, 'Empirics for Growth and Distribution: Stratification, Polarization and Convergence Clubs', *Journal of Economic Growth* 2, no. 1 (1997): 27–59.

46. James Davies, Susanna Sandstrom, Anthony Shorrocks and Edward Wolff, *The World Distribution of Household Wealth* (Tokyo: World Institute for Development Economics Research of the United Nations University, 2006). See also en.wikipedia.org/inequality. Accessed on 01/04/2020.

47. Andre Gunder Frank, *Capitalism and Underdevelopment in Latin America: Historical Studies of Chile and Brazil* (New York: Monthly Review Press, 1969).

48. Andre Gunder Frank, *Latin America: Underdevelopment and Revolution* (New York: Monthly Review Press, 1970).

49. Samir Amin, *Imperialism and Unequal Development* (New York: Monthly Review Press, 1977); Andre Gunder Frank, *Dependent Accumulation and Underdevelopment* (London: Macmillan, 1978).

50. Andre Gunder Frank, 'Revolution in Eastern Europe: Lessons for Democratic Social Movements and Socialists?' *Third World Quarterly* 12, no. 2 (1990): 36–52.

51. Frank, *Capitalism and Underdevelopment in Latin America*; Karl Marx, *A Contribution to the Critique of Political Economy* (Moscow: Progress Publishers, 1970); Samir Amin, *Delinking: Towards a Polycentric World* (London: Zed Books, 1990).

52. Andre Gunder Frank, *World Accumulation, 1492–1789* (London: Macmillan, 1978).

53. Immanuel Wallerstein, 'The West, Capitalism, and the Modern World-System', *Review* 15, no. 4 (1992): 561–619.

54. Ibid. See also Ernest Aniche and Victor Ukaegbu, 'Structural Dependence, Vertical Integration and Regional Economic Cooperation in Africa: A Study of Southern African Development Community', *Africa Review* 8, no. 2 (2016): 108–19.

55. Immanuel Wallerstein, *Historical Capitalism* (London: Verso, 1983).

56. Immanuel Wallerstein, *The Modern World-System I: Capitalist Agriculture and the Origins of the European World-Economy in the Sixteenth Century* (New York: Academic Press, 1974); Aniche and Ukaegbu, 'Structural Dependence, Vertical Integration and Regional Economic Cooperation in Africa'.

57. Immanuel Wallerstein, *The Modern World-System III* (San Diego: Academic Press, 1989).

58. Immanuel Wallerstein, *World-Systems Analysis: An Introduction* (Durham: Duke University Press, 2004).

59. Milanovic, 'Global Inequality Recalculated and Updated'. See also Stiglitz, *The Price of Inequality*.

60. Mark Pearson, 'Trade Facilitation in the COMESA-EAC-SADC Tripartite Free Trade Area', and Sean Woolfrey, 'Industrial Development in the Tripartite Free Trade Area', In *Free Trade Area – towards a New African Integration Paradigm?* eds. Trudi Hartzenberg et al. (Stellenbosch: TRALAC, 2012); Ernest Aniche, 'Problematizing Neo-functionalism in the Search for a New Theory of African Integration: The Case of the Proposed Tripartite Free Trade Area (T-FTA) in Africa', *Developing Country Studies* 4, no. 20 (2014): 128–42; Ken Kalu and Ernest Aniche, 'China-African Economic Relation: A Double-Edged Sword for Africa', *African Journal of Economic and Sustainable Development* 7, no. 4 (2020): 374–90.

61. Ron Sandrey and Taku Fundira, 'Intra-industry Trade: An Examination of South Africa and the BRICS' (working paper, TRALAC, Stellenbosch, 2012); Woolfrey, 'Industrial Development in the Tripartite Free Trade Area'.

62. Aniche and Ukaegbu, 'Structural Dependence, Vertical Integration and Regional Economic Cooperation in Africa'.

63. Simon Mevel and Stephen Karingi, 'Deepening Regional Integration in Africa: A Computable General Equilibrium: Assessment of the Establishment of a Continental Customs Union', (Selected paper for presentation at the Seventh African Economic Conference, Kigali, Rwanda, October 30–2 November 2012).

64. AUC and UNECA, *Boosting Intra-African Trade: Issues Affecting Intra-African Trade* (Addis Ababa: AUC, 2012).

65. Ibid.

66. Ernest Aniche, 'Post-neo-functionalism, Pan-Africanism and Regional Integration in Africa: Prospects and Challenges of the Proposed Tripartite Free Trade Area (T-FTA)', in *State and Development in Post-independent Africa*, eds. Samuel Oloruntoba and Vusi Gumede, 155–74 (Austin, TX: Pan-African University Press, 2018).

67. Mevel and Karingi, 'Deepening Regional Integration in Africa'.

68. Ibid.

69. Woolfrey, 'Industrial Development in the Tripartite Free Trade Area'.

70. Tsidiso Disenyanai, *Towards an EAC, COMESA and SADC Free Trade Area: Issues and Challenges* (Johannesburg: South African Institute of International Affairs, 2009); Aniche, 'Problematizing Neo-functionalism in the Search for a New Theory of African Integration'.

71. Ibid.

72. Ibid. See also Woolfrey, 'Industrial Development in the Tripartite Free Trade Area'.

73. Disenyanai, *Towards an EAC, COMESA and SADC Free Trade Area.*

74. Echezona, *International Politics in Post-Cold War Era.*

75. Aniche, 'Problematizing Neo-functionalism in the Search for a New Theory of African Integration'.

76. Aniche, 'Post-neo-functionalism, Pan-Africanism and Regional Integration in Africa'.

77. Note that these conflicts have rendered Africa a crisis or troubled region. For detail analysis, see Ernest Aniche, 'The Brexit: A Massive Setback for European Union and a Lesson for African Integration. *Chinese Political Science Review* 5, no. 1 (2020): 13–30; Ernest Aniche, 'Pan-Africanism and Regionalism in Africa: The Journey so Far', in *Pan-Africanism, Regional Integration and Development in Africa*, ed. Samuel Oloruntoba, 17–38 (New York: Palgrave Macmillan, 2020); Ernest Aniche, 'From Pan-Africanism to African Regionalism: A Chronicle', *African Studies* 79, no. 1 (2020): 70–87, doi: 10.1080/00020184.2020.1740974.

78. Note also that to ensure good governance, there is need for a detribalized leader (not a nepotistic leader or a religious or ethnic champion) with the political will to carry out effective national policies of national integration, national unity and nation-building or even state-building. On this, see Ibid.

79. Note that this exempt or exclude regional security cooperation or integration of security affairs at regional level (post-nationalism) at this first stage of this two-staged theoretical approach which must operate *pari passu* with neo-nationalism. For more detailed explanation on this, see Aniche, 'Post-neo-functionalism, Pan-Africanism and Regional Integration in Africa'.

80. It should be noted that achieving industrialization and national development through economic nationalism requires not just patriotic leaders but also emergence of developmental elites to replace the present crop of rentier, neo-patrimonial, prebendal and predatory elites with political and economic will to enforce the mercantilist policies. For more clarification on this, see Aniche, 'The Brexit: A Massive Setback for European Union and a Lesson for African Integration'.

81. Ibid.
82. Aniche, 'Pan-Africanism and Regionalism in Africa'.
83. Jude Okafor and Ernest Aniche, 'Deconstructing Neo-functionalism in the Quest for a Paradigm Shift in African Integration: Post-neo-functionalism and the Prognostication of the Proposed Continental Free Trade Area in Africa', *IOSR Journal of Humanities and Social Sciences* 22, no. 2 (2017): 60–72.

BIBLIOGRAPHY

Aghohowa, Julius. 'The Marginality of Developing Member Countries in IMF's Policy Implementation Process: An Explanation'. *African Political Science Review* 1, no. 1 (2000): 51–81.

Akpuru-Aja, Aja. *Selected themes in International Economic Relations: Understanding Trends of Globalization and Regionalization*. Enugu: Rhycee-Kerex Publishers, 2001.

Amin, Samir. *Imperialism and Unequal Development*. New York: Monthly Review Press, 1977.

Amin, Samir. *Delinking: Towards a Polycentric World*. London: Zed Books, 1990.

Aniche, Ernest. *A Modern Introduction to Political Science*. Onitsha: Desvic Publishers, 2009.

Aniche, Ernest. 'Problematizing Neo-functionalism in the Search for a New Theory of African Integration: The Case of the Proposed Tripartite Free Trade Area (T-FTA) in Africa'. *Developing Country Studies* 4, no. 20 (2014): 128–42.

Aniche, Ernest. 'The "Calculus" of Integration or Differentiation in Africa: Post-neo-functionalism and the Future of African Regional Economic Communities (RECs)'. *International Affairs and Global Strategy* 36 (2015): 41–52.

Aniche, Ernest. 'Post-neo-functionalism, Pan-Africanism and Regional Integration in Africa: Prospects and Challenges of the Proposed Tripartite Free Trade Area (T-FTA)'. In *State and development in Post-Independent Africa*, edited by Samuel Oloruntoba and Vusi Gumede, 155–74. Austin, TX: Pan-African University Press, 2018.

Aniche, Ernest. 'The Brexit: A Massive Setback for European Union and a Lesson for African Integration'. *Chinese Political Science Review* 5, no. 1 (2020): 13–30.

Aniche, Ernest. 'Pan-Africanism and Regionalism in Africa: The Journey so Far'. In *Pan-Africanism, Regional Integration and Development in Africa*, edited by Samuel Oloruntoba, 17–38. New York: Palgrave Macmillan, 2020.

Aniche, Ernest. 'From Pan-Africanism to African Regionalism: A Chronicle'. *African Studies* 79, no. 1 (2020): 70–87, doi: 10.1080/00020184.2020.1740974.

Aniche, Ernest and Victor Ukaegbu. 'Structural Dependence, Vertical Integration and Regional Economic Cooperation in Africa: A Study of Southern African Development Community'. *Africa Review* 8, no. 2 (2016): 108–19.

Asobie, Assisi. *Re-inventing the study of International Relations: From State and the State Power to Man and Social Forces*. Nsukka: University of Nigeria Press, 2007.

Atkinson, Anthony. *The Economics of Inequality*. Oxford: Clarendon Press, 1983.

Atkinson, Anthony. *Inequality: What Can Be Done*? Massachusetts: Harvard University Press, 2015.

AUC and UNECA. Boosting intra-African Trade: Issues Affecting Intra-African Trade. Addis Ababa: AUC, 2012.

Birdsall, Nancy. *Why Inequality Matters in a Globalizing World*. Helsinki: UNU-WIDER Annual Lecture, 2005.

Brennan, Samantha. 'Feminist Ethics and Everyday Inequalities'. *Hypatia* 24, no. 1 (2009): 41–159.

Cornia, Giovanni. 'The Impact of Liberalization and Globalization on Income Inequality in Developing and Transitional Economies'. Working Paper No. 14, International Labor Office, Geneva, 2003.

Davies, James, Susanna Sandstrom, Anthony Shorrocks and Edward Wolff. *The World Distribution of Household Wealth*. Tokyo: World Institute for Development Economics Research of the United Nations University (UNU-WIDER), 2006.

Disenyanai, Tsidiso. *Towards an EAC, COMESA and SADC Free Trade Area: Issues and Challenges*. Johannesburg: South African Institute of International Affairs (SAIIA), 2009.

Doob, Christopher. *Social Inequality and Social Stratification in US Society*. New Jersey: Pearson Education, 2013.

Easterly, William. 'Inequality Does Cause Underdevelopment: Insights from a New Instrument'. *Journal of Development Economics* 84, no. 2 (2007): 755–76.

Echezona, Nduba. *International Politics in post-Cold War Era*. Awka: Meks Publishers, 1998.

Frank, Andre Gunder. *Capitalism and Underdevelopment in Latin America: Historical Studies of Chile and Brazil*. New York: Monthly Review Press, 1969.

Frank, Andre Gunder. *Latin America: Underdevelopment and Revolution*. New York: Monthly Review Press, 1970.

Frank, Andre Gunder. *Dependent Accumulation and Underdevelopment*. London: Macmillan, 1978.

Frank, Andre Gunder. *World Accumulation, 1492–1789*. London: Macmillan, 1978.

Frank, Andre Gunder. 'Revolution in Eastern Europe: Lessons for democratic social movements and socialists?' *Third World Quarterly* 12, no. 2 (1990): 36–52.

Galbraith, James. *Inequality and Instability: A Study of the World Economy just before the Great Crisis*. New York: Oxford University Press, 2012.

Gilbert, Dennis. *The American Class Structure in an Age of Growing Inequality*. Los Angeles: Pine Forge Press, 2011.

Goldstein, Joshua and Jon Pevehouse. *International Relations*. New York: Pearson Longman, 2008.

Goldthorpe, John. 'Analyzing Social Inequality: A Critique of Two Recent Contributions from Economics and Epidemiology'. *European Sociological Review* 26, no. 6 (2010): 731–44.

Igwe, Obasi. *Politics and Globe Dictionary*. Enugu: Jamoe, 2002.

Hongbo, Wu. *Inequality Matters*. New York: UN Department of Economic and Social Affairs World Social Situation, 2013.

Kalu, Ken and Ernest Aniche. 'China-African Economic Relation: A Double-Edged Sword for Africa'. *African Journal of Economic and Sustainable Development* 7, no. 4 (2020): 374–90, doi: 10.1504/AJESD.2020.10027708.

Kuznets, Simon. 'Economic Growth and Income Inequality'. *American Economic Review* 45 (1955): 1–28.

Lancee, Bram and Herman van de Werfhorst. 'Income Inequality and Participation: A Comparison of 24 European Countries'. Discussion Paper No. 6, Amsterdam Centre for Inequality Studies, GINI, Amsterdam, 2011.

Litchfield, Julie. 'Inequality: Methods and Tools'. In *Inequality, Poverty, and Socio-economic Performance*. Washington, DC: World Bank, 1999.

Love, Joseph. 'Raúl Prebisch and the Origins of the Doctrine of Unequal Exchange'. *Latin American Research Review* 15 (1980): 45–72.

Mandel, Hadas. 'Winners and Losers: The Consequences of Welfare State Policies for Gender Wage Inequality'. *European Sociological Review* 28, no. 2 (2012): 241–62.

Marx, Karl. *A Contribution to the Critique of Political Economy*. Moscow: Progress Publishers, 1970.

McKay, Andrew. 'Inequality Briefing: Defining and Measuring Inequality'. Briefing Paper 1, Overseas Development Institute (ODI), London, 2002.

Mevel, Simon and Stephen Karingi. 'Deepening Regional Integration in Africa: A Computable General Equilibrium: Assessment of the Establishment of a Continental Customs Union'. A selected paper for presentation at the 7th African Economic Conference, Kigali, Rwanda, October 30–November 2, 2012.

Milanovic, Branko. 'True World Income Distribution, 1988 and 1993: First Calculation Based on Household Surveys Alone'. *The Economic Journal* 112, no. 476 (2002): 51–9.

Milanovic, Branko. *Worlds Apart: Measuring International and Global Inequality*. Princeton: Princeton University Press, 2005.

Milanovic, Branko. 'Global Inequality and the Global Inequality Extraction Ratio: The Story of the Past Two Centuries'. World Bank Policy Research Working Paper 5044, Washington, DC, 2009.

Milanovic, Branko. *Global Income Inequality: The Past Two Centuries and Implications for 21st Century*. Washington, DC: World Bank, 2011.

Milanovic, Branko. 'Global Inequality Recalculated and Updated: The Effect of New PPP Estimates on Global Inequality and 2005 Estimates'. *Journal of Economic Inequality* 10, no. 1 (2012): 1–18.

Milanovic, Branko and Shlomo Yitzhaki. Decomposing World Income Distribution: Does the World Have a Middle Class? *Review of Income and Wealth* 48, no. 2 (2002): 155–78.

Morgenthau, Hans. *Politics among Nations: The Struggle for Power and Peace*. New York: Alfred A. Knopf, 1978.

Nnoli, Okwudiba. *Introduction to Politics*. Ibadan: Longman, 1986.

Okafor, Jude and Ernest Aniche. 'Deconstructing Neo-functionalism in the Quest for a Paradigm Shift in African Integration: Post-neo-functionalism and the Prognostication of the Proposed Continental Free Trade Area in Africa'. *IOSR Journal of Humanities and Social Sciences* 22, no. 2 (2017): 60–72.

Okeke, Vincent and Ernest Aniche. 'World Bank and Public Sector Reforms in Nigeria (1999–2007)'. *International Journal of Development Studies* IV, no. II (2012): 1–10.

Okeke, Vincent and Ernest Aniche. 'Internal Political Environment of Nigerian Foreign Policy and Implementation of Citizen Diplomacy under Yar'Adua/Jonathan Administration (2007–2011): A Linkage Political Approach'. *American Journal of Social Issues and Humanities* 4, no. 1 (2013): 72–83.

Ortiz, Isabel and Matthew Cummins. 'Global Inequality: Beyond the Bottom Billion – a rapid Review of Income Distribution in 141 Countries'. UNICEF Social and Economic Policy Working Paper, New York, 2011.

Ostry, Jonathan, Andrew Berg and Charalambos Tsangarides. *Redistribution, Inequality, and Growth*. Washington, DC: IMF, 2014.

Pearson, Mark. 'Trade Facilitation in the COMESA-EAC-SADC Tripartite Free Trade Area'. In *Free Trade Area – towards a New African Integration Paradigm?*, edited by Trudi Hartzenberg et al. Stellenbosch: TRALAC, 2012.

Piketty, Thomas and Emmanuel Saez. 'Income Inequality in the United States, 1913–1998'. *Quarterly Journal of Economics* CXVIII (2003): 1–39.

Prebisch, Raul. 'Commercial Policy in the Underdeveloped Countries'. *American Economic Review* 49 (1959): 251–73.

Quah, Danny. 'Empirics for Growth and Distribution: Stratification, Polarization and Convergence Clubs'. *Journal of Economic Growth* 2, no. 1 (1997): 27–59.

Sandrey, Ron and Taku Fundira. 'Intra-industry Trade: An Examination of South Africa and the BRICS'. TRALAC Working Paper, Stellenbosch, 2012.

Sawhill, Isabel. 'Do We Face a Permanently Divided Society?' In *The Economics of Inequality, Poverty, and Discrimination in the 21st Century*, edited by Robert Rycroft. Washington, DC, Baltimore: University of Maryland, 2012.

Sen, Amartya. *Inequality Re-examined*. Oxford: Oxford University Press, 1995.

Sen, Amartya and James Foster. *On Economic Inequality*. Oxford: Oxford University Press, 1997.

Sernau, Scott. *Social Inequality in a Global Age*. Thousand Oaks, CA: SAGE, 2013.

Stiglitz, Joseph. *The Price of Inequality: How Today's Divided Society Endangers Our Future*. New York: W.W. Norton & Company, 2012.

Stockhammer, Engelbert. 'Rising Inequality as a Root Cause of the Present Crisis'. Working Paper No. 282, Political Economy Research Institute (PERI), Massachusetts, 2012.

Svizzero, Serge and Clem Tisdell. 'Income Inequality between Skilled Individuals'. *International Journal of Social Economics* 30, no. 11 (2003): 1118–30.

Toye, John and Richard Toye. 'The Origins and Interpretation of the Prebisch-Singer Thesis'. *History of Political Economy* 35, no. 3 (2003): 437–67.

Wallerstein, Immanuel. *The Modern World-System I: Capitalist Agriculture and the Origins of the European World-Economy in the Sixteenth Century*. New York: Academic Press, 1974.

Wallerstein, Immanuel. *Historical Capitalism*. London: Verso, 1983.

Wallerstein, Immanuel. *The Modern World-System III*. San Diego: Academic Press, 1989.

Wallerstein, Immanuel. 'The West, Capitalism, and the Modern World-System'. *Review* 15, no. 4 (1992): 561–619.

Wallerstein, Immanuel. *World-Systems Analysis: An Introduction*. Durham: Duke University Press, 2004.

Weeden, Kim and David Grusky. 'The Three Worlds of Inequality'. *American Journal of Sociology* 117, no. 6 (2012): 1723–85.

Woolfrey, Sean. 'Industrial Development in the Tripartite Free Trade Area'. In *Free Trade Area – towards a New African Integration Paradigm?*, edited by Trudi Hartzenberg. Stellenbosch: TRALAC, 2012.

Wright, Quincy. *The Study of International Relations*. New York: Appleton-Century-Crofts, 1955.

Chapter 12

Trade Institutions, Trade Regimes and Challenges of Food Security in West Africa

Emeka C. Iloh, Ifeanyi P. Maduechesi and Chukwuemeka V. Muoneke

INTRODUCTION

Extant literature has blamed the low level of intra-regional trade in West Africa, especially in food staples, on poor road infrastructure, non-tariff and other administrative barriers, problems associated with the transfer of funds across countries, especially those with different monetary systems, growing insecurity and corruption on the part of border officials, customs and police personnel.[1] Others have blamed it on the failure to comply with regional agreements, inadequate implementation of programmes, non-coordination among countries, inadequate infrastructural and telecommunication systems, high cost of transportation, as well as protracted and cumbersome customs processes.[2] Extant literature has, therefore, largely overlooked the role of preferential agreements within the framework of the World Trade Organization (WTO) in this regard. Thus, this chapter tries to establish a nexus between these preferential agreements and intra-regional food trade in West Africa with the intention of determining how these agreements have undermined intra-West African trade on food staples, and by extension, food security in the sub-region. This will be done by examining the level of intra-regional food trade in West Africa since the establishment of the WTO in 1995 as well as the relevant preferential agreements allowed within the framework of the WTO.

The WTO permits extra-organizational agreements and partnerships. In other words, member states can engage in other mutually beneficial trade agreements with other states while retaining their memberships of the global trade body. West African countries have largely explored these preferential trade partnerships with food exporters and importers from outside the region for the supply and purchase of food staples. This has substantially affected intra-regional trade in agricultural and food products. Intra-regional food trade is fundamental for regional food security because it allows movement of food from surplus areas to deficit areas[3] as against diversion of trade to other regions which undermines food security. So, for several reasons which include need to have access to larger markets, opportunities to earn foreign exchange and impediments to inter-state movement of goods created by some countries in the sub-region, many West African countries prefer to trade with countries outside the sub-region, and consequently have entered into some form of preferential trade agreements with them. For instance, according to Staatz, Dembélé, Kelly and Adjao, Senegal once signed a five-year pact with India which guaranteed the importation of rice from India.[4] Many other West African countries have entered into such agreements in form of partnerships with foreign countries, blocs and regions.

This chapter, therefore, examines two of these preferential trade arrangements. The first is the Economic Partnership Agreements (EPAs) between the European Union (EU) and the African, the Caribbean and the Pacific (ACP) countries of which West Africa is a part. The second is the African Growth and Opportunity Act (AGOA) between the United States and eligible sub-Saharan African (SSA) countries. The idea is to examine the impacts of these partnerships on intra-regional food trade in West Africa as well as how the impact affects food security in the sub-region.

INTRA-REGIONAL FOOD TRADE IN WEST AFRICA

World Bank has argued that regional trade integration can have substantial impact on food security.[5] It can achieve this by connecting food producers to food consumers across countries, cushioning the negative impacts of occasional national food shortfalls and of increasing global food prices. In other words, food security within a region or among countries in a region could be enhanced if food producers trade across borders. West African countries and cities have long been engaging in intra-regional trade before the WTO was established in 1995. This trade dates back to the era of caravan trade before the colonization of the region.[6] For instance, long-distance trade flows between countries in the Sahel region and those in the coastal areas have been going on for a long period of time and they are often driven by ethnic and social ties. During the earliest period of this trade, staples such as cereals, animals (livestock) and cowpeas were being exported from the Sahelian region to the coastal region. There were also flows of cereals from the coast towards the northern part of West Africa, and countries and cities in the Sahel and coastal areas were importing fruits, tubers and vegetable from the Guinea savannah zone.[7] Thus, even before inter and intra-national trade were formalized and streamlined through the instrumentality of the WTO, West African countries have been trading amongst themselves, albeit informally, without state or supra-national involvement. In other words, serious intra-regional trade flows have been in existence for several years before institutional mechanisms were put in place to administer trade across borders.

Before the WTO, there has been an attempt in West Africa to create an institutional framework to regulate trans-border trade, with its main focus on promoting regional trade in agriculture and improving food security in the sub-region. The framework is the Permanent Interstate Committee to Combat Drought in the Sahel (CILSS), created in 1973 and which has nine countries in West Africa as members. These countries include The Gambia, Mali, Burkina Faso, Niger, Guinea Bissau, Cape Verde, Chad, Mauritania and Senegal. It was, in fact, a regional effort aimed at combating drought and desertification as well as promoting food security through the promotion of regional cooperation, policy coordination and capacity building.[8] Since its creation, CILSS has been providing both empirical research and fora for policy discussions for the purpose of promoting regional trade in agricultural products throughout the West African sub-region. It has also gotten the nod of ECOWAS to assist in leading the same efforts for the whole of the ECOWAS community.

An analysis of intra-regional food trade in West Africa reveals that north-south flows dominate the trade corridor.[9] This flow is mainly trade in livestock, originating from the northern part of the sub-region to the southern part. Thus, livestock flows from Chad, Niger, Mali, Benin, and Burkina Faso into Nigeria; from Cote d'Ivoire and Burkina Faso into Ghana; from Burkina Faso and Mali into Cote d'Ivoire; from Mali into Guinea; and from Mauritania into Senegal. On the other hand, cereals, roots and tubers flow from Nigeria into Niger; from Benin into Nigeria, Niger and Togo; and from Burkina Faso into Niger, Mali and Ghana. They also flow from Cote d'Ivoire into Burkina Faso, Mali, Guinea and Ghana; from Mali into Mauritania and Senegal; from Senegal into Guinea; and from Sierra Leone to Guinea. This is illustrated in figure 12.1.

Trade in food staples accounts for less than 10% of the value of intra-regional trade in West Africa.[10] About sixty-five metric tons of grains are annually produced in West Africa, but less than 3% of this is traded within the sub-region, while more than six million tons are imported from outside the region annually. As regards livestock, cross-border trade in the sub-region covers less than five million heads of livestock, when nearly 200 million heads covering all species are produced annually. This forces countries in West Africa to depend on international markets for about 45% of their animal protein needs.[11] Other staples such as tubers and roots do not also fare better as they equally circulate poorly within the sub-region.

Figure 12.1. Food staples trade flows in West Africa. *Source*: CILSS (2014).

Despite these given figures, it is indeed difficult to ascertain the level of food trade that takes place between and among all countries within West Africa. This is because as Keyser has noted, most of the trade in food staples that go on across borders in the sub-region do take place informally outside the legal system. According to him, small-scale traders constitute a greater percentage of all transactions going on across borders in West Africa where about 70% of intra-regional food trade among member states of ECOWAS is unrecorded.[12] World Bank also notes that most of the trade in food staples in West Africa does not reflect in official trade statistics.[13] This is because the preponderance of unofficial trade channels permits eversion of formal border posts through the many roads that connect countries. The Bank reports that in the Republic of Benin alone, there are about 171 informal trade crossing points, compared to about thirty official border posts. Citing the United States Agency for International Development (USAID), Josserand equally notes that about 66–80% of intra-regional trade in food staples in West Africa is not recorded officially.[14]

Hence, the World Bank notes that going by official figures, intra-regional food trade amounts to between US$ 750 million and US$ 1 billion and about 79% of ECOWAS intra-regional trade.[15] Livestock represents the bulk of these figures, with maize and millet following in that order. Burkina Faso, Mali and Niger rank as the largest exporters of livestock in the sub-region while Nigeria is the largest exporter of cereals and cassava. Nigeria, Ghana, Côte d'Ivoire and Senegal are also the largest importers of livestock from other West African countries while Niger, Senegal and Burkina Faso import maize the most. Benin, Ghana and Niger are the largest importers of sorghum and millet from other West African countries.[16] Most of these staples are smuggled into neighbouring West African countries where the prices of such commodities are higher. For instance, more than 10% of cocoa beans produced in Cote d'Ivoire are smuggled across the border into Ghana where prices of the commodity are more attractive.[17] This informal cross-border trade happens partly as a result of practices of some business men and companies, who choose to bypass formal institutions and procedures to avoid bottlenecks, reduce transit delays, ease border crossing and minimize the deterioration of perishable goods.

Keyser notes that most of this cross-border food trade in West Africa involves movements ranging from mere cross-border transactions between extended families and members of an ethnic group to trade dealings along traditional corridors which in some cases stretches over thousands of kilometres and covers numerous border posts.[18] For instance, traders in the Ashaiman market in Ghana travel as far as to the northern part of Togo about twice in a month to buy twenty to fifty bags of cowpea which they sell back home to consumers and to the other local traders in the market. Also, in most years, Niger and Mali import between 20,000 and 40,000 tons of maize from Burkina Faso. Depending on the level of demand, Burkina Faso also exports lesser volumes to Ghana, Benin and Togo.[19] There is also the trade route for maize between Techiman in Ghana and Niamey in Niger which stretches over 1100 kilometres across two borders. Another trade corridor exists between Kano in Nigeria and Dakar in Senegal (stretching over 3600 kilometres across four borders) where large volumes of sorghum move from the former to the later. Tomatoes and onions also travel across borders and are sold in regional markets.[20] The relevance of these transactions notwithstanding, the overall volume of intra-regional trade on food staples in the sub-region is considerably small and clearly below its potential.

Table 12.1 shows the percentage of ECOWAS imports of basic food staples from member countries in 2001 and 2016.

Table 12.1 shows that generally, these food staples imported into West Africa came from outside the sub-region. Only very few were imported from the sub-region. More worrisome is the fact that apart from fish and poultry meat, more of the other food staples (wheat, rice, sorghum and maize) were imported from ECOWAS countries in 2001 than they were in 2016. In other words, as the years rolled by, West African countries depended more on the rest of the world for wheat, rice, sorghum and maize than they depended on fellow West African countries. Thus, in 2001, while 3.5% of rice imported into West Africa originated from the sub-region, only 0.2% originated from West Africa in 2016. Likewise, while West Africa supplied itself 41% of

Table 12.1. ECOWAS imports of basic foods, by region, 2001 and 2016 (in percentages)

Product	2001		2016	
	ECOWAS	Rest of World	ECOWAS	Rest of World
Fish and other Aquatic Edibles	6	94	10	90
Poultry Meat	1	99	2	98
Wheat	0.3	99.7	0.1	99.9
Rice	3.5	96.5	0.2	99.8
Sorghum	41	59	13	87
Maize	15.5	84.5	3	97

Source: Authors' calculation based on ITC (2018) data.

all imported sorghum in 2001, the quantity went down to 13% in 2016. In the same vein, for maize, while 15.5% of all the staple imported into West Africa in 2001 originated from the sub-region, a mere 3% originated from the sub-region in 2016. Virtually all imported wheat into West Africa within the period came from outside the sub-region.[21]

Table 12.2 shows that food importation into West Africa is largely dominated by exporters from outside the sub-region.

WEST AFRICAN COUNTRIES' PREFERENTIAL AGREEMENTS WITHIN THE WTO FRAMEWORK

The ECOWAS Treaty and the ECOWAS Agricultural Policy (ECOWAP) are a reflection of an agreement among policy makers in the sub-region on the need to strengthen regional integration and trade for the purpose of taking the advantage of the complementarities that come from the various agro-ecological conditions and consumption patterns in West Africa. However, as AfDB and FAO have noted, in terms of trade policy, ECOWAS does not have an officially endorsed document analogous to ECOWAP which contains the objectives and vision for the development of trade in West Africa.[22] Instead, what could pass as ECOWAS' trade policies are derived from several regulatory documents and programmes which regulate different aspects of trade within the Community as well as how the Community manages its trade relations with the outside world. One of the most significant of these texts is the ECOWAS Trade Liberalization Scheme (ETLS).[23] As regards ECOWAS trade relations with countries outside the Community, they are governed by the multilateral and bilateral agreements ECOWAS member states have entered individually with those states. One significant example of these bilateral or multilateral agreements is the West African individual countries' trade relations with the EU through the now-expired EU/ACP accords and

Table 12.2. Trade flows for three strategic commodities into ECOWAS countries

			Maize					
	Rice		*Seed*		*Maize Products*		*Cassava*	
Period	*From ECOWAS*	*From rest of World*	*From ECOWAS*	*From rest of World*	*From ECOWAS*	*From rest of World*	*From ECOWAS*	*From rest of World*
1997–2000	2.511	307.002	1.829	13.936	155	5.232	59	45
2001–2004	8.500	719.620	5.086	18.863	457	13.779	21	222
2005–2008	14.757	1.470.369	3.106	45.839	563	29.102	77	721
2009–2012	28.712	3.161.592	N/A		9.397	81.287	N/A	N/A
2013–2016	39.719	2.852.260	N/A		9.008	116.944	N/A	N/A

Source: Extracted from Elbehri et al. (2013), 30–31; calculations based on ITC (2018) data.

their successor, the EPAs. The second is their trade relations with the United States through the AGOA.

ECOWAS as an organization is not a member of the WTO, though its member countries, with the exception of Liberia, are all members of the world trade governing body. What this means is that it cannot negotiate in the WTO on behalf of its members as the EU, for instance, does for its own members. This has two major implications for West African countries' trade relations with the rest of the world. The first is that countries that make up the Community do enter preferential trade relations with other countries outside the sub-region without recourse to the ECOWAS Common External Tariff (CET). In other words, member countries, irrespective of their commitments to ECOWAS, are exporting and importing goods to and from third countries as a result of bilateral agreements they have with these countries, with serious implications for intra-regional trade in the sub-region. The second implication of non-membership of ECOWAS in the WTO is that because each country in the sub-region negotiated its own terms and was admitted into the WTO on individual basis, there are no uniform terms of accession amongst these countries, especially with regard to openness to international trade, as seen in their different bound tariffs for different goods. For instance, for cereals, the level of openness is shown in the wide range of bound tariffs for these staples that the respective ECOWAS member countries accented to when joining the WTO. Thus, the level of openness for cereals ranges from as low as 15% for Cote d'Ivoire and as high as 150% for Nigeria. This would not have been the case if member states of ECOWAS had negotiated and joined the WTO as a bloc. The differences in bound tariffs are shown in figure 12.2.

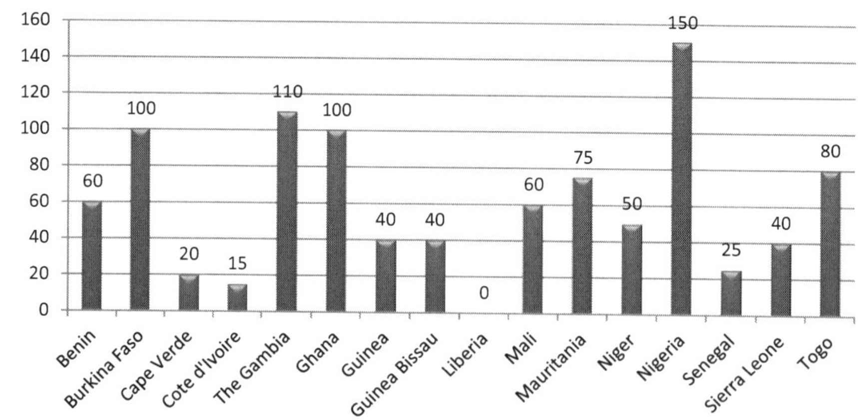

Figure 12.2. Bound agricultural tariffs for cereals in the ECOWAS under the Uruguay Round (percentage). ***Source*: AfDB and FAO (2015), 327.**

With regard to West African countries' trade relations with the EU under the EPAs, member states of ECOWAS gave the ECOWAS Commission their mandate to jointly negotiate with the West African Economic and Monetary Union (WAEMU) Commission for a regional EPA for West Africa (including Mauritania that is not a member of ECOWAS). The agreement for this Community-wide EPA was signed with the EU in October 2014. Prior to this period, trade relations between ECOWAS member states and the EU were on a country-by-country basis under what could be described as bilateral trade agreements. The EPAs arose from the Cotonou Agreement of 2000 which replaced the Lomé Conventions between ACP countries and the European Community. The Cotonou Agreement is meant to cover the period between March 2000 and February 2020. The Agreement was, however, revised in 2001 and 2010 in order to take into account some changes that have occurred in issues of security and regional integration.[24] The Cotonou Agreement replaced the Lomé Conventions to include reciprocal, WTO-compatible EPAs. The later was non-reciprocal (it was based on a system of preferences), and as a result, was not WTO-compliant. Under the Cotonou Agreement with the reciprocal arrangements, some products coming from ACP states would receive duty-free, quota-free (DFQF) access to the EU markets immediately. On the other hand, preferential access to ACP markets for EU products is phased in over a period up to twenty-five years. All these make it attractive to West African countries to have preference in trading with the EU to trading internally within the sub-region.

However, the Cotonou Agreement effectively expired on February 29, 2020, bringing an end to a trade framework between the EU and the seventy-nine-country bloc of ACP states. In anticipation of the end of the Cotonou Agreement, there was a launching of negotiations for a new EU-ACP partnership in New York in September 2018. The future agreement intends to focus separately on the three regional pillars that make up the ACP. Thus, ACP countries will have separate agreements with the EU. With respect to Africa in particular, the EU is already exploring new forms of partnerships, with the hope of taking it to 'another level', as well as initiating an international cooperation between the two continents 'based on rules-based multilateralism'.[25] On the other hand, there are also calls for Africa to quit any form of partnership with the EU. Stout is of the view that the EU does not treat its African counterpart, the African Union, as an equal partner, and as such, it is Africa's turn to quit the EU after Brexit. He notes that it is obvious that the EU would want to extend the terms, but African political leaders should reconsider whether it is wise for them to remain in a partnership that is antithetical to their development goals, an arrangement that is averse to the African integration project and which does not also respect them as equal partners.[26]

Table 12.3. West African countries' eligibility for AGOA, 2001–2017

	2001	*2002*	*2003*	*2004*	*2005*	*2006*	*2007*	*2008*	*2009*	*2010*	*2011*	*2012*	*2013*	*2014*	*2015*	*2016*	*2017*
Benin	X	X	X	X	X	X	X	X	X	X	X	X	X	X	X	X	X
Burkina Faso					X	X	X	X	X	X	X	X	X	X	X	X	X
Cape Verde	X	X	X	X	X	X	X	X	X	X	X	X	X	X	X	X	X
Cote d'Ivoire		X	X	X							X	X	X		X	X	X
Gambia			X	X	X	X	X	X	X	X	X	X	X	X	X	X	X
Ghana	X	X	X	X	X	X	X	X	X	X	X	X	X	X	X	X	X
Guinea	X	X	X	X	X	X	X	X	X		X	X	X	X	X	X	X
Guinea Bissau	X	X	X	X	X	X	X	X	X	X	X	X		X	X	X	X
Liberia							X	X	X	X	X	X	X	X	X	X	X
Mali	X	X	X	X	X	X	X	X	X	X	X	X		X	X	X	X
Mauritania	X	X	X	X	X		X	X		X	X	X	X	X	X	X	X
Niger	X	X	X	X	X	X	X	X	X		X	X	X	X	X	X	X
Nigeria	X	X	X	X	X	X	X	X	X	X	X	X	X	X	X	X	X
Senegal	X	X	X	X	X	X	X	X	X	X	X	X	X	X	X	X	X
Sierra Leone	X	X	X	X	X	X	X	X	X	X	X	X	X	X	X	X	X
Togo								X	X	X	X	X	X	X	X	X	X

Source: Extracted from the United States International Trade Commission (2014; 2018).
Key: X= Eligible for AGOA

For the AGOA, it was signed into law by former President Clinton on 18 May 2000 as part of the Trade and Development Act of 2000. The Congress, in its policy statement, gave its support to the Act:

> Encouraging increased trade and investment between the United States and sub-Saharan Africa . . . reducing tariff and nontariff barriers and other obstacles to sub-Saharan African and United States trade . . . expanding United States assistance to sub-Saharan Africa's regional integration efforts.[27]

AGOA provides countries in SSA a duty-free access to U.S. markets after meeting certain conditions. It strengthens the existing U.S. trade programmes by enlarging the scope of the (duty-free) gains formerly obtainable only under the Generalized System of Preferences (GSP).[28] As shown in table 12.3, all West African countries are beneficiaries of AGOA, though some countries lost the benefit in certain years for failing to meet the conditions of the programme.

Under AGOA, beneficiaries have duty-free access to the U.S. markets on products such as crude petroleum, agricultural products, manufactured products, natural resources and textiles/apparels. The implication of the above is that as long as West African countries meet with the conditions (as they have always met) of AGOA, they have free access to the U.S. markets to export agricultural products which include food staples. Unlike the EPAs that were negotiated jointly under the auspices of the ECOWAS and WAEMU Commissions, AGOA is a bilateral scheme between the U.S. government and each of the benefitting countries on individual basis. For several reasons which include unnecessary road blocks, lack of infrastructure and restrictions on free movement of goods and persons (even in a free trade area), West African countries have preferred trading with the United States under the AGOA arrangement than trading with regional neighbours, thereby undermining intra-regional trade, especially in food staples. As Oluwafemi et al. have noted, since the commencement of the agreement on AGOA, there has been obvious growth in the export of products under AGOA from African countries to the United States. Thus, the United States' preferential imports from countries under AGOA have risen impressively.[29]

EFFECTS OF PREFERENTIAL AGREEMENTS ON INTRA-REGIONAL FOOD TRADE IN WEST AFRICA

A proper understanding of the effects of preferential trade arrangements between the EU and West African countries will stem from appreciating the importance of EU to West Africa in terms of trade. To start with, West Africa is the biggest region of all ACP regions that negotiated an EPA in terms of trade, accounting for over 40% of all EU-ACP trade. Second, West Africa is not only the EU's biggest trading partner in SSA, but the EU is the largest trading partner of West Africa. Third, for West Africa's agricultural products such as textiles, agribusiness and fisheries, the EU is the main export destination.[30] While the EU is the main destination for West Africa's exports, West Africa represents a negligible market for EU exports as less than 1% of total EU exports are destined towards the ECOWAS region.[31] The EPAs ECOWAS countries had with the EU led to rapid trade creation effects for EU producers and exporters, the largest benefits for the EU accruing from its growing trade with Ghana, Côte d'Ivoire Nigeria and Senegal.

However, the most important effect of these trade arrangements with West African countries is that these arrangements have taken away trade from the sub-region. As ECA, 2005[32] has observed, these arrangements have led to substantial trade diversion from intra-regional trade among countries in West Africa, especially as it concerns Burkina Faso, Benin, Côte d'Ivoire and Ghana. In a Sustainability Impact Assessment (SIA) on the EPAs which was commissioned by the EU, the results indicated that with regard to food security, imported agricultural goods from the EU constituted an obstacle to local food production.[33]

As regards the effects on specific products, trade in milk and dairy products in West Africa has been hugely affected as a result of the EPAs. Milk production is an essential part of pastoralist livelihoods among the countries in the Sahel region of West Africa, which are the biggest producers of milk in the sub-region. As in 2005, milk represented the largest share of West African food imports from the EU (about 17%), and this has been on the increase. As a result of this increasing dependence on imports for local consumption, the consequent fall in demand for locally-produced milk has resulted in the decline in intra-regional trade in milk, forcing local producers out of business. On poultry meat, apart from Nigeria and Senegal that have banned its importation, there has been an increasing importation of poultry meat from the EU into West Africa from the time of GSP to the period of EPAs with dire consequences for local production and food security. The SIA results also showed that with the lowering of tariffs in ACP countries (as EPA demanded), EU exports of poultry food to West Africa expanded greatly, and this threatened local poultry production in West Africa. This came with serious implications not only for employment in the sub-region but also for production for the local regional market as well as for food security. The case of Ghana is very instructive in this context. The domestic market in Ghana supplied 95% of Ghana's poultry requirements in 1992 (pre-WTO and pre-EPA era), but by 2002, it provided only a dismal 11%.[34]

With regard to wheat and wheat flour, trade relations between the EU and countries in West Africa have resulted in a total trade effect of 12.5%. Again, Ghana experienced the largest shift in its import structure, where EU exports increased by 36.5%. On the other hand, Mauritania witnessed only a slight increase of 3.5%. On trade diverted away from West Africa, Benin and Niger diverted 18% and 16.5%, respectively, of their previously non-EU imports to the EU.[35] On tomato concentrate, exports of that commodity from the EU into Senegal jumped from 64 tons to 5348 tons between 1994 and 1996, limiting Senegal's importation of that product from other West African countries. As a result, not only have rural Senegalese tomato farmers been side-lined by that process, but also intra-regional trade has been adversely affected as neighbouring countries such as Mali and The Gambia similarly received the vast share of their demand through EU channels.[36] Table 12.4 illustrates U.S. agricultural trade profile with ECOWAS countries from 2007 to 2017.

One major reason why the main focus of West Africa's export destinations are outside the sub-region and continent is because currently, there are no trade preferences between Africa's regional integration communities. In other words, there are no attractions to export to neighbouring African countries as there are in exporting to Europe, United States and other destinations. For instance, in March 2001, as a Generalized System of Preferences (GSP) arrangement, the Everything-But-Arms (EBA) initiative was adopted by the European Community. The idea was to grant preferential access to the EU market to the Less Developed Countries (LDCs).[37] With the exception of arms and ammunition, EBA granted all products from LDCs (including West African countries) a duty-free access to EU markets, with no form of quantitative restriction. However, banana, rice and sugar were exempted from this initiative initially but were also later granted a duty-free quota-free access in January 2006, September 2009, and July 2009, respectively. This preference enabled many SSA countries to export their products to EU markets without much restriction. Such preferences are lacking in West Africa, thereby limiting intra-regional and intra-continental trade.

Table 12.4. Agricultural trade profile between the United States and ECOWAS, 2007–2017 ('000 dollars)

	2007	*2009*	*2011*	*2013*	*2015*	*2017*
US Exports to ECOWAS Countries	914,103	987,670	3,295,243	1,102,407	841,427	727,837
US Imports from ECOWAS Countries	91,837	161,310	1660	6711	12,129	88

Source: Extracted from Oluwafemi et al (2012: 30); authors' calculations based on ITC (2018) data.

A second example, as noted earlier, is the AGOA. It is a non-reciprocal trade preference programme which allows certain products from eligible SSA countries to enter U.S. markets without any form of duty being imposed on them.[38] It offers trade preferences to SSA countries that have adopted trade, investment and economic reforms as enshrined in the act. It is also intended to complement foreign aid to the benefitting countries. The most immediate benefit SSA countries derive from AGOA is the enlarged product set it covers under the Generalized System of Preferences (GSP), as well as the export of textile and apparel products which have tariff-and quota-free access to the U.S. markets.[39]

Promoting intra-regional trade is, therefore, fundamental for food security in West Africa. According to Terpend, the sub-region has experienced various food crises: between 1997 and 1998, 2002, and from 2004 to 2005.[40] There is also the food crisis of 2007/2008. In many ways, these food crises have shown the importance of intra-regional food trade. The most important is that the crises created new incentives for intra-regional trade because it allowed food-deficit countries to turn to neighbouring countries to fill their food deficit. For example, during the 2002 food crisis, Burkina Faso helped Niger to restock its safety reserves. This was made possible because of incentives provided by intra-regional trade. Also, during the 2004/2005 food crisis, food traders from Niger relied on food supplies from Ghana and Benin for the purchase of some staples such as maize. Burkina Faso also depended on Mali for importation of cereals after the food crisis of 1997/1998. Regional trade is, therefore, very important in enhancing food security. It allows movement of food from surplus areas to deficit areas. It also leads to efficiency gains as producers gain access to larger markets and can thus benefit from economies of scale within the sub-region. Hence, any constraints to intra-regional trade have severe implications for regional food security. Thus, it is certain that trade that is diverted from West Africa to the outside world through preferential trade arrangements has reduced both the quantity and value of trade that takes place within the sub-region, with negative implications for food security in the sub-region.

CONCLUSION AND RECOMMENDATIONS

This chapter demonstrated that preferential trade arrangements between West African countries and the EU and the United States have diverted food trade from West Africa to other parts of the world, thereby undermining intra-regional food trade in West Africa. It also revealed that the existence of preferential agreements within the framework of the WTO undermined intra-regional food trade in the sub-region. The analysis showed that food trade is often diverted to the EU and the United States under the EPAs and the AGOA arrangements. The effect of this has been that intra-regional food trade in the West African sub-region is adversely affected as countries in the sub-region prefer trading with the outside world because it offers them larger markets and other good incentives. Food security in West Africa becomes the ultimate victim as food staples can no longer move from food-surplus countries to food-deficit countries within the sub-region.

On the basis of the foregoing, therefore, this chapter concludes that the existence of preferential agreements within the framework of the WTO undermines intra-regional food trade in West Africa, thereby exacerbating food insecurity within the sub-region. Consequently, the chapter recommends as follows:

1. West African countries should aim at food self-sufficiency instead of food self-reliance. This will help the sub-region become less dependent on the food trade policies of Third World countries. In other words, West African countries will become immune from the changes and modifications in export and import policies on food staples of other countries.
2. As a corollary to the aforementioned text, national governments in West Africa should invest more in the agricultural sector so as to increase food availability as well as beef up the food production system in the sub-region, especially the innovation of family/smallholder farming. Reliance on international trade that is obviously biased against their food needs is not a strategy that can be sustained.
3. West African countries should urgently do away with discriminatory external tariffs and also lower the level of intra-regional tariffs that create trade barriers amongst themselves. It is these trade barriers that encourage trade diversion to the outside world thereby undermining intra-regional trade in the sub-region, with dire consequences for food security.
4. ECOWAS should fast track efforts to becoming a customs union, which is a prerequisite for a regional economic bloc to become a member of the WTO. If it becomes a full member, ECOWAS can negotiate in the WTO on behalf of all of its member countries as the EU does. There are several benefits of negotiating as a bloc, which includes having a stronger voice in the international economic system.

NOTES

1. African Development Bank (AfDB) and Food and Agriculture Organization (FAO), *Agricultural Growth in West Africa: Market and Policy Drivers* (Rome: AfDB and FAO, 2015).

2. Food and Agriculture Organization, *Why Has Africa Become a Net Food Importer? Explaining Africa Agricultural and Food Trade Deficits* (Rome: FAO, 2012).

3. Jeske van Seters, Dolly Afun-Ogidan and Francesco Rampa, 'Regional Approaches to Food Security in Africa: The CAADP and Other Relevant Policies and Programs in ECOWAS' (discussion paper, no. 128d, European Center for Development Policy Management, Maastricht, 2012).

4. John Staatz, Niama Dembélé, Valerie Kelly and Ramziath Adjao, 'Agricultural Globalization in Reverse: The Impact of the Food Crisis in West Africa', Background paper prepared for the Geneva Trade and Development Forum, Crans-Montana, 17–20 September 2008.

5. World Bank, *Africa Can Help Feed Africa: Removing Barriers to Regional Trade in Food Staples* (Washington DC: World Bank, 2012).

6. AfDB and FAO, *Agricultural Growth in West Africa*. See also Bio Goura Soulé, 'West African Cross-Border Trade: Trends and Opportunities', *Bridges Africa* 7, no. 4 (2008): 18–21.

7. Ibid.

8. Staatz et al., 'Agricultural Globalization in Reverse'.

9. 'Comité Permanent Inter-Etats de Lutte contre la Sécheresse dans le Sahel, or Permanent Interstate Committee for Drought Control in the Sahel (CILSS)', *Cross-Border Trade Flow of Agricultural Products in West Africa* (Ouagadougou: CILSS, 2014).

10. Soulé, 'West African Cross-Border Trade: Trends and Opportunities'.

11. Ibid.

12. John Keyser, 'Regional Trade of Food Staples and Crop Inputs in Africa', in *Trade Policy and Food Security: Improving Access to Food in Developing Countries in the Wake of High World Prices* eds. Ian Gillson and Amir Fouad, 158–88 (Washington DC: The World Bank, 2015).

13. World Bank, *Connecting Food Staples and Input Markets in West Africa: A Regional Trade Agenda for ECOWAS Countries* (Washington DC: World Bank, 2015).

14. Henri Josserand, 'Assessment of Volumes and Value of Regionally Traded Staple Commodities' (Paper prepared for the Food across Borders Conference, Accra, 29–31 January, 2013).

15. World Bank, *Connecting Food Staples and Input Markets in West Africa*.

16. Ibid.

17. Soulé, 'West African Cross-Border Trade'.

18. Keyser, 'Regional Trade of Food Staples and Crop Inputs in Africa'.

19. Ibid.

20. Ibid.

21. Aziz Elbehri, Jonathan Kaminski, Suffyan Koroma, Massimo Iafrate and Marwan Benali, 'West Africa Food Systems: An Overview of Trends and Indicators of Demand, Supply, and Competitiveness of Staple Food Value Chains', in *Rebuilding West Africa's Food Potential*, ed. Aziz Elbehri, 3–39 (Rome: FAO/IFAD, 2013).

22. AfDB and FAO, *Agricultural Growth in West Africa*.

23. Ibid.

24. United States Department of Commerce, *U.S. Trade with sub-Saharan Africa, January–December 2014* (Washington DC: United States Department of Commerce, 2014).

25. Josep Borrell and Jutta Urpilainen, 'Africa and the European Union: A Partnership for the Future', *The Cable News*, 2019.

26. Brian Stout, 'It's Africa's Turn to Leave the European Union', 2020. https://foreignpolicy.com/2020/02/10/african-union-european-union-trade.

27. United States Department of Commerce, *U.S. Trade with sub-Saharan Africa.*

28. Edun Adetunji Oluwafemi, Khikmatullo Kudratov, Bah Abdoulaye Oury, Oji-Okoro Izuchukwu and Abba Abubakar Shehu, 'African Growth and Opportunity Act (AGOA) and Economic Community of West African States (ECOWAS) Regional Trade: Challenges and Prospects', *Journal of African Studies and Development* 4, no. 1 (2012): 25–36.

29. Ibid.

30. European Commission, *West Africa: Trade Picture* (Brussels: European Commission, 2019), https://ec.europa.eu/trade/policy/countries-and-regions/regions/west-africa.

31. Christoph Pannhausen, *Economic Partnership Agreements and Food Security: What Is at Stake for West Africa?* (Bonn: German Development Institute, 2006).

32. Ibid.

33. Ibid.

34. Inter Press Service, *The Chilling Effect of Frozen Poultry Imports* (Rome: Inter Press Service, 2006). http://www.ipsnews.net/news.asp?idnews.

35. Pannhausen, *Economic Partnership Agreements and Food Security.*

36. United Nations Conference on Trade and Development, *The Least Developed Countries Report* (New York: United Nations & UNCTAD, 2002).

37. United Nations Conference on Trade and Development, *The African Growth and Opportunity Act: A Preliminary Assessment* (New York: United Nations & UNCTAD, 2003).

38. Brock Williams, *African Growth and Opportunity Act (AGOA): Background and Reauthorization* (Washington, DC: Congressional Research Service 7–5700, 2015).

39. UNCTAD, *The African Growth and Opportunity Act.*

40. Noelle Terpend, *An Assessment of Knowledge about Trade and Markets Related to Food Security in West Africa* (Rome: United Nations World Food Program, 2006).

BIBLIOGRAPHY

African Development Bank (AfDB) and Food and Agriculture Organization (FAO). *Agricultural Growth in West Africa: Market and Policy Drivers*. Rome: AfDB and FAO, 2015.

Borrell, Josep and Jutta Urpilainen. 'Africa and the European Union: A Partnership for the Future'. *The Cable News*, 2019. https://www.thecable.ng/africa-and-the-european-union-a-partnership-for-the-future?

Comité Permanent Inter-Etats de Lutte contre la Sécheresse dans le Sahel, or Permanent Interstate Committee for Drought Control in the Sahel (CILSS). *Cross-Border Trade Flow of Agricultural Products in West Africa*. Ouagadougou: CILSS, 2014.

Elbehri, Aziz, Jonathan Kaminski, Suffyan Koroma, Massimo Iafrate and Marwan Benali. 'West Africa Food Systems: An Overview of Trends and Indicators of Demand, Supply, and Competitiveness of Staple Food Value Chains'. In *Rebuilding West Africa's Food Potential*, edited by Aziz Elbehri, 3–39. Rome: FAO/IFAD, 2013.

European Commission. 'West Africa: Trade Picture'. Brussels: European Commission, 2019. https://ec.europa.eu/trade/policy/countries-and-regions/regions/west-africa.

Food and Agriculture Organization. *Why Has Africa Become a Net Food Importer? Explaining Africa Agricultural and Food Trade Deficits*. Rome: FAO, 2012.

Inter Press Service. *The Chilling Effect of Frozen Poultry Imports*. Rome: Inter Press Service, 2006. http://www.ipsnews.net/news.asp?idnews=32293.

International Trade Center. *Trade Map – International Trade Statistics*. Geneva: ITC, 2018. https://www.trademap.org/tradestat/Country_SelProductCountry_TS.aspx?

Henri Josserand. 'Assessment of Volumes and Value of Regionally Traded Staple Commodities'. Paper prepared for the Food across Borders Conference, Accra, 29–31 January 2013.

Keyser, John. 'Regional Trade of Food Staples and Crop Inputs in Africa'. In *Trade Policy and Food Security: Improving Access to Food in Developing Countries in the Wake of High World Prices*, edited by Ian Gillson and Amir Fouad, 158–88. Washington DC: The World Bank, 2015.

Oluwafemi, Edun Adetunji, Khikmatullo Kudratov, Bah Abdoulaye Oury, Oji-Okoro Izuchukwu and Abba Abubakar Shehu. 'African Growth and Opportunity Act (AGOA) and Economic Community of West African States (ECOWAS) Regional Trade: Challenges and Prospects'. *Journal of African Studies and Development* 4, no. 1 (2012): 25–36.

Pannhausen, Christoph. *Economic Partnership Agreements and Food Security: What Is at Stake for West Africa?* Bonn: German Development Institute, 2006.

Soulé, Bio Goura. 'West African Cross-Border Trade: Trends and Opportunities'. *Bridges Africa* 7, no. 4 (2008): 18–21. http://www.ictsd.org/bridges-news/bridges-africa/news/west-african-cross-border-trade-trends-and-opportunities

Staatz, John, Niama Dembélé, Valerie Kelly and Ramziath Adjao. 'Agricultural Globalization in Reverse: The Impact of the Food Crisis in West Africa'. Background paper prepared for the Geneva Trade and Development Forum, Crans-Montana, September 17–20, 2008.

Stout, Brian. 'It's Africa's Turn to Leave the European Union'. 2020. https://foreignpolicy.com/2020/02/10/african-union-european-union-trade/

Terpend, Noelle. *An Assessment of Knowledge about Trade and Markets Related to Food Security in West Africa*. Rome: United Nations World Food Program (WFP), 2006.

United Nations Conference on Trade and Development. *The Least Developed Countries Report*. New York: United Nations & UNCTAD, 2002.

United Nations Conference on Trade and Development. *The African Growth and Opportunity Act: A Preliminary Assessment*. New York: United Nations & UNCTAD, 2003.

United States Department of Commerce. *U.S. Trade with sub-Saharan Africa, January-December 2014*. Washington, DC: United States Department of Commerce, 2014.

van Seters, Jeske, Dolly Afun-Ogidan and Francesco Rampa. 'Regional Approaches to Food Security in Africa: The CAADP and Other Relevant Policies and Programs in ECOWAS'. ECDPM Discussion Paper, No 128d., European Center for Development Policy Management (ECDPM), Maastricht, 2012.

Williams, Brock. *African Growth and Opportunity Act (AGOA): Background and Reauthorization*. Washington, DC: Congressional Research Service 7–5700, 2015.

World Bank. *Africa Can Help Feed Africa: Removing Barriers to Regional Trade in Food Staples*. Washington, DC: World Bank, 2012.

World Bank. *Connecting Food Staples and Input Markets in West Africa: A Regional Trade Agenda for ECOWAS Countries*. Washington, DC: World Bank, 2015.

Index